THAI STREET FOOD

authentic recipes, vibrant traditions

DAVID
THOMPSON

with photography by
EARL CARTER

TEN SPEED PRESS
Berkeley

CONTENTS

INTRODUCTION

It's all about the food. Even a fleeting visit to Thailand can leave you in no doubt of this. Walking down the street – almost any street in Thailand – you can only be struck by the variety of stalls (sometimes literally) and amazed at the variety of food. Thais are obsessed by food, talking and thinking about it, then ordering and eating it. Markets brim with produce and snacks. Streets often seem more like busy restaurant corridors than major thoroughfares for traffic.

Much of Thai culture expresses itself through food. It sits happily at the centre of all occasions and celebrations: births, weddings, making merit, dispensing generosity and repaying obligations. Food is integral to the Thais. Its diversity and profusion clearly shows the importance of food and eating in their daily lives.

There are two distinct parts to the Thai culinary repertoire. Firstly, there is food eaten with rice (arharn gap kao), which forms the basis of the meal proper. This encompasses the largest variety of Thai cooking: salads, curries, soups and relishes, all of which are eaten with rice, the heart of the meal. Several dishes are put on the table along with rice and are shared, family style. Thais consider this style of food to be traditionally Thai: it is what is served and eaten in the home, and is what they mean when they talk about food. The other main component is single-plate food (arharn jarn dtiaw), which is literally just that, with the dish normally plated in individual portions intended for one person. Although once it arrives, it might well be shared by friends. Unlike regular Thai food, this food may be eaten by itself – that is, it is not always eaten with rice. Originating in the markets and then later finding its way onto the streets as an occasional meal or snack, these noodles, pastries and other complex desserts, and deep-fried and braised dishes are unlikely to be prepared at home. And it is this diverse and distinctive food that is the subject of this book.

Thai Street Food offers a glimpse into the vibrant world of Thailand's streets and markets, following the sweep of time as day slips into night, and the people and food change accordingly. It contains a small selection of a few of my favourite recipes – it is by no means an exhaustive survey. It depicts the beguiling Thai food culture at its source, in the markets. There is a nod to history as the development of street food in Thailand is tracked. For me, it is vital to understand the past in order to make sense of the culinary mosaic that comprises street food. It may not help you cook better or yield tastier results, but it will give more meaning to what you do.

The book traces the traditional rhythm of the day, from morning to night, a progression that is often refreshingly different from the pace of modern life. Each chapter contains the food you are likely to find at that time. But like so much of Thai culture, these dishes are not easily confined and many can be found throughout the day, much as food stalls spread beyond the market out onto the streets and into the night.

°

In many ways, food from the markets and streets is the most accessible of all Thai food. Stalls and vendors fill the street, making it a delicious obstacle course. It is also the easiest of Thai cooking to enjoy and eat – not just for the Thais but for the stumbling visitor too. Even though it is prepared fresh every day and packed up every night, such vending feels as if it has withstood the test of time.

Pervasive as it now is, street food is a relatively recent addition to the Thai culinary landscape. Despite the prominence of hawker food among Chinese migrant communities in Bangkok in the early twentieth century, it was really only in the 1960s, perhaps slightly earlier, that street food came to the fore, gradually spilling out onto the streets as Thais left their family homes and farms and moved to the cities in search of new, more lucrative jobs in emerging industries.

Traditionally Thais ate at home, staying within the orbit of the family and its food. As farmers working the land they had little need or desire to leave their farms. Only when it was necessary did they eat outside the home – at markets, during temple festivals and village celebrations. Sometimes itinerant hawkers came to them, plying their wares: necessary items that could not be made or grown, such as salt, shrimp paste (gapi), charcoal, simple pieces of equipment, plates and the like, as well as some prepared food.

While farmers rarely strayed from home, women often did – and headed towards the market to barter and trade surplus produce for required items. Along the way some of the more enterprising traders sold food, portable snacks to those who gathered at the markets. Women have always played a large role in the markets and on the streets. Rarely have men intruded – they were farmers, soldiers, bureaucrats and monks, and often regarded such financial acumen with disdain, thinking it somehow improper. Historically and culturally women have always had a greater freedom to pursue trade.

These women of the market (mae khaa) banter to barter! They are full of character and sass, and love nothing more than to have a chat, bitch and play – with one another and with passing trade. Polite Thais modestly decline such rambunctious fun but smile inwardly, possibly considering a response but constrained by convention. A hallmark of Thai culture is the delight in a well-turned phrase, a graceful aside, incisive good-humoured repartee – and it is in the markets and on the streets where this is most freely expressed. It's enjoyed as much as the transaction itself. Sometimes more so, it seems.

Thai markets are as vivacious as the Thais and their food. They provide pleasure and materials for living. You can pick up food at every stage of preparation: from raw and straight from the fields (live, cleaned, cut and sliced), through assembled packages of raw ingredients, to finished dishes to take home or to eat then and there. But the market is more than a place that feeds the body. There is always a coffee shop where men will sit, read the newspapers, talk about affairs and, naturally, gossip. Women, on the other hand, go to the markets to shop, spending more time than they ought and as much time as they like, having a chat and maybe even a gossip too.

Traditionally the market was the place where people met, talked and exchanged information. Until recently people, if they lived within walking distance, went to the market once a day, sometimes twice. It was an important centre in society, second only to the temple. It was a lifeline to the outside world. Sadly this role of the marketplace is changing. Fewer people shop there now, and Bangkok's burgeoning middle class often prefers the newer supermarkets with their Western ways. While the supermarkets are doubtlessly more hygienic, they contain little of the atmosphere, the welcome or the quality of fresh ingredients.

○

Within the market there is a strong bond between the stallholders, who spend much of their day – most of their life – with their neighbours, chatting, sleeping, selling, occasionally working and always looking forward to eating, safe in the knowledge that the food will be good and robustly flavoured: real Thai market food. They can be certain of its quality.

Often the finest food comes from the most humble operations, such as one veteran noodle-seller I first encountered in Phetchaburi, to the south-west of Bangkok. Surrounded by bamboo baskets in which she totes all her food, and a few small stools on which her customers sit, eat and chat, she sells only one dish, kanom jin noodles dressed with pineapple and dried prawns, a dish she has been selling for the last 30-odd years. She's never used a fridge, let alone a freezer – there's simply no need. Her dish is based on local ingredients, with everything freshly purchased each day from the nearby market: good pineapples, dried prawns, green mango and chillies. She starts about 5 a.m., going to the market before returning home to do the simple preparation necessary. She'll probably offer some food to passing monks on their dawn alms collection, then at about 9 a.m. she'll head back to her street corner. She opens about 10 a.m. and generally runs out of food in the early afternoon. She knows all of her customers, some of them for years – they've grown old together. Most come at least once a week, but they'll often stop by for a chat on a daily basis. They are attuned to each other, as she is to the market and its food. That's why her noodles are so good. She, and a legion of hawkers like her, face their customers every day, so they can ill afford to obtain a poor reputation. And that's why the good people of the market can expect a satisfying meal.

○

The other major influence on Thai street food has been the wave of Chinese migration that accompanied the transformation of the Kingdom of Siam into modern Thailand. There have been Chinese merchants, adventurers and coolies in Thailand for hundreds of years, but during the nineteenth and especially the early twentieth century, the development of Bangkok was fed by Chinese coolies. Seeking to escape the hardship and poverty that was afflicting the south-eastern seaboard of their country, they came to try their luck in a new land. Some stayed for only a few years, but others settled, finding work on the wharves, in factories and in market gardens. Housed in communal accommodation, the Chinese could not eat at home, so they ate on the streets or canalside, in the fields and the factories. Their food was the basic, peasant food of their home regions: noodles, rice congee, pork offal and braises infused with five-spice powder. Among the Chinese there was less demarcation of roles, with men often becoming involved in food and its commercial preparation. There was often little choice for these immigrants and their offspring as many occupations were closed to them.

The Chinese brought with them hawkers, mendicant sellers of food. They carried their wares in two baskets supported by a bamboo pole slung across their shoulders. Most of the food they carried was prepared and cooked, as it was easier to serve and would keep more successfully in the tropical heat. They walked the streets and tracks and patrolled the land. Their sweep was small, determined by the weight of their baskets. They really could only carry enough for half a day – besides, the food would only last that long.

As the pace of modernisation accelerated, canals were dug to open up new areas and allow produce, rice, charcoal, sugar, to be brought easily into the city and its merchants. Main roads were non-existent and the tracks that did wind their way through the land became unusable during the rainy season. Small communities settled along the canals, and boats plied the waterways, supplying people with ingredients, household goods and simple prepared food. On board might be noodle soups, snacks and sweets, together with the equipment to prepare and serve them: a small, smouldering charcoal stove beneath a pot of simmering stock, and some bowls and utensils, which would be washed in the canals.

But as Bangkok grew, the modern city was established and streets began to supersede the waterways. Bamboo poles and baskets fell by the wayside, replaced by a cart (plaeng loy) that was better equipped to serve large communities, factories, building sites. Late one afternoon in Suphanburi, a small town in the heart of the central plains, I encountered the perfect example of such an operation. I had sought shelter in an old wooden market – a dark, cool and quiet place seemingly overlooked by time as it sat half in the shade, lapsing into disuse. But with the appearance of a woman of perhaps sixty slowly pushing a large rickety trolley, the marketplace came back to life, restored by the prospect of something to eat. Her cart was filled with pots and bowls full of curries and noodles, rice and a large wooden pestle and mortar for making salads.

At first I was a bit dismissive, thinking decent food unlikely in such a forgotten place. Having already had lunch, I could afford such indifference! Gradually people emerged from the surrounding shophouses and ordered their meal: one had a green curry with some leftover kanom jin noodles, another had some crunchy and still-warm spring rolls. Intrigued, I sampled a red curry spooned over rice and a green papaya salad (som dtam) with some salted beef on the side. Everything was exemplary, wonderful and richly seasoned – she'd been cooking these dishes every day for some forty years and it showed. Uncommonly good though this food was, I don't think her talent was unusual; there are just so many fine cooks preparing food in Thailand. She stayed and chatted, longer than she ought, seeing the delight in my eyes and possibly sniffing another sale (she had some desserts, you see – and yes, she was right, I succumbed to a few little dainties) before moving on to continue along her route.

About forty years ago, around the same time as this market woman and her trolley started out, 'made to order' (dtam sang) stalls began to appear, where raw food was cooked in woks over charcoal burners – or, later, gas jets. These stalls catered to the needs of an influx of Thai workers who had left their homes and paddy fields to move into a newly developing world of factories and workshops. In the city, they were housed in communal dormitories with few facilities. Lacking the means to cook for themselves but having the cash to pay for meals, these uprooted people looked to the streets for simple, portable and affordable food. The ready availability of cheap ice allowed the more established hawker to set up shop and chill raw produce through the afternoon into the night: trays were filled with food to tempt a tired Thai and make a worthwhile and happy conclusion to a long day's work. Plastic bags also became available and this meant that a greater variety of food, including soups and curries, could be taken away. Sometimes these stalls became so successful that the operator bought a nearby property, turning in his or her wheels and setting up shop.

Curry shops started up in much the same way, although some authorities believe that the dishes offered by these stalls mirrored the offerings made to monks: from such a meal, enterprising women began to provide similar dishes to passers-by. These stalls sprang up near thoroughfares, crossroads, markets and large communities, wherever customers were likely to be. Some became more permanent while others remained ad hoc, set up in front of the cook's house.

As the Chinese and their descendants moved out of their enclave in Chinatown and into the wider community, they brought noodle shops with them – and the popularity of these stalls among the Thai paralleled Chinese integration into Thai society and culture. The first generation of hawkers became ensconced and now a second generation has followed, staking their claim on the streets as they begin their rise to more established businesses.

Increasingly over the last twenty years, traditional Thai dishes, such as nahm prik relishes, hot and sour soups and salads of all kinds, are finding their way onto the streets and into night markets. Such food was once the preserve of home cooks and was seldom seen on the streets, but its appearance reflects the fact that Thais are working longer hours and are increasingly relying on prepared food. Who can blame them? The food is good, fresh and so convenient. The streets cater to modern Thais – everything that was à la carte is on the carts now.

∘

When I first went to Thailand in the 1980s there was a certain opprobrium surrounding people who regularly brought dinner home for their families, rather than cooking it themselves. They were considered irresponsible, and their family was considered quite unfortunate to have to rely on the cooking of strangers. The women were referred to as 'plastic-bag housewives', since they returned home after work laden with a multitude of plastic bags filled with dinner. However, times have changed and now there are few people, at least in Bangkok, who spend all day at home preparing food. Most urban Thais work outside the home and have little time to prepare food as their grandparents once did. But few are to be pitied as they partake of the bounty of the streets.

In any provincial town, and in many crowded areas of Bangkok, there is always a place – a corner or two, a few blocks or a square – that is brightly lit well into the night. These are the night markets of Thailand and they are filled with people, food and noise, as flames lick around woks and wood smoke from charcoal grills lingers in the still night air. Dtam sang stalls are among the brightest and busiest, but there will also be noodle stalls offering their wares in steaming soups or briskly stir-fried, and curry shops with an array of colourful curries in trays. Other stalls will be selling Muslim pastries, madtarbark and roti; elsewhere, fish cakes will be fried to order. Cooks develop different dishes to attract customers. A good place is always busy, with tables clustered around the cook and his or her stand. These precincts are all about eating and pleasure. They contain everything that lures a Thai out: good food, people, atmosphere and laughter – the Thai world on a plate. It really is all about the food.

MOR

NING

THE MORNING STARTS EARLY IN THAILAND. Well before dawn, markets all over the country open. Around dawn, monks leave their temples and make their morning rounds to collect their culinary alms. At some stage almost every Thai will contribute: it is part of their religious obligation. Wisely the monks will often head to where there are the most people – the markets – to give the faithful an opportunity to make merit. While many people prepare and cook food specifically for the monks, some purchase food for them – and of course the stallholders offer food, as they too want to improve their karmic lot. Curries and sweets are the most popular dishes to give, along with kanom jin noodles and bags of cooked rice, but anything edible can be given. As the monks return to their temples, the day's business begins. ◦ Most markets start in the cool of the morning and close by lunchtime. The market slowly fills with people unpacking their goods and setting up their stalls. A little later the early shoppers arrive. These hours can be quite flexible. I have been to one in the remote north-west of the country that closed around 9 a.m., and to another in Chiang Mai that only began in the middle of the afternoon. But it is mainly in the morning when they bustle with shoppers and jostling trolleys, with workers who whistle or click their tongues to alert stragglers that they are in the way. ◦ The stalls are usually arranged in a recognisable order, with each type of stall clumped together. For instance, fruit and vegetables are often at the centre of the market. The produce is displayed with tender care and refreshed throughout the day with regular splashes of water. Familiar staples like garlic, lemongrass, galangal, ginger and kaffir lime and of course chillies of all kinds are there. More exotically, there are bundles of aquatic acacia with their fluffy roots, fresh turmeric, apple and pea eggplants, betel leaves, and basils holy, lemon and Thai. But this is only a small part of the cornucopia. ◦ Nearby are stalls laden with small plastic bags

Previous page: Monks go on their dawn rounds in Samut Sakhon, on the coast south-west of Bangkok.

that contain everything a cook needs: white pepper, dried chillies, sugar, tamarind pulp, cumin and coriander seeds; fish, soy and oyster sauces. A lot of commercial products are also creeping onto the stalls, including prepared lime juice, chilli pastes and canned coconut cream. But in sight is the coconut stall – a blessing for all determined cooks. The fresh coconuts are cut in half then grated and pressed to order, yielding a succulent fresh cream very different from its canned cousins. ○ Down one of the aisles there is a fish stall, selling the most pert, clear-eyed fish: sea bass or barramundi, red emperor, red spot whiting, glorious squid and live prawns and crabs. There is always a tub of live fish, usually freshwater catfish and serpent-head fish. Very often one or two of the beasts will have escaped and be wriggling across the floor. These fish are killed and cleaned as required. Prawns and crabs are sold still kicking. Even in the smallest markets, the quality of seafood is outstanding. ○ Meat, pork, beef and poultry take the sidelines, having been introduced quite late into the diet due to the Buddhist prohibition on the taking of life. Those who consume meat circumvent this by saying that the beast is already dead. Even now, though, few Thais are butchers; mostly they are of Chinese descent. ○ Near the exit there is often a small stand where caged finches or bowls of small fish and eels are for sale. Mercifully they are not for eating. They are bought to be released in a nearby river or canal to earn merit and expiate the sins after a day's shopping, eating or just plain living. ○ In every market there are always three or four stands selling prepared food. Stallholders seldom leave their posts in case they miss a sale. The nearby vendors will often drop off a plate of stir-fried noodles, some kanom jin noodles or rice topped with curry, some Thai cup cakes or sweets like sticky rice pikelets. The spicier dishes might come as a surprise to some as welcome tastes for so early in the morning, but many of these people have been up for several hours and their palates are well and truly awake.

อาหารเช้าและของว่าง
BREAKFAST AND MORNING SNACKS
ARHARN CHAO LAE KORNG WANG

The sounds of the morning announce the breaking day: dogs begin to scratch and roam, cars and bikes rev up their engines and people stir as they prepare themselves for the day ahead. The rhythmic clunking of pestles in mortars can be heard.

Already the market is up and running, busy with cooks and hawkers shopping for their provisions and diligent housewives hankering for a chat. People are on the streets, heading off to work or simply out for a stroll, and they will pick up a snack or two on the way. Their breakfast snacks, though, are nothing like the Western meal – perhaps some Thai cup cakes, a few pieces of deep-fried bread to have with coffee and friends, or maybe a bag of warm sticky rice pikelets to dip into on the way back from the markets.

As the morning starts in earnest, school kids hit the streets, often three or four piled on a single bike, and they need something to make the prospect of school more palatable. A few yellow sugar plant puddings – picked up from a stall that's little more than a large metal steamer with a small side tray – should sweeten the learning process.

However, the almost always sunny morning doesn't mean sweet treats alone. A shophouse opens out to the street and on a bench some stretched dough will be proving, ready to be deep-fried while people wait to take away this bread to eat while it is still fresh, hot and crunchy.

Modern Bangkok heads to work at a hectic pace: women riding pillion – sitting side-saddle on motorbikes, defying any known laws of cosmetics and physics as they apply their make-up elegantly and precisely, at the same time balancing plastic bags filled with snacks to have on their way or at the office. Buses huff and puff and roar forth; traffic gnarls as the temperature rises and the modern world and its pressures ensue.

The market, however, follows a different pace – it is never so intense, it never loses it humour, its humanity. After all, its very raison d'être is to supply the community with the stuff of living: food, laughter, interaction, contact, life in the Thai manner.

Well inside the market, old ladies sit in the shade and cool – a few of them might be chewing on betel nut, which stains their lips an ancient red. They will be dexterously wrapping sticky rice with various toppings in banana leaves that will be exchanged for some baht, a bit of banter and a story or two. The market is at its busiest, brightest and best at this time, as shoppers set about their daily tasks, gossiping, laughing, buying and eating.

○ Sticky rice pikelets (see page 44) ready to go at Samut Sakhon market, south-west of Bangkok.

MAKES 40 CAKES OR 20 PAIRS,
ENOUGH FOR 4–5

BATTER

small pinch of lime paste
125 g (4 oz) rice flour
1 scant teaspoon arrowroot flour
1½ tablespoons cooked jasmine rice
¼ cup grated coconut
2 tablespoons thick coconut cream
good pinch of salt

TOPPING

3–4 tablespoons white sugar
pinch of salt
1 cup coconut cream
2 tablespoons chopped spring (green)
    onions – optional
2 tablespoons boiled corn kernels – optional
2 tablespoons steamed cubed taro – optional

grated coconut wrapped in muslin (cheesecloth)
    or a little vegetable oil, for greasing moulds

Thai cup-cake moulds

There are a few tricks to making these little fiends. Firstly, you must have the correct mould, which is a heavy pan with small rounded wells and a lid. These may be available at Thai specialty shops; otherwise any heavy non-stick, round-bottomed mould can be used. It must be well seasoned, otherwise it will be difficult to extract the cooked cakes. Season the pan by filling each well with some freshly grated coconut, possibly coconut from which cream has already been extracted. Heat the mould over a very gentle heat for an hour or two. Let it sit over the flame as the oil seeps out of the coconut. Don't worry if it goes brown and toasty, as long as it doesn't burn. Once done, wipe out the coconut, then rub and clean the wells to make sure every bit is removed. Never, ever wash the mould – it will destroy the seal, virtually guaranteeing the cup cakes will stick. Before adding the batter, rub the inside of each well with some grated coconut wrapped in muslin (cheesecloth) to oil them and help to prevent the cakes from sticking. Plain oil will do. The wells must be smeared with oil or coconut before and after each use. After every third use, it is wise to re-seal the mould with grated coconut.

KANOM KROK

THAI CUP CAKES

These wonderful cakes are eaten throughout the day – and they deserve to be. They are addictive . . . although cakes is perhaps not a true description of these crisp, golden-skinned wafer cups with soft and creamy centres. Be careful when they just come out as when they are fresh and hot, the centres are molten. But I suspect that won't stop you from being compelled to eat several; I certainly am.

- First make the batter. Dissolve the lime paste in ¾ cup of water and wait for about 15 minutes until it has completely precipitated. Drain off and reserve the lime water, discarding the sludgy residue.
- Mix the rice and arrowroot flours together with 2–3 tablespoons of plain water. Knead to a slightly wet, dough-like consistency. Add a further 2–3 tablespoons of plain water bit by bit to make a thick batter. Leave the batter to rest, covered, for an hour or so.
- Meanwhile puree the rice, grated coconut and ½ cup of the lime water in an electric blender until smooth. (Keep the remainder of the lime water for later use.) Add the coconut cream, the salt and perhaps a little more lime water, then continue to blend until a fine batter is achieved – it should be quite runny but able to coat the back of a spoon. Make sure there are no lumps whatsoever; if there are, the cakes are bound to stick. Leave to the side to settle for a few hours at room temperature or refrigerate overnight.
- Bring the batter to room temperature before using. It will probably be necessary to lighten and dilute it with a tablespoon or two of the remaining lime water, but do not add too much otherwise the cooked cup cakes will be overly crisp and brittle.
- Now make the topping by mixing the sugar, salt and coconut cream together in a bowl, stirring until completely dissolved. Put this to the side.
- Heat the cup-cake pan over a low–medium heat for 4–5 minutes until quite hot – ideally over gas, but without the flames touching the base of the mould (a cake ring should be able to assist with this). Grease each well with some grated coconut wrapped in muslin or a little vegetable oil, then pour batter into each sizzling well until it is three-quarters full. Cover with a lid and cook over a low–medium heat until the cup cakes are just beginning to set around the edges – this should take about 3–4 minutes but it depends on the thickness of the mould and the heat underneath it. Carefully pick up the hot pan and swirl it in a circular motion to redistribute the batter so that it thinly lines each well to the top. Don't worry if a little, or a lot, splashes onto the shoulder of the mould, it can be cut away later.
- Return to the heat and let any batter from the sides of the wells settle back in the centre. Cover once again and allow the batter to cook until it is just beginning to set. Gingerly add a tablespoon or two of the coconut cream topping to each cake – each well should be almost filled – then cover and let it cook for a few moments. This is the time to add a pinch of either chopped spring onions, boiled corn kernels or steamed taro to the mix, if using, just as the topping begins to thicken. Cover once more and continue to cook until the edges of the cakes are golden and the centre is slightly but not overly set.
- With a small knife, cut around the edge of each well and remove the cup cakes carefully with a Chinese soup spoon. Use the point of the spoon to lift the cup cake away from the mould, gently prising the edges of the cup cake from the well, then working your way down until the cake lifts away from the mould.
- If the first batch of cup cakes are not crisp enough, then stir a tablespoon or two of the remaining lime water into the batter. Just be careful not to add too much or the flavour of the batter will be diluted. If, on the other hand, the cup cakes are too brittle, then stir in a few tablespoons of coconut cream. Repeat until all the batter and topping is used, greasing the wells in between batches.
- Serve as single cup cakes or as culinary Siamese twins in pairs.

about ½ teaspoon salt

1 tablespoon white sugar

½ teaspoon bicarbonate of ammonia
    (baking ammonia) *or* 1 teaspoon bicarbonate
    of soda (baking soda)

2 cups sieved plain (all-purpose) flour –
    more as needed

about 2 teaspoons vegetable oil

plenty of vegetable oil, for deep-frying

sugar or dipping custard (see below), to serve

Bicarbonate of ammonia

Although not essential, bicarbonate of ammonia makes the bread extra crunchy, golden and light when cooked. As the bread cooks there is often a pronounced aroma of ammonia but this dissipates leaving no residue, merely a slightly bitter yet agreeable after-taste. It is sometimes called hartshorn and occasionally chemists stock it, as do some Middle Eastern, Greek and Scandinavian grocery shops; it can also be found online. Do not use normal ammonia – it is poisonous. Bicarbonate of soda can be used as an alternative (double the amount), but the resulting bread will not be as nutty, burnished and crunchy.

+ DIPPING CUSTARD

3–4 pandanus leaves

2 egg yolks

pinch of salt

3 cups coconut cream

1½ cups white sugar

2 tablespoons cornflour (cornstarch)

3 tablespoons tapioca flour

½ cup milk

Wash and drain the pandanus leaves. Finely chop the leaves, then puree them in an electric blender with as little water as possible. Strain, pressing against a sieve to extract as much of the very green and grassy pandanus water as possible. Set aside.

Mix the egg yolks with the salt, coconut cream and sugar in a bowl. Combine the flours in a separate small bowl and stir in the milk, then work this into the egg yolk mixture. Strain into a small pan.

Heat over a very low heat, stirring constantly, until thickened and cooked. This should take about 20 minutes. Stir in the pandanus water and simmer for a minute or so before taking off the heat and allowing to cool.

PAA TONG GOY

DEEP-FRIED CHINESE BREAD

Every morning in every market there is always a crowd milling around this stall, waiting for freshly cooked bread. Throughout the morning, a man, usually of Chinese descent, rolls and assembles the bread then deep-fries the pieces before they are served and sold, usually by his wife. They should be eaten promptly since they become stale quite quickly – within an hour or so. But there is little chance of this since they taste so good and the line of waiting people is long.

If there is a place to sit, then coffee – of a very Thai variety, based on chicory and condensed milk – is served. Strangely enough, a glass of black tea is usually served with the coffee, as it helps to wash away its bitter sweetness. Some places offer a glass of sweetened soy milk. There is always a newspaper and an opinion or two passed around. While some like to dip their bread into the coffee there is usually a bowl of white sugar on the table and the bread can be rolled in it, if preferred. I prefer it. Sometimes a small bowl of light coconut custard coloured and perfumed with pandanus is offered too. It's the right way to start the day.

Much later in the day, this bread is also cooked and eaten as an accompaniment to rice congee and its various garnishes (see page 306).

- In a large bowl, mix the salt, sugar and bicarbonate with 1 cup of water, stirring until dissolved. Pour the flour into a large bowl. Make a well in the centre, then add a few tablespoons of the prepared water. Work to make a loose, dry crumb then gradually incorporate the remainder of the water as well as the oil, kneading well after each addition. While kneading, occasionally gather the dough into a ball, pick it up and slap it several times, to stretch the gluten. When all is added, continue to knead and slap for at least 5 minutes – longer is better – to arrive at a silken, smooth, soft yet quite wet dough. The dough must be quite wet – if it is too dry, this will inhibit the puffing of the bread as it cooks.
- Cover and leave to prove and ferment slightly in a warm, airy place for 6–8 hours or longer, until the dough has almost doubled in size and slowly springs back when pressed.
- On the streets, the dough is patted and knocked back then slowly and gently stretched into long rectangular strips about 20 cm × 5 cm × 5 mm (8 in × 2 in × ¼ in). Home cooks might prefer to roll the dough into the required shape. Make sure the surface and the rolling pin are dusted with plenty of flour to help prevent the dough from sticking. Leave to rest and prove for about 10 minutes, covered with a slightly damp cloth.
- Now cut into smaller strips, each piece about 5 cm × 2 cm (2 in × 1 in). Brush the centre of a piece with a little water and top with another piece, pressing the middle sections lightly together. Repeat with the remaining strips. Some cooks use a skewer dusted with flour to do this, lifting one piece of the dough and pressing it against the other piece in the middle to secure the pair.
- Pour the deep-frying oil into a large, stable wok or a wide, heavy-based pan until it is about two-thirds full. Heat the oil over a medium–high flame until a cooking thermometer registers 180–190°C (350–375°F). Alternatively, test the temperature of the oil by dropping in a cube of bread – it will brown in 10–15 seconds if the oil is hot enough.
- Deep-fry the bread 4 or 5 pieces at a time until puffed, floating and golden. Turn each piece constantly during the deep-frying, to ensure that the dough puffs up then cooks and colours evenly. Experienced street cooks will deep-fry as many as 20 in a batch, but I have found that 4 or 5 at a time is enough to handle. Most cooks in Thailand will use a pair of large, long chopsticks to turn the pieces of bread – you can too, or a long-handled pair of tongs will do the trick. As each batch is cooked, lift out with chopsticks or tongs and drain on paper towels. Use a fine strainer to scoop out any scraps, which would taint the oil, and repeat until all of the shaped and cut dough is used.
- Serve warm with a bowl of sugar or some dipping custard and a newspaper, and pepper with some gossip.

SERVES 2

2 heads (ears) corn
1–2 pandanus leaves, knotted
1 cup grated coconut – ideally from
    a semi-mature coconut
good pinch of salt, to taste
1 tablespoon sesame seeds, roasted
3 tablespoons white sugar

ข้าวโพดคลุก

KAO PORT KLUK

CORN WITH GRATED COCONUT AND SESAME SEEDS

This is a simple and traditional snack, which is eaten at any time but mostly early in the day. Trays of woven bamboo keep the boiled corn warm and ready to serve. Sometimes a few pandanus leaves line these trays to perfume the corn and the surrounding air. A few stalls might vary this dish and sell steamed sugar bananas cooked and dressed the same way as the corn.

While any coconut will work with this dish, the ideal coconut to use is what is known in Thailand as a mapraow teun teuk – one that is neither fully mature nor too young – but they are hard to find. I call them teenagers. The flesh of this coconut is yielding yet still flavoursome, and it is generally the best for grating, especially for desserts. The coconut is cleaved in half then grated as needed. Like all fresh coconut, it needs to be used quite quickly, as it will begin to sour after only a few hours. To prolong its life, the grated coconut can be steamed for 2–3 minutes with a sprinkle of salt – often on those same bamboo trays – although this does soften its texture and reduce its creamy taste. This process is also beneficial if using the more commonly available mature coconut, with its firmer flesh, in order to achieve a similar quality to the teenager nut.

- Husk the corn and boil in plenty of salted water with the pandanus leaves until tender – about 10 minutes. It could take longer, depending on the quality and freshness of the corn. When ready, take out and allow to cool before paring off the kernels.
- Mix the coconut with the salt, then stir into the corn. Lightly crush the sesame seeds, mix with the sugar and sprinkle over the corn and coconut.

MAKES ABOUT 15

½ cup mung bean flour
½ cup black sticky rice flour or white sticky rice flour
good pinch of lime paste
¼ cup white sugar
good pinch of salt
1 cup grated coconut – ideally from a semi-mature
    coconut (see page 42)

แป้งจี่ข้าวเหนียว
BLAENG JII KAO NIAW

STICKY RICE PIKELETS

These gorgeous little breakfast dainties are good enough to bring a smile to the face as the day begins. Almost always, it is young girls who make this sweet snack, and they are sold throughout the day. A flat grillplate is used to gently cook the pikelets. Sometimes the batter is spooned onto the surface to make irregular free-form pastries, but often small cake rings are used to give them a uniform shape. There are two variations of this confection: one made with black sticky rice flour, the other with the more common white sticky rice flour. Both are made from their ground grains, which impart either a red-wine or toasty golden colour to the pikelets. This flour also gives the pikelets their chewy, nutty qualities. The mung bean flour, which is made from mung beans (the small olive-green beans that germinate to produce bean sprouts), imparts a light crispness. All of these flours are available in most Asian food shops.

o Combine the flours then gradually work in about ¼ cup of water, kneading well to produce a firm dough – you may not need all the water. Cover with plastic film then rest it overnight in the refrigerator.

o The next day, dissolve the lime paste in ¼ cup of water and wait for about 15 minutes until it has completely precipitated. Drain off and reserve the lime water, discarding the sludgy residue. Remove the dough from the refrigerator and knead the dough to return it to room temperature. Work in the lime water, sugar and salt, followed by the freshly grated coconut. By now, the pikelet mixture should have a similar consistency to thick pancake batter.

o Spoon onto a clean flat grillplate (griddle) or non-stick frying pan over a low heat, allowing a large spoonful of batter for each pikelet. After 5 minutes turn the pikelets over, then after another 5 minutes flip once more and cook for a final 5 minutes.

o These are best eaten while still warm, but can be quickly reheated – if they last that long!

SERVES 3–4

1 cup white sticky rice
1 large banana leaf – about 1 metre
    (3 feet) in length
2 sugar bananas
small bowl of white sugar

BOILED STICKY RICE AND BANANA

When the sticky rice is wrapped and boiled in banana leaves it takes on a green hue, but most surprising of all is that the sugar banana turns a dark red. It is important to have a bowl of sugar ready for dipping and rolling slices of the cooled rice – some stalls also add a pinch of roasted sesame seeds to the sugar.

- Rinse the sticky rice and soak overnight in plenty of water.
- Trim the banana leaf and wipe both sides with a damp cloth, then cut into three roughly 35 cm (14 in) squares and wipe once again. Place one square on a board, shiny side facing down. Place the next leaf on top, shiny side facing up, at right angles to the one underneath. Place the third one on top, again at right angles to the one beneath it. Now turn the leaves around so that two of the bottom leaf's corners point to 9 and 3 o'clock.
- Drain the rice, then spoon half of it onto the prepared banana-leaf squares, in a horizontal line across the centre.
- Peel the bananas and trim the top and bottom. Place the bananas head to tail on the rice, then cover with the remaining rice.
- Lift the corners of the banana leaves at 6 and 12 o'clock up and over the rice, bringing them together and lifting slightly to give the banana-leaf roll a rounded base. Fold the joined leaves over to make a 2 cm (1 in) fold, then repeat several times to tighten into an open-ended cylinder. To close the end, fold each side down in turn to make a triangle, exactly as you would when wrapping a parcel with paper. Fold this up and over the cylinder, then pick up the cylinder and stand it on its sealed end, pressing lightly to secure it. Repeat with the other end.
- Tie a piece of twine around one end, being sure to cover the overlapping triangle, and knot tightly. Tie the other end, then tie two loops of twine around the middle to hold everything firmly in place.
- Bring a large pan of water to the boil. Add the banana-leaf roll and simmer, covered, for about 45 minutes, then remove and leave to cool. Cut into slices before peeling off the banana leaf, then dip in sugar and eat.

MAKES 10

1–2 pandanus leaves
450 g (14 oz) cassava
scant ½ cup very finely grated coconut
3–4 tablespoons white sugar, to taste
pinch of salt, to taste
1 tablespoon arrowroot flour – optional
¼ cup jasmine water (see page 358)
    or coconut cream or water

+ BANANA-LEAF CUPS

To make banana-leaf cups, cut 20 rectangular pieces of banana leaf, each roughly 10 cm × 6 cm (4 in × 2½ in), and wipe each side with a damp cloth. Place two pieces together, shiny sides facing out, one on top of the other, with the grain running parallel. Make a light 3 cm (1¼ in) fold along the lower narrower end, bringing up the edge to form one side of the cup. Bring the bottom right-hand corner across and down over the side of the cup to form a tight corner. Secure with a small tooth-pick or staple. Repeat with the other three corners to make an open box or cup approximately 5 cm × 2 cm (2 in × 1 in). Make the remaining cups then set aside, covered with a damp cloth.

ขนมมันสำปะหลัง

KANOM MANSAPALANG

STEAMED CASSAVA CAKES

These are delicious and nutty little dainties: they are sweet and perfumed, with a wonderful texture. Cassava cakes come in two varieties: one light green, coloured with pandanus water; and a paler version containing perfumed water. Often they are steamed in banana-leaf cups secured with small toothpicks (actually these are tiny, more like splinters), although staples are now a common alternative. The method for making banana-leaf cups is described here, but oval friand moulds are a pragmatic alternative for those of us who are not as nimble-fingered as the girls at the markets.

- Rinse and chop the pandanus leaves, then blend with ¼ cup of water until pureed. Pass through a fine sieve, pressing the pulp insistently to extract as much of the vivid green water as possible. Set aside.
- Peel the cassava, then rinse and cut into quarters. Rinse once again before grating very finely – there should be about 1 cup. Combine the grated cassava with ⅓ cup of the coconut (grated as finely as the cassava – chop it with a knife to break it down further, if necessary), the sugar, salt and arrowroot flour (if using). Work and knead until the sugar has dissolved, then divide the mixture into two lots. Stir the pandanus water into one half; stir the jasmine water, coconut cream or water into the other half. Divide the pale-green batter among 5 banana-leaf cups, oval friand moulds or muffin tins, then divide the other batter among the remaining 5 cups or moulds.
- Place in a steamer and steam for about 20 minutes or until firm and translucent. Sprinkle the remaining grated coconut over the cassava cakes, then steam for another minute before removing from the heat. Leave to cool.
- Unmould the cakes to serve – although if you've toiled over the banana-leaf cups, I suggest you leave the cakes in them so your handiwork can be admired.

SERVES 6

1 cup sugar plant (luk dtarn) puree
1 cup rice flour
1 cup coconut cream
¾ cup white sugar
good pinch of salt
1½ teaspoons baking powder
15–20 cup-cake cases (paper liners) about
    5 cm (2 in) in diameter and 3 cm (1¼ in) deep
3–4 tablespoons grated coconut – ideally
    from a semi-mature coconut (see page 42)

YELLOW SUGAR PLANT PUDDING

The Palmyra sugar plant or toddy palm grows around the Gulf of Thailand. Its sap is used to make a variety of palm sugar or sometimes fermented to make a rum-like drink that is truly lethal. The tree's leathery black-skinned fruit has golden-yellow flesh, which is extracted and washed to produce a rich and aromatic pulp. This preparation is sold in the markets and forms the base for this wonderful snack. The fresh pulp is not too common even in Thailand – it must be ordered – but jars of the prepared paste are available in Thai and Asian supermarkets.

Traditionally these puddings were steamed in small circular moulds fashioned from dried sugar palm or banana leaves, but more modern cooks use little plastic cups or cup-cake cases.

The best coconut for garnishing these steamed sweets is a soft, slightly immature coconut called mapraow teun teuk (see page 42). Of course normal coconut can be used – just grate it more finely and sprinkle it over the puddings a minute before they are taken from the steamer.

- Combine the sugar plant puree with ½ cup of water. Work for a moment, making sure the water is mixed throughout the puree, which can be slightly fibrous. Wrap in rinsed muslin (cheesecloth) and hang to drain overnight – there is no need to refrigerate it – suspended above a large bowl to collect the liquid, which will be considerable. (The puree will reduce by as much as two-thirds in volume, leaving a thick paste.)
- The next day place the rice flour in a large bowl and stir in ¼ cup of water, mixing gently at first then working well to incorporate. Knead the dough for a minute then let it rest, covered with plastic film, for at least an hour.
- Gently heat the coconut cream in a small pan with the sugar and salt, stirring until dissolved. Allow to cool.
- Now add ⅓ cup of the sugar plant paste and all of the baking powder to the rice flour dough. Work together and knead for 3–4 minutes to form a soft, crumbly dough. Work in the cooled seasoned coconut cream, adding a few tablespoons at a time and stirring well to produce a smooth, golden, pancake-like batter that coats the back of a spoon. Cover and leave to prove slightly in a warm and airy place – this can take anywhere between 2 and 6 hours. When it has swelled and thickened somewhat and smells a little yeasty, then it is ready.
- Fill a metal steamer with plenty of water and bring to the boil. Spoon enough of the batter into each cup-cake case to two-thirds fill it. Place in the steamer, wipe the lid before putting it on, and steam over a medium heat for 5 minutes, then lower the heat and continue to steam for another 7–10 minutes. When they are ready, they should have puffed up like a sponge cake and be springy to the touch.
- Take the sweets from the steamer, sprinkle with the grated coconut and allow to cool. Remove the cup-cake cases and eat.

Overleaf: Steamed cassava cakes (left), Yellow sugar plant pudding (middle), Boiled sticky rice and banana (right).

2¼ cups white sticky rice

¾ cup black sticky rice

3–4 pandanus leaves for steaming – optional

WHITE DRESSING

¾ cup white sugar

1 tablespoon salt

1 cup coconut cream

GOLDEN DRESSING

½ cup coconut cream

½ cup white sugar

1 tablespoon salt

2 tablespoons sliced turmeric *or* 2 tablespoons
   saffron water made by steeping a good pinch
   of saffron in 2 tablespoons of water then
   straining before use

PRAWN TOPPING

150 g (5 oz) raw prawns (shrimp) in their shells

1 heaped tablespoon cleaned and chopped
   coriander roots

½ teaspoon salt

¼ teaspoon white peppercorns

1 tablespoon vegetable oil

½ cup finely grated coconut

2 tablespoons shaved palm sugar,
   plus 2 teaspoons extra

2 tablespoons white sugar

pinch freshly ground white pepper, if necessary

1–2 tablespoons shredded kaffir lime leaves –
   about 12 leaves

1 tablespoon chopped coriander

COCONUT TOPPING

½ cup shaved palm sugar

¼ cup coconut cream

½ cup tightly packed grated coconut

CUSTARD TOPPING

1 duck egg or 2 chicken eggs – about ¼ cup

½ cup coconut cream

¼ cup shaved palm sugar

pinch of salt

1 pandanus leaf, cut into 4 or 5 lengths

SEASONED COCONUT CREAM

1 tablespoon rice flour

2 cups coconut cream

⅓ cup white sugar

1 heaped teaspoon salt

1 pandanus leaf, knotted

KAO NIAW SAHM SII

THREE TYPES OF STICKY RICE

The surprising interplay of sweetness, saltiness and richness captures the complexity of seasoning in Thai food. These parcels of rice are descended from the palaces of Siam but have found a happy place on the street stalls of Thailand, where women prepare these sweetmeats to sell.

It does take some time to assemble all the components of this dish but, as with many things that require effort, it repays in the taste obtained. In the markets, smiling old girls make the effort and their work makes it a simple pleasure to buy and eat these treats. At home, however, you may wish to make it easier by preparing only one or two types of rice, completing this culinary trifecta once you've become addicted or at least seasoned. But whether one, two or all three, you really should try it.

- Separately rinse the white and black sticky rice in several changes of water. Measure out 2 cups of the white rice into a bowl. In another bowl, mix the remaining ¼ cup of white rice with the black rice. Cover both with plenty of water and leave to steep for several hours – overnight is even better.

- Drain the white sticky rice and place in a steamer over water at a rolling boil with the pandanus leaves in it, if using. White sticky rice can be placed directly into the steamer – only a little should fall through the holes – but for those who are cautious, the steamer can be lined with some rinsed muslin (cheesecloth). Steam for about 45 minutes or until the rice is cooked. Check that the inner part of the mound is cooked as well. Make sure there is plenty of water in the bottom; steamers do have a tendency to burn!

- While the white rice is steaming, make the two coconut-cream dressings. For the white dressing, add the white sugar and salt to the coconut cream and stir until dissolved. It should taste rich, sweet and salty, and it should have a matt white sheen. Divide this mixture in half: one half will be used with the white sticky rice, and the other with the combined black and white rice.

- Make the golden dressing. Combine the coconut cream with the sugar and salt. Add the turmeric or saffron water and leave to infuse for about 30 minutes or longer.

- When the white sticky rice is cooked, take it out of the steamer and divide into two lots. Put the first half into a small bowl then stir in half of the prepared white dressing. Cover and leave in a warm place while you prepare the rest of the rice and toppings.

- Put the second lot of steamed white rice into another small bowl and stir in the golden dressing. Cover and leave in a warm place.

- Replenish the pan under the steamer with plenty of water, retaining the pandanus leaves. Line the steamer with muslin (cheesecloth) – the bran layer of black sticky rice prevents it from clumping together as it cooks, making it more likely to fall through the holes. Drain the combined black and white sticky rice, place in the steamer and steam over a rolling boil for about 1 hour.

- Meanwhile make the toppings. For the prawn one, peel and devein the prawns. Squeeze the heads to drag out as much tomalley as possible, and reserve. Mince the prawn meat finely – there should be about 100 g (3 oz). Using a pestle and mortar, pound the coriander roots with the salt and white pepper to make a fine paste. Heat the oil and fry the paste over a medium heat until aromatic – about 3, maybe 4 minutes – stirring constantly to prevent it from catching. Then add the prawns and their tomalley and continue to fry over medium heat until just cooked. Add the grated coconut and fry, stirring often. After 4–5 minutes, when the coconut is softened and fragrant, add the palm and white sugars and simmer until absorbed. It may need an additional teaspoon or two of palm sugar, and a little pepper and salt, but be careful not to over-season – as it cools, the salt will become more obvious. It should be pungent but not aggressively so. Finish by adding the shredded kaffir lime leaves and sprinkling with the chopped coriander. The topping should taste pleasingly salty, rich, sweet and peppery, and be fragrant from the kaffir lime leaves and coriander.

Thais manage to fold, form and encase items in banana leaves with such skill it's infuriating. The gals can even wrap and natter at the same time. Here's the method they follow – but should you find, as I do, that such nimbleness eludes, then simply serve the rice and topping spooned onto plates.

1 roll of banana leaves, about 2 metres (6 feet)
about 20 toothpicks or very small thin
   bamboo skewers

Cut the banana leaves into strips approximately 25 cm × 12 cm (10 in × 5 in). You will need about 20 strips altogether, allowing for a few trials and some errors. Trim and round all of the corners. Wipe each side with a damp cloth.

It may be wise to practise the following method using a matchbox or similar first, in order to become familiar and comfortable with what is actually quite a simple process, despite my long and clumsy description of it.

Pick up the first banana-leaf strip and lay it across one hand, shiny-side up. Slightly cup your palm and, with it, the leaf. Place the matchbox or whatever it might be in the centre. Imagine a line running down the middle of the leaf. Place the thumb and index finger of the other hand on each side of that line about two thirds of the way along the banana leaf. Pinch them and the leaf together, then lift the right half of the leaf up and towards the centre over the matchbox (or later, the rice). There should be folds on either side of the base of the leaf as it bends. Place the package on the bench, then slightly press the thumb and index finger onto the matchbox to hold it as you repeat the pinching and folding process. Secure the package with a toothpick.

Try this a few times before starting with the rice. Place 2–3 tablespoons of one type of rice in the centre of the prepared banana leaf, then drizzle with a little seasoned coconut cream and finish with about 2 teaspoons of the appropriate topping. Fold as outlined above.

Every person should receive three packages, each filled with a different kind of rice and their respective topping. In the markets you can order them individually, having one, two or three types.

- For the coconut topping, melt the palm sugar in a pan, then add the coconut cream and simmer for 3–4 minutes over a medium heat until it has reduced by about a third and bubbles quite heavily. Add the grated coconut and simmer for another 10 minutes, until the coconut is tender but a little wet. It should taste sweet and rich.

- For the custard topping, combine the eggs with the coconut cream, sugar and salt. Add the pandanus, squeezing to extract a slight perfume and mashing the eggs to make a custard. Pass through muslin (cheesecloth) or a fine sieve into a heatproof bowl that will fit in the steamer, then leave to rest for 20–30 minutes, skimming off any bubbles that rise to the surface.

- Now go back to the combined black and white sticky rice in the steamer. Check to see if the grains are slightly tender, testing the inner part of the mound as well. Once the rice is cooked, put it in a bowl and stir in the prepared golden coconut dressing. Cover and leave in a warm place.

- Replenish the pan under the steamer with water and return to the boil. Skim any foam from the surface of the custard then steam it over a medium heat for 10 minutes. When checking on it, be sure to wipe the lid of the steamer dry of any condensation, as any water that drips onto the custard will mar it. After 10 minutes, the custard should be beginning to bulge, bubble slightly and have a few wrinkles at its centre. Turn the heat down to low and steam for a further 5 minutes. When cooked – that is, slightly firm to the touch – remove and leave to cool.

- Meanwhile, prepare the seasoned coconut cream. In a small pan, make a slurry by mixing 2 or 3 tablespoons of water into the rice flour. Stir in the coconut cream, sugar, salt and pandanus leaf. Heat over a medium heat, then simmer for 3–4 minutes, stirring constantly, until thickened. It should taste rich, salty and sweet.

- Now it can be eaten – you certainly deserve something after all this work! Each type of rice is drizzled with a little seasoned coconut cream before its topping is added: the white rice is eaten with the custard topping, the golden rice with the prawn topping, and the black rice with the caramelised coconut.

Overleaf: Three types of sticky rice

BATTER

small pinch of lime paste
½ cup coconut cream
¼ cup rice flour
¼ cup mung bean flour
good pinch of salt
¼ teaspoon turmeric powder
½ teaspoon vegetable oil
1 small stalk lemongrass, cleaned
    and bruised – optional

PRAWN AND COCONUT FILLING

2 coriander roots, cleaned and chopped
pinch of salt
2 garlic cloves, peeled
a few white peppercorns
2–3 tablespoons vegetable oil
½ cup finely minced raw prawns (shrimp)
2–3 tablespoons prawn tomalley – optional
a generous ½ cup grated coconut – ideally
    from a semi-mature coconut (see page 42)
1 tablespoon white sugar
2 tablespoons shaved palm sugar, or more
    to taste
good pinch of salt
2–3 tablespoons fish sauce
½ teaspoon ground white pepper

vegetable oil, for frying

GARNISH

1 cup bean sprouts, washed and
    drained – trimming their tails is a refined option
3–4 tablespoons finely cubed yellow bean curd,
    about 150 g (5 oz) – the same amount of firm
    bean curd is a good alternative
1 heaped tablespoon shredded salted radish –
    the sweet and salty variety – rinsed and dried
1 heaped tablespoon chopped spring
    (green) onions
1 heaped tablespoon chopped coriander
1 heaped tablespoon coarsely ground
    roasted peanuts

+ CUCUMBER RELISH

¼ cup white sugar
½ cup white vinegar
about 1 teaspoon salt
½ cup sliced cucumber
¼ long red chilli, deseeded and chopped
½ cup sliced red shallots
1 tablespoon coarsely chopped coriander

Simmer the sugar with the vinegar, salt
and ¼ cup of water. When the sugar has
dissolved, remove from the heat and allow
to cool.

    Just before serving, stir in the cucumber,
chilli, shallots and coriander.

KANOM
BEUANG YUAN

CRISPY PRAWN AND TURMERIC WAFERS

This snack was originally brought to Thailand by the Vietnamese (yuan is an old Thai term for Vietnamese). The wafers are cooked in a quite small wok – about half the size of a normal wok. Some versions of the recipe make thick opaque wafers by adding a little egg to the batter, however I prefer the translucent thinness of this version. It is slightly harder to make, but the result is alluring.

- To make the batter, dissolve the lime paste in ¾ cup of water and wait for about 15 minutes until it has completely precipitated. Drain off and reserve the lime water, discarding the sludgy residue.
- Work a few tablespoons of the coconut cream into the rice and mung bean flours in a large bowl. Knead in the salt and turmeric powder, then work in the remainder of the coconut cream and ½ cup of the lime water, followed by the oil. Stir with the bruised lemongrass stalk (if using), leaving it in the batter to infuse. Set aside to rest for at least 30 minutes, to allow the flour to swell and the batter to thicken slightly.
- Meanwhile, make the filling. Using a pestle and mortar, make a paste by pounding the coriander roots with the salt, garlic and peppercorns. In a small, heavy-based pan, fry the paste in the oil until fragrant, then add the minced prawns, tomalley (if using) and the coconut. Season it with the sugars, salt, fish sauce and pepper, then add 2–3 tablespoons of water and simmer for about 10 minutes until rich, aromatic and quite dry. The coconut must be cooked and tender and still a little moist. If it's not, then add a few more tablespoons of water and continue to simmer. The paste should taste salty, sweet and quite peppery. It should be highly seasoned, in fact overly so if tasted alone.
- Stir the batter to re-incorporate the thick floury part that will have settled at the bottom of the bowl. The batter must be thin, even film-like in its transparency. Almost without exception, it will be necessary to add a few more tablespoons of lime water. Allow the batter to rest for a few minutes afterwards, to ensure that the extra lime water reacts with the batter so the wafers won't be too soft and soggy.
- Heat a small, well-seasoned wok over a low heat. (I have seen a few cooks use a non-stick wok.) Add a few tablespoons of oil and swirl it around the whole of the wok. Drain the excess oil then wipe dry with a paper towel.
- Let the wok cool just slightly before pouring a ladle of batter – about 3 tablespoons – into the wok and swirling it around. Place on the heat. Pour in another ladle of batter, trying to cover some of the areas not covered by the first ladle. However, there is no need to cover all the wok's surface: a few holes add to the wafer's charm. There should be quite a thin covering, with the thickest part in the centre, at the bottom of the wok.
- Gradually move the wok around, making sure each part of the wafer has its moment over the heat – the wafer should begin to colour slightly and lift at the edges. Be patient. Do not attempt to lift the wafer too soon, otherwise it will never become crisp. As the edges start to crisp and crinkle slightly, pry the wafer away from the wok with a small spatula, sliding it around, if possible. As the batter cooks, the aroma of the flour and turmeric will become apparent.
- Pour about 1 tablespoon of oil down around the sides of the wafer and continue cooking until it bubbles, becoming golden, aromatic and crunchy. If the wafer is not crispy, then stir another tablespoon or two of the lime water into the batter and start again.
- Turn down the heat slightly, then add a good pinch of the bean sprouts and crumble over about a tablespoon of the prawn and coconut filling. Cook for a moment until the bean sprouts are slightly wilted, then add a couple of cubes of bean curd and a little salted radish.
- After a few moments, when the filling is warmed through, sprinkle with a pinch each of spring onions, coriander and peanuts. Fold the wafer over the filling and lift out from the wok.
- Wipe the wok of any excess oil and repeat until all the batter is used. There should be around 5 wafers, with enough batter to allow for a few mistakes.
- Serve with a bowl of cucumber relish.

PASTRY

1 cup rice flour

¼ cup tapioca flour, plus a few
    tablespoons more for dusting

2 tablespoons sticky rice flour

large pinch of salt

3 tablespoons vegetable oil

FILLING

400 g (12 oz) Chinese chives, cut into
    1 cm (½ in) lengths – about 6 cups

4 tablespoons vegetable oil

1–2 tablespoons finely chopped garlic, to taste

pinch of salt

about 1 teaspoon white sugar

2–3 tablespoons light soy sauce

pinch of ground white pepper

1 banana leaf – optional

vegetable oil, for frying

1–2 tablespoons garlic deep-fried in oil
    (see page 358) – optional

soy and chilli sauce (see below), to serve

+ SOY AND CHILLI SAUCE

4 tablespoons dark soy sauce

1 tablespoon light soy sauce

a drizzle of sesame oil – optional

1 tablespoon white vinegar

1 long orange or red chilli, chopped

To make the sauce, combine all the
ingredients with 1–2 tablespoons of
water – it should taste dark, rich and salty.

KANOM
GUI CHAI

CHINESE CHIVE CAKES

This white fleshy dough is straight from China: the combination of flours (all of which can be found in Chinese grocers) and the cooking technique mean that the pastry is rich, silken and satisfying. Here it is wrapped around sharp garlic-flavoured Chinese chives, but the stuffing can also be made from shredded bamboo with dried prawns (see page 182) or with yam beans (see page 183).

Once the cakes are formed, they can either be steamed straight away or refrigerated for a day, as long as they are covered with plastic film. Once steamed, they may be eaten as they are, though you'd be well-advised to let them cool for a moment first. However, I find they are better if they are shallow-fried until golden – on the streets Thai cooks use large heavy cast-iron griddles for this. Whichever way you decide to eat the cakes, they should always be accompanied by some smoky and dark soy sauce with a few chopped chillies.

- First make the pastry. Mix the flours together with the salt. Work in the oil, then add 1½ cups of water and work to form a thick but quite wet dough. Put the pastry in a pan or brass wok and stir constantly over quite a low heat. You may need to resort to a whisk if the flour begins to clump. Do not let it catch. When the pastry is half cooked – it will start to become very sticky and take on an opaque sheen – remove from the heat and allow to cool for a few minutes.
- Cast a few tablespoons of the extra tapioca flour on a board, scrape the dough onto it and work the flour into the warm pastry for about 5 minutes, until it is comparatively firm and clean to the touch. Be careful not to use too much flour as it will make the finished pastry heavy. Roll into 10 balls, each approximately 4 cm (1½ in) in diameter, and rest, covered with a clean damp cloth, for at least 10 minutes.
- For the filling, wash the cut Chinese chives in water then drain them well. Heat the oil in a wok or pan and fry the garlic with the salt until it is beginning to colour, then add the chives. When wilted, season with sugar, soy sauce and white pepper. Make sure the filling is well seasoned but not too salty. Allow to cool.
- Lightly knead each pastry ball between the fingers, then press out on a board or plate, one at a time, into thin discs that are very slightly thinner at the edges and about 10 cm (4 in) in diameter. Place a pastry disc on the palm of one hand and spoon 2 heaped tablespoons of the filling into the centre, making sure there is no excess liquid. Lift the edges of the pastry up and over then fold and crimp together, working your way around and pushing the pinched edges up into the centre – custom dictates that there should be 10 folds. Pinch the edges together in the centre, twist them together, then press down and seal. Each chive cake should be about 5 cm (2 in) in diameter. Keep covered with a damp cloth. Repeat with the remaining pastry balls and filling.
- Steam for 15 minutes on a banana leaf or baking (parchment) paper – it could take a little longer, depending on your steamer and the heat under it. Remove and smear with a dash of oil then return to the steamer for another minute or so. Lift out, smear with oil once again then allow to cool for a moment before serving.
- Often, however, the cakes are reheated by shallow-frying them in some oil until golden, as those pictured opposite have been. If doing so, let the cakes cool somewhat after steaming – this will help to stop them from sticking as they fry. Heat a heavy frying pan until quite hot then pour in 2–3 tablespoons of oil. Add the cakes and shallow-fry over a low–medium heat, shaking the pan and gently shuffling the cakes to prevent them from sticking. Allow the cakes to colour lightly before turning with a spatula. Turn them two or three times until they are lightly coloured on all sides, making sure they do not get too brown. Remove and drain on paper towels.
- Sprinkle the cakes with a little deep-fried garlic in oil, if desired, and serve with a bowl of soy and chilli sauce.

เส้นขนมจีน
KANOM JIN NOODLES
SEN KANOM JIN

These silken noodles are entwined around the culture and community of the Thais. In the past kanom jin were only prepared and eaten at times of celebration, such as the ordination of a monk, the celebration of a marriage, the building of a house, the installation of a spirit house or any event associated with making merit that monks attend. Some people believe that the strands of noodles are similar in appearance to the white twine that monks wrap around the wrist after a blessing, and so kanom jin are seen as an auspicious part of the festive meal. They are still a part of the culinary conclusion to many such rites today – although about 80 years ago, maybe longer, they left the realms of ceremony and started to be enjoyed with no further meaning than for their own delicious sake in the markets and streets of Thailand. Kanom jin are mainly eaten in the daytime. Most ceremonies take place in the morning, in order for the participants to be able to feed the monks by midday, after when the monks must abstain from eating. By custom then, the noodles became associated with late morning.

Traditionally the making of kanom jin was laborious, and this meant that their production was confined to times when several people could be mustered to produce them: a large household and friends or a whole village could then make light work of this strenuous process. A large wooden mortar with a long pestle, a large wok or two and, most importantly, a large cotton bag with a brass sieve attached were needed. Firstly raw long-grain rice was steeped and left to ferment slightly for up to seven days before being pureed to a sticky mass. This dough was blanched, kneaded and then extruded through a sieve into a large cauldron of boiling water. Finally the noodles were rinsed in several changes of warm water and rolled into skeins. The traditional method of making these noodles was time consuming, to say the least.

Quite understandably then, kanom jin were reserved for special occasions. Now however these noodles are made by machines, with little ceremony attached. The slightly fermented rice is kneaded into a paste before being pressed and blanched. An altogether easier process, which means that the noodles are now everyday fare available in the market. The ivory-coloured strands of spaghetti-like rice noodles are rolled and bundled together into an alluring tussle, before being eaten with various sauces and accompanied by vegetables.

Kanom jin stalls open early – in the south and in marketplaces, some are on the go around dawn. Mostly however, stalls open during the morning and are closed by mid-afternoon. There are exceptions, of course, and as culinary habits evolve and change, these ever-popular noodles will no doubt be eaten throughout the day and well into the night. The stalls themselves are very simple affairs with a line of aluminium or terracotta pots filled with sauces. Most stalls sell three or four varieties of sauce to accompany the noodles, although smaller ones may specialise in just one kind.

The most traditional companion to kanom jin noodles is nahm yaa, a thick spicy sauce made from freshwater fish, dried chillies, shallots, garlic, lemongrass and grachai (wild ginger). In Thai folklore, one goes with the other like love and marriage; peasants say, in their earthy way, that kanom jin is the woman and nahm yaa is the man – the noodles beckon welcomingly on the plate.

But nahm yaa is not the only sauce. Equally popular, and perhaps more acceptable to the Western palate, is one called nahm prik. A rich and smoky sauce made from grilled chillies, shallots and garlic, thickened with mung beans, it has evolved into a rich and luscious sauce with chilli jam offsetting the nutty, earthy taste of the mung beans. This sauce is always eaten with an array of vegetables, some battered and deep-fried.

Kanom jin are the only noodles the Thais eat with curries, usually ones made with coconut cream – in fact, mainly red or green in all their variations. Notably however, the curries are almost never oily: even when the regular version of the curry is meant to have a healthy sheen of oil, it is modified so that it has only the faintest dappling of oil when eaten with these noodles. I know of no rich, Muslim-style curries that are served with kanom jin. (Maybe this is due to the noodles originally being associated with Buddhist rituals.) When eaten with coconut-based curries, the noodles are rarely accompanied with any additional vegetable garnish, so necessary with nahm yaa and its ilk.

Once the sauce is chosen, it is spooned over two or three loosely coiled skeins of noodles. The noodles are always eaten at Thai room temperature; the sauces, however, are best served slightly warm, or hotter in chillier climes. And so the dish is placed in front of the diner. There is always a tray or several bowls containing assorted vegetables and herbs, which are picked and torn before being mixed through the noodles. Fresh, blanched, pickled or dried, these are essential companions to the dish, giving it its final character. The fresh vegetables are vital, as they offer contrasting tastes and textures to the soft noodles and their sauce. Each region has its own preference for vegetables and herbs, according to the style of sauce and the season. Local vegetables growing nearby may be collected, while others are purchased in the market. Bean sprouts are perennial favourites for most styles of sauce, and lemon basil is a firm partner to nahm yaa in all its forms. Shredded and rinsed pickled mustard greens and boiled eggs are also commonplace on the stand.

Kanom jin are eaten with a spoon and fork, which are dragged across the plate to cut the noodles into bite-sized strands or clumps, at the same time mingling them with the sauce and herbs. Often a second plate of noodles is ordered, topped with the requisite sauce and finished with assorted herbs. Some customers like to order two sauces with their noodles, if two varieties are on offer – a spicy one and a sweet one, say a nahm yaa and a nahm prik, which they will mix together with vegetables.

○ Weighing skeins of fresh kanom jin noodles.

200 g (6 oz) serpent-head fish (plaa chorn),
    Murray cod or zander, on the bone

NAHM YAA PASTE

4 dried long red chillies, deseeded, soaked
    in water for 15 minutes then drained

3 dried bird's eye chillies

good pinch of salt

½ tablespoon sliced galangal

1½ tablespoons coarsely chopped lemongrass

4 tablespoons chopped grachai (wild ginger)

6 red shallots, peeled

6 garlic cloves, peeled

50 g (2 oz) plaa insiri kem (Spanish mackerel)
    or plaa gulao (tropical threadfin perch)

2½ cups coconut cream

pinch of salt

pinch of white sugar

pinch of roasted chilli powder – optional

2–3 tablespoons fish sauce, to taste

2–3 stalks grachai (wild ginger), peeled

2 bird's eye chillies (scuds)

600 g (1¼ lb) fresh kanom jin noodles
    or 500 g (1 lb) dried kanom jin noodles,
    reconstituted

ACCOMPANIMENTS

sprigs of lemon basil

trimmed bean sprouts

finely sliced snake (yard-long) beans or runner
    beans – regular green beans or the more
    exotic wing beans can also be used

sliced pickled mustard greens

medium-boiled eggs

raw or boiled bitter melon – be sure to scrape
    out the white pith and seeds, rub with salt
    and leave for 20 minutes

shredded banana blossoms

deep-fried dried bird's eye chillies

KANOM JIN NAHM YAA

FISH AND WILD GINGER SAUCE
WITH KANOM JIN NOODLES

This is kanom jin's most common accompanying sauce. Nahm yaa means medicinal water or liquid – a name that may have come from the terracotta pot in which the sauce is cooked and often served, one very similar to those in which folk medicines were decocted. There are many variations of the sauce, but one essential, defining ingredient is grachai, which is used in a surprising amount, comprising as much as 20 per cent of the nahm yaa paste. Indeed some authorities believe that the term nahm yaa comes from the use of this pungent, sometimes therapeutic rhizome – it certainly has a medicinal taste.

Thais consider the best fish for this dish to be plaa chorn (serpent-head fish). This robust fish is sold live and thrashing; however, once the purchase is made, it is soon despatched and handed over. It is a malevolent-looking fish with a head that looks like a snake, giving it its English name. But beneath its dark scaly skin lies gloriously rich, firm, clean and sweet flesh, which lends the nahm yaa sauce just the right texture. Since it is rarely available fresh outside Thailand, I suggest using freshwater fish such as farmed Murray cod or perch, or in Europe pike or zander.

Plaa insiri kem (Spanish mackerel) and plaa gulao (tropical threadfin perch) are salted dried fish that have a rich, dark and slightly fermented flavour. Frankly, they are somewhat musty and high in odour; however, don't be put off, as they give a rich round base to the finished dish that other, more immediately agreeable dried fish do not. The dish is much less satisfying without these. Both types of salted fish are readily available in Asian shops in the dried fish section: the plaa insiri may be sold in a jar under oil, while the gulao hangs in a piece. They can also be found online.

This sauce improves markedly if left to mellow for a few hours. In Thailand the sauce is often served at room temperature, just like the noodles – and given the average daytime temperature, this is a good thing.

- Poach the fish in 4 cups of water with all the nahm yaa paste ingredients. When the fish is cooked, remove it and set aside. Continue simmering the aromatics until they are tender – about 5 minutes. Strain, keeping the poaching liquid. Allow the fish and aromatics to cool.

- Meanwhile, wrap the plaa insiri kem or plaa gulao in foil or banana leaf, then grill for several minutes until even more aromatic. Do not let it char, as this will make the fish and consequently the sauce bitter.

- Using a pestle and mortar, pound the cooked aromatics to a fine paste, then add the grilled salted fish and combine well. Transfer the paste to a bowl and set aside. Lift the flesh from the bones of the poached fish, place in the mortar and pound to a light, fluffy puree. Stir this into the paste in the bowl: it should be thick and aromatic.

- Simmer 2 cups of the coconut cream with 2 cups of the reserved poaching liquid and a pinch of salt until slightly thickened but not separated. Add the paste, stirring until it has dissolved, then simmer gently until fragrant – this could take as long as 20 minutes. Moisten with some more of the poaching liquid or water if it threatens to separate or seems too thick. Season the sauce with sugar, chilli powder and fish sauce, to taste. Simmer for a few more minutes, then add the remaining ½ cup of coconut cream.

- Finally, using a pestle and mortar, pound the grachai with the scuds to a fine paste and stir into the sauce. Check the seasoning: it should taste rich, hot and salty, and be fragrant with grachai and redolent of the fish. Adjust as necessary. The sauce improves if left to stand for half an hour before serving.

- When serving, wrap each skein of noodles around four fingers to form a loose coil and place in a bowl, allowing a generous two skeins per person. Spoon the sauce over the noodles, being generous with it too. Serve with a few of the suggested accompaniments. Try to make sure you have some lemon basil and bean sprouts – both are almost essential.

SERVES 4

1 fresh bamboo shoot – about 200–300 g (6–9 oz)

FISH DUMPLINGS

200 g (6 oz) featherback fish (plaa graai), pike,
   perch, kingfish or Spanish mackerel fillet,
   skin removed
about 1 teaspoon salt
3–4 ice cubes

GREEN CURRY PASTE

pinch of coriander seeds, roasted
pinch of cumin seeds, roasted
10 white peppercorns
a little mace or, at a pinch, nutmeg
10–20 green bird's eye chillies (scuds)
1 long green chilli, deseeded
good pinch of salt
2 tablespoons chopped red shallots
2 tablespoons chopped garlic
1½ tablespoons chopped lemongrass
2 teaspoons chopped galangal
½ teaspoon finely grated kaffir lime zest
1 teaspoon cleaned and chopped coriander roots
½ teaspoon chopped turmeric
1 tablespoon chopped grachai (wild ginger)
½ teaspoon Thai shrimp paste (gapi)

1½ cups coconut cream
3 tablespoons fish sauce – more or less, to taste
2 cups coconut milk
about 1 cup chicken stock or water, as required
1–2 stalks lemongrass – optional
2–3 kaffir lime leaves, torn
2 tablespoons shredded grachai (wild ginger)
2 long red or green chillies, seeds retained
   or removed as preferred
1–2 bird's eye chillies (scuds), pounded
handful of Thai basil leaves
600 g (1¼ lb) fresh kanom jin noodles
   or 500 g (1 lb) dried kanom jin noodles,
   reconstituted

ขนมจีนแกงเขียวหวานลูกชิ้นปลา

KANOM JIN GENG
KIAW WARN LUK CHIN PLAA

GREEN CURRY OF FISH DUMPLINGS, BAMBOO AND BASIL WITH KANOM JIN NOODLES

Green curries are among the most popular curries to serve with kanom jin. Just take care not to make the curry oily; it should also be slightly thicker than a regular green curry that is eaten with rice. In Thailand, fish dumplings are usually bought ready prepared at the market – few make their own. However, outside the country, few of us are lucky enough to have a market so well stocked. Some places may have fish puree for sale, but be careful of its quality. An easy alternative is to finely slice the fish rather than making it into dumplings. In up-country Thailand, minced catfish is a popular option in any case.

A few quartered apple eggplants, picked pea eggplants or some trimmed baby corn are alternatives to the bamboo. If using any of these ingredients, simmer the curry for a couple of minutes after adding them.

- Peel the bamboo shoot by stripping off the hard and fibrous outer layers to reveal the white shoot. Trim off the coarse base of the shoot, being careful of the dark hairs, as they can irritate the skin. Wash well then steep in salted water. Cut the bamboo into rough batons, place in a pan and cover with plenty of salted water. Bring to the boil and simmer for a minute. Drain, cover with more salted water and bring back to the boil. Simmer for a minute, then carefully lift out a piece and taste – it should be nutty and pleasingly bitter. If it is unpalatably so, blanch again then let it cool in the water. The bamboo can be prepared ahead of time, as it keeps well for several days in the refrigerator.
- To make the fish dumplings, puree the fish flesh to a fine paste in a small food processor. (As an optional refinement, pass the fish through a fine sieve to remove any fibres, then return the fish to the food processor and blend once again to develop the protein as much as possible.) Add the salt and then, one at a time, the ice cubes, processing until the fish has a silken sheen and a firm, resilient texture. Transfer the fish to a bowl and, using wet hands, gather it into a ball and slap it against the sides of the bowl to further develop the protein until it becomes even firmer – about a minute or so.
- Have a large bowl of iced water to the side. Using wet hands, scoop up a ball of the fish that can be comfortably held in the palm of the hand. Roll it smooth, then squeeze some of the paste through the thumb and index finger to form an elongated oval, bringing the finger and thumb together to pinch the dumpling. Scoop off a small ball – about 1 cm (½ in) – with the index and middle fingers of the other hand; the more scrupulous may want to use a spoon to do this. Some cooks refine this process by rolling the ball to smooth it, but I prefer a rougher finish. Drop the ball into the bowl of iced water. Repeat with the rest of the fish.
- Almost fill a large wok or pan with water then heat to barely simmering – about 60°C (140°F). Poach the fishballs until they float to the surface, then continue cooking for another 10 minutes. Carefully lift them out and immerse in iced water. When they are completely cooled, drain well.
- To make the curry paste, in a dry, heavy-based frying pan, separately roast the coriander and cumin, shaking the pan, until aromatic. Grind to a powder using an electric grinder, along with the peppercorns and the mace or nutmeg. Using a pestle and mortar, pound the chillies with the salt, then add the remaining ingredients in the order they are listed, reducing each one to a fine paste before adding the next. Alternatively, puree the ingredients in an electric blender. You will probably need to add a little water to aid the blending, but try not to add more than necessary, as this will dilute the paste and alter the taste of the curry. Halfway through, turn the machine off and scrape down the sides of the bowl with a spatula then turn it back on and whiz the paste until it is completely pureed. Include any seeds, flowers or buds you find when cleaning the basil in the paste as well. Finally, stir in the ground spices.
- Heat 1 cup of the coconut cream and simmer for a moment. Add the curry paste and continue to simmer for 5 minutes, or until fragrant and slightly oily, stirring regularly to prevent it catching. Don't let the coconut cream separate too much: add a little water if it threatens to do so. Season with the fish sauce, moisten with the coconut milk and stock or water, then simmer gently for a further 5 minutes. I like to add a piece or two of lemongrass as it simmers, to help perfume the curry, removing them before serving. Add the kaffir lime leaves and the prepared bamboo, then add the fish dumplings, grachai and red or green chillies. Finish with the remaining ½ cup of coconut cream, the pounded scuds and the Thai basil, then leave to rest and ripen for several minutes.
- When serving, wrap each skein of noodles around four fingers to form a loose coil and place in a bowl, allowing a generous two skeins per person. Spoon the curry over the noodles.

NAHM PRIK PASTE

1 heaped tablespoon mung beans

3 bamboo skewers, soaked in water for 30 minutes

4 red shallots, unpeeled

4 garlic cloves, unpeeled

5 slices galangal

½ teaspoon Thai shrimp paste (gapi)

pinch of salt

1 coriander root, cleaned and chopped –
      about 1 teaspoon

3 tablespoons chilli jam (see opposite)

6 medium-sized raw prawns (shrimp),
      rinsed but not peeled

1 cup coconut cream

2 tablespoons shaved palm sugar

1–2 tablespoons tamarind water, to taste,
      plus 1 tablespoon extra

1 tablespoon fish sauce – more or less, to taste

1 kaffir lime, cut in half and seeds removed

2–3 tablespoons kaffir lime juice

1 tablespoon deep-fried shallots

1 tablespoon deep-fried garlic

5–10 deep-fried dried bird's eye chillies, to taste

600 g (1¼ lb) fresh kanom jin noodles
      or 500 g (1 lb) dried kanom jin noodles,
      reconstituted

ACCOMPANIMENTS

sprigs of Thai basil

trimmed bean sprouts

shredded banana blossom

deep-fried dried small chillies, with stems
      attached

sliced raw vegetables, such as green beans
      and cucumber

deep-fried vegetables (see opposite)

ขนมจีนน้ำพริก

KANOM JIN NAHM PRIK

PRAWN AND CHILLI JAM WITH KANOM JIN NOODLES

This rich and sweet sauce became popular in the nineteenth century. The oldest recipes are made with a large amount of ground mung beans, an unusual ingredient in Thai cooking. Some Thai cooks now substitute peanuts for the beans, while others mix whole or coarsely ground peanuts through the finished sauce. Peanuts alone, I'm afraid, do not offer the complexity that the beans give; however, they are undoubtedly more readily available in Thailand.

   This version is adapted from a recipe by Gobgaew Najpinij, a retired teacher from the Suan Dusit culinary college in Bangkok. It is slightly unusual in using chilli jam in the paste, but this creates a suave result. Older recipes use roasted chilli powder fried in oil, which is then added to the simmering paste. Kaffir limes are a defining seasoning and taste, giving a slightly bitter and aromatic tartness. However, they can be difficult to find so regular limes can be used, but it will be at some cost to the final outcome. This is a rich and luxurious sauce. It needs to be simmered for at least 15 minutes, and often quite a bit longer, until it has a nutty, meaty aroma from the mung beans.

- First make the paste. Soak the mung beans in plenty of cold water for about 30 minutes, then drain and let them dry for a while. Dry-fry them in a wok or pan, stirring and tossing throughout, until they are roasted and nutty. Grind to a fine powder with a pestle and mortar or an electric grinder, then set aside.

- Thread the shallots onto one bamboo skewer, the garlic onto another and the galangal onto a third. Wrap the shrimp paste in foil or banana leaf. Grill the skewers until the skin of the shallots and garlic is somewhat charred and the flesh tender. Simply flash the galangal as it will burn much quicker. The wrapped shrimp paste will take a little longer, but take care not to scorch it. Let everything cool before peeling the shallots and garlic and chopping the galangal. Using a pestle and mortar, pound these ingredients with the salt and the coriander root to a smooth paste. Stir in the ground mung beans and chilli jam. Scoop out this paste and put it into a small bowl.

- Bring 1 cup of salted water to the boil and poach the prawns until cooked. Remove the prawns (reserving the poaching liquid) and allow to cool before peeling and deveining them. Using a pestle and mortar, pound the prawn meat to a somewhat coarse paste. Strain the poaching liquid.

- Bring the coconut cream and ½ cup of the reserved poaching liquid to the boil and stir in the nahm prik paste. Simmer for about 10 minutes or so before seasoning to taste with the sugar, tamarind water and fish sauce. Add the kaffir lime halves. Taste the developing flavours: it should taste smoky, rich, salty and sweet. Continue to simmer until it is fragrant and its surface is dappled with oil: it must smell and taste cooked, nutty from the mung beans and rich from the chilli jam. Add the prawns, stir to prevent them clumping, then simmer until the film of oil returns to the surface – this should take another 5 minutes or so. During the cooking, it will probably be necessary to add a little water or poaching liquid if the sauce becomes too thick or oily.

- When the sauce is ready, stir through the extra tamarind water and the kaffir lime juice. It should now taste fragrantly sour, salty and sweet, yet slightly bitter and nutty. Sprinkle with most of the deep-fried shallots, garlic and chillies.

- To serve, wrap each skein of noodles around the fingertips to form a scroll and place in a bowl, allowing two skeins per person. Spoon over a generous amount of the nahm prik sauce, then sprinkle with the remaining deep-fried shallots, garlic and chillies. Serve with a few of the suggested accompaniments.

+ CHILLI JAM

Chilli jam is versatile. It is not only used as a component of nahm prik sauce but it can also be used as the basis for a stir-fry, to finish a hot and sour soup (dtom yam) or as a component in a salad dressing. As it lasts indefinitely in the refrigerator, I suggest you double this recipe and have it on hand. It will come in useful.

MAKES ABOUT ½ CUP

vegetable oil, for deep-frying
1 cup finely sliced red shallots
½ cup finely sliced garlic
2 slices galangal – optional
¼ cup dried long red chillies, deseeded, soaked in water for 10 minutes then drained and chopped
2 tablespoons dried prawns (shrimp), rinsed and dried
2–3 tablespoons shaved palm sugar
3 tablespoons thick tamarind water
good pinch of salt *or* about 1 tablespoon fish sauce

Pour the deep-frying oil into a large, stable wok or a wide, heavy-based pan until it is about two-thirds full. Heat the oil over a medium–high flame until a cooking thermometer reads 180°C (350°F). Alternatively, test the temperature of the oil by dropping in a cube of bread – it will brown in about 15 seconds if the oil is hot enough.

Deep-fry the shallots, garlic, galangal (if using) and chillies separately until the shallots and garlic are golden and the chillies crisp. Allow to cool. Using a pestle and mortar, pound the shallots, garlic and chillies, along with the galangal and dried prawns, to a fine paste. Alternatively, puree the ingredients in a food processor, moistening with some of the oil used for deep-frying (up to ½ cup) to facilitate the blending.

Transfer the mixture to a small saucepan and bring to the boil, moistening with 2–3 tablespoons of the deep-frying oil if none has already been added. Season with the palm sugar, tamarind water and salt or fish sauce. Simmer for a minute or so until it thickens a little, stirring regularly – but do not leave it over the heat for too long, otherwise the sugar may burn.

The resulting chilli jam should taste smoky, oily, sweet, sour and salty. It should be thick with a good layer of oil on the surface.

+ DEEP-FRIED VEGETABLES

BATTER
smallest pinch of lime paste
½ cup rice flour
2–3 tablespoons coconut cream
½ teaspoon salt

100 g (3 oz) Siamese watercress (water spinach), cleaned and cut into 3 cm (1¼ in) lengths
10 or so betel leaves, trimmed
50 g (2 oz) Asian pennywort, cleaned and stalks trimmed
6 snake (yard-long) beans, trimmed and cut into 3 cm (1¼ in) lengths
vegetable oil, for deep-frying

First make the batter. Dissolve the lime paste in ¼ cup of water and wait for about 15 minutes until it has completely precipitated. Drain off and reserve the lime water, discarding the sludgy residue.

Knead the flour with 2–3 tablespoons of plain water until quite firm. Rest for 30 minutes. Add the coconut cream, salt and 2–3 tablespoons of the lime water and combine to make a pancake-like batter. This can be made a few hours in advance and kept covered, but it may be necessary to dilute it with a little extra lime water or coconut cream as the flour swells and the batter thickens.

Prepare the vegetables, washing and draining them well.

Pour the deep-frying oil into a large, stable wok or a wide, heavy-based pan until it is about two-thirds full. Heat the oil over a medium–high flame until a cooking thermometer reads 180°C (350°F). Alternatively, test the temperature of the oil by dropping in a cube of bread – it will brown in about 15 seconds if the oil is hot enough.

Stir the batter, adding a tablespoon or two of lime water, if necessary, to restore it to a pancake-like consistency.

Working in batches, dip the vegetables in the batter, then deep-fry them until they are a light golden colour. Drain on paper towels.

The vegetables can be eaten hot or at room temperature – more likely the latter when on the streets.

Overleaf: Prawn and chilli jam with kanom jin noodles

DRESSING

1 cup white sugar

1 teaspoon salt

4 tablespoons fish sauce

5–6 bird's eye chillies (scuds), pounded
    or finely sliced

squeeze of lime juice

1 cup coconut cream

good pinch of salt

600 g (1¼ lb) fresh kanom jin noodles
    or 500 g (1 lb) dried kanom jin noodles,
    reconstituted

2 cups finely chopped pineapple, from
    about ¼ pineapple

1 cup shredded young ginger

1 cup shredded green mango, from
    about 1 small green mango

2–3 tablespoons sliced garlic – young,
    new-season garlic is best

½ cup coarsely ground dried prawns

5 or so bird's eye chillies (scuds), chopped –
    more or less, to taste

dash of fish sauce

KANOM JIN SAO NAHM

PINEAPPLE AND DRIED PRAWNS WITH KANOM JIN NOODLES

This is a clean, refreshing dish that was originally devised about 150 years ago, to be offered to monks in the hot season. However, it is now served in markets throughout Thailand year-round, especially during hot weather. It is particularly popular where pineapples are grown, around Phetchaburi and a little farther south.

All the ingredients are served at room temperature and a spoonful of each item – as much or as little as desired – is sprinkled over the noodles.

Some stalls offer variations such as tart, green hog apples (makrok) or sour cucumbers (madan) in place of the green mango, according to the season and the region. Some fancy cooks will even add some sour snakeskin pears (salak). I have come across old recipes that propose pomelo too, but I have never seen this on the streets.

- First make the dressing by simmering the sugar with 1 cup of water, the salt, fish sauce and scuds for a few minutes until slightly reduced. Remove from the heat and add the lime juice. As it cools, the dressing will thicken a little. It should taste quite sweet and salty and just a little tart and spicy. Allow to cool completely.
- Simmer the coconut cream with the pinch of salt until slightly thickened but not separated. Put to the side to cool.
- To serve, wrap each skein of noodles around the fingertips to form a scroll and place in a bowl, allowing two skeins per person. Top with the pineapple, ginger, green mango and sliced garlic. Spoon over the dressing and sprinkle with the ground dried prawns and chillies. Drizzle over a dash of fish sauce.
- To finish, spoon over the simmered coconut cream.

SAUCE

2 fresh long red chillies, deseeded

1–2 bird's eye chillies (scuds)

good pinch of salt

2 small coriander roots, cleaned

1 large garlic clove, peeled

⅓ cup white sugar

⅓ cup white vinegar

RED CURRY PASTE FROM PHETCHABURI

5 dried long red chillies

10 dried bird's eye chillies

good pinch of sea salt

1 tablespoon chopped galangal

2 tablespoons chopped lemongrass

1 teaspoon finely grated kaffir lime zest

1 tablespoon chopped grachai (wild ginger)

2½ tablespoons chopped garlic

1 teaspoon Thai shrimp paste (gapi)

300 g (9 oz) kingfish or Spanish mackerel fillet

small pinch of shaved palm sugar – optional

2 tablespoons fish sauce – or more, to taste

1 chicken egg – or, more authentically, ½ duck egg

2 heaped tablespoons finely sliced green, snake (yard-long) or wing beans

1 tablespoon finely shredded grachai (wild ginger)

6–8 kaffir lime leaves, finely shredded

pinch of salt

pinch of roasted chilli powder – optional

vegetable oil, for deep-frying

1–2 dried long red chillies

handful of holy basil or Thai basil leaves

600 g (1¼ lb) fresh kanom jin noodles
    or 500 g (1 lb) dried kanom jin noodles, reconstituted

sliced cucumber, to serve

ขนมจีนทอดมัน
ปลาเพชรบุรี

KANOM JIN TORT MAN PLAA PHETCHABURI

FISH CAKES FROM PHETCHABURI WITH KANOM JIN NOODLES

This is an unusual dish using kanom jin. It is generally found only around Phetchaburi, which lies on ancient trade routes to the south-west of Bangkok. Phetchaburi has a wonderful bustling old town, with a market that spills out along its roads every morning. Fish cakes are a popular market snack and, about 60 or 70 years ago, an inventive cook from the town combined them with kanom jin noodles.

The fish most commonly used for fish cakes in Thailand is the freshwater featherback fish (plaa graai). Its flesh has a firm springy quality when pureed, which gives the fish cakes their characteristic texture. However, around Phetchaburi and along the coast, a saltwater fish is also used, making kingfish or Spanish mackerel the best choice. Although most recipes say it is best to deep-fry fish cakes at quite a high heat, I find it is better to do so at a medium one. It ensures the cakes are tender and reduces their tendency to become rubbery as they cool.

- First make the sauce. Using a pestle and mortar, pound the chillies with the salt, coriander roots and garlic. Transfer to a small saucepan and simmer with the sugar and vinegar and ⅓ cup of water to make quite a thick syrup. It should taste sweet and sour and a little hot. If it seems too thick or tastes slightly undercooked, then add a little more water and simmer for a moment. Set aside. This can be made well in advance and refrigerated; it will keep for several days.

- Next make the curry paste. Nip off the stalks of the dried long red chillies then cut along their length and scrape out the seeds. Soak the chillies in water for about 15 minutes until soft. Drain the soaked chillies, squeezing to extract as much water as possible, then roughly chop them. Rinse the dried bird's eye chillies to remove any dust. Using a pestle and mortar, pound the chillies with the salt, then add the remaining ingredients in the order they are listed, reducing each one to a fine paste before adding the next. Alternatively, puree the ingredients in an electric blender. You will probably need to add a little water to aid the blending, but try not to add more than necessary, as this will dilute the paste and alter the taste of the curry. Halfway through, turn the machine off and scrape down the sides of the bowl with a spatula, then turn it back on and whiz the paste until it is completely pureed. Transfer to a bowl and set aside.

- Mince the fish flesh. Traditionally, the flesh is scraped away from the skin with the edge of a spoon. Place the fish in the mortar and pound until it is sticky yet firm. Have a bowl of salted water nearby to clean the pestle if the fish sticks to it too much. Or, for the more modern cook, the fish may be blended in a food processor. Return the curry paste to the mortar – or add it to the processor – and work it into the fish, then season with the sugar and fish sauce. Add the egg and work until everything is thoroughly incorporated. Stir in the beans, grachai and lime leaves.

- Check the seasoning. I try it raw, but the more squeamish can deep-fry a little to test the seasoning. It may need a little salt and chilli powder. Using slightly wet hands, shape the fish cake mixture into 2–3 cm (1–1¼ in) discs. An alternative is to gather large pinches of the mixture using fresh basil leaves.

- Pour the deep-frying oil into a large, stable wok or a wide, heavy-based pan until it is about two-thirds full. Heat the oil over a medium–high flame until a cooking thermometer registers 180ºC (350ºF). Alternatively, test the temperature of the oil by dropping in a cube of bread – it will brown in about 15 seconds if the oil is hot enough. Deep-fry the dried chillies until crisp and burnished, then lift out and drain on paper towels. Briefly deep-fry the basil leaves – be careful, as they can splatter when added to the oil. Set aside to drain.

- Now deep-fry the fish cakes – only a few at a time, turning them once or twice to promote even cooking. When they float to the surface and are slightly puffed and beginning to colour, continue to fry for a few more moments to ensure they are completely cooked. Drain on paper towels. Repeat with the remaining fish cakes.

- When serving, wrap each skein of noodles around four fingers to form a loose coil and place in a bowl, allowing a generous two skeins per person. Spoon over the sauce and sprinkle with the deep-fried chillies and basil. Serve with slices of cucumber.

NO

ON

เชียง

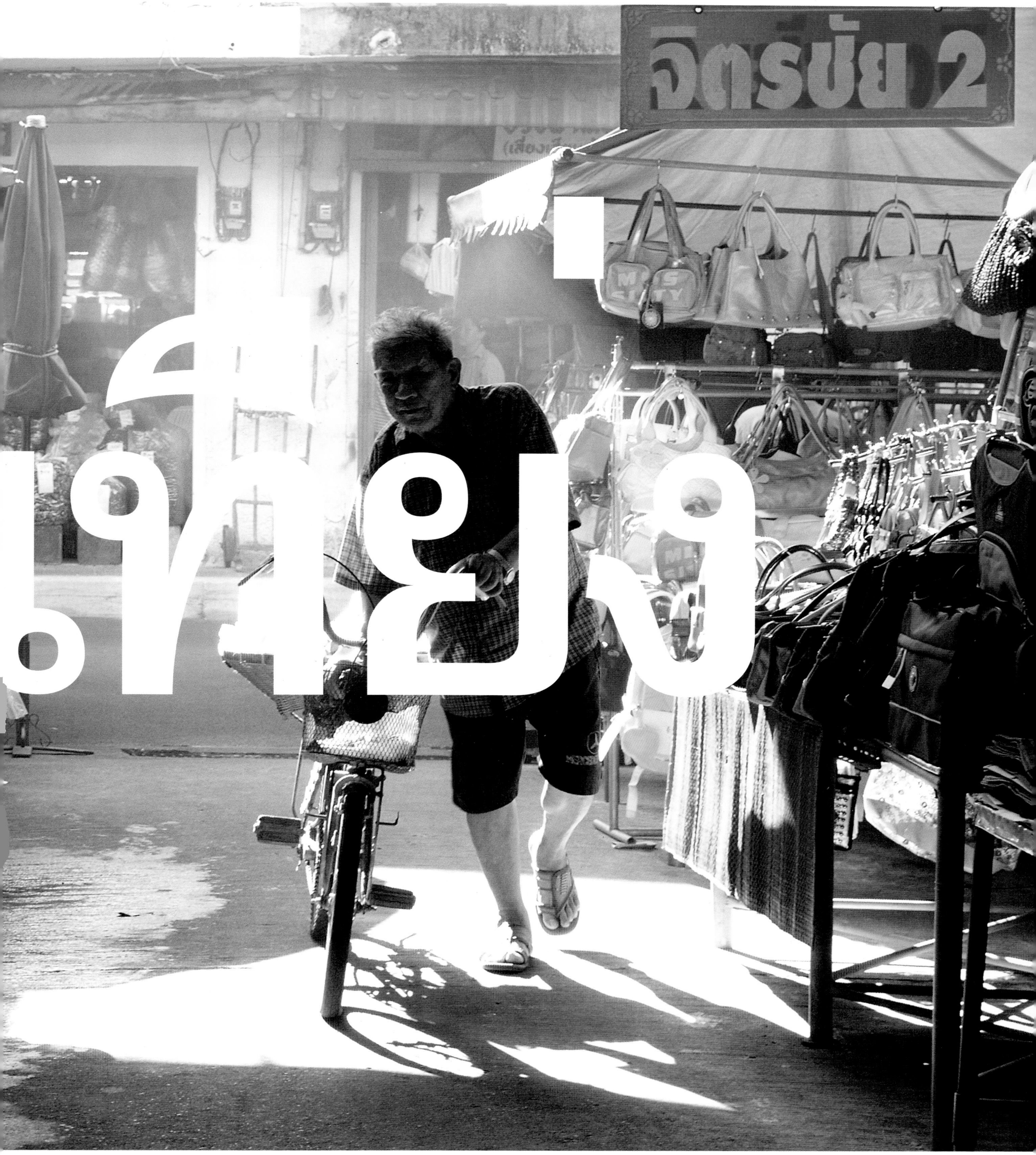

AS THE DAY HEATS UP, the markets fall into a lull. Most of the business is done, and much of the produce is sold. A few stalls remain open to serve latecomers and sell the remainder of their goods – all the locals know when the markets operate and which place will still have food late into the day. In the middle of the day, when it is infernally hot, a torpor creeps into the market. Covers are drawn, lights are dimmed, cats sleep and stallholders snooze. ○ It is not the end of the culinary day, though. As early as 10 a.m., the streets begin to fill with food vendors as they roll out their carts in preparation for the lunch and afternoon crowds. Noodle shops open up their shutters and owners peep out into the hectic streets, wondering what the day will bring. Their stocks begin to simmer and, behind the scenes, perhaps some meat is being roasted, ready to be hung invitingly behind glass panes later. Batches of dumplings are made, and coriander and spring onions are chopped. More kanom jin noodles are rolled and placed on banana leaves; lemon basil, bean sprouts and other vegetable garnishes are washed and trimmed; and the sauces are cooked and poured into waiting terracotta jars. Curry shops display their pyrotechnic wares, with golden pineapple, sour orange, and green and red curries filling trays and bowls to the brim. Small grills are stoked and smoke begins to rise as satays, pork skewers or marinated chickens gently cook. Heavy cast-iron pans are heated, ready to fry crispy mussel omelettes or plump yam bean cakes.

Previous page: The markets are a cool haven from the torrid midday sun – this large market in Chanthaburi contains many welcome delights.

○ Sweet treats start to be seen too – and this brings joy to the Thai's heart. Trays of vivid green pandanus cake, steamed in the early morning, sit cool and settled, waiting to be consumed. A bowl of pandanus noodles with black sticky rice might help to quell the growing heat of the day. One of the best carts that rolls out to see the harsh light of day is the one containing fruit – it's more of a glass display case on wheels really. It is filled with ice to chill down its luscious contents: small sweet pineapple, smooth-tasting papaya or crisp succulent green mango. The fruit is peeled and, when an order is received, sliced up into bite-sized slithers. You'll always be asked if you want 'prik gap gleua' – that is, some salt mixed with chilli powder and the odd bit of ground dried prawn – into which to dip the pieces of fruit. ○ All seems to spill out from the mouth of the markets and onto the surrounding streets. As the day progresses, the stalls move farther away from the markets, often leaving them altogether as they stretch into adjacent alleyways. Large colourful umbrellas offer shade from the sun, and shelter from the rain – a kaleidoscopic canopy for myriad tastes. In the modern business centre of Bangkok, the stalls segue into malls – located in the basement or on the upper floors of skyscrapers. Sanitary, air-conditioned and safe, they are a perfect way for the more inexperienced to sample street food. But they offer little of the colour and chaos, full flavours and sheer exuberance that are to be found in the tasty world of the street.

อาหารกลางวัน
LUNCH
ARHARN GLANG WAN

Lunch is a fast affair. Around midday battalions of office and factory workers pour into the streets, searching for food. For most Thais, lunchtime means heading towards the local market or to a favoured stall to see what's on the carts. It is when there is the greatest variety of food available: curries, noodles, salads and sweets. Snacks abound for those who can't wait or have little time – spring rolls, prawn cakes and irresistible grilled pork skewers are ready to go. There will still be the remnants of the morning's snacks available, with the possibility of some early afternoon traders wheeling out their wares.

But being Thai, most will allow themselves at least an hour for the pursuit of lunch. Every Thai will have a mental map of good places to eat – nearby there are bound to be several exemplary if unprepossessing shops or stands offering good food, making the day's foray worthwhile. Perhaps fried rice with crab, salted fish, cured pork or a little shredded chicken tossed in a battered old wok by an equally time-worn old cook. Or a stall seasoning steamed rice with shrimp paste, then serving it with various garnishes, such as sweet pork, eggs, green mango and a side plate of refreshing vegetables to make a very Thai lunch. Another place will sell a rich and meaningful green curry of braised beef with a terrifying amount of Thailand's favourite chillies, scuds, served with some freshly made roti. There will be several noodle stalls too, with one or two no doubt selling the noodle dish par excellence, pat thai.

A large wooden pestle and mortar will indicate the stand that sells green papaya salad (som dtam). This sweet and sour dish of the shredded fruit with dried prawns, tomatoes, beans and chillies is the favourite fast food of north-easterners who have come to work in the city. And then of course there are the sweets . . .

Such favoured places are often found along the narrow side alleys that sprout off the main street, many of them too small to go anywhere. Few cars can squeeze down them, but they are congested nonetheless – jammed full with stools, stalls, spluttering motorbikes and diners – for they lead to lunch. The vendors are primed and at the ready, waiting for the horde's onslaught.

During the lunch hour it is wise not to disturb Thais. It is also street-smart to avoid the food alleys, which can become frantically busy. The midday meal is taken quite seriously and, since time is short, quite urgently too. This is one time when it is better not to get in the way of the otherwise-patient Thais! By 2 p.m. the rush of lunch is done and it is safe to wander once again.

Some of the early openers begin to wind up their day and wearily wend their way home. They close when they run out of food, since they usually only prepare enough for the day, ensuring that everything is fresh, made for that day alone. Their day finishes with lunch.

○ Before school, after school or shirking it, noodles are de rigueur.

FILLING

5 small dried shiitake mushrooms, rinsed

1 teaspoon oyster sauce or light soy sauce

50 g (2 oz) dried glass (bean thread) noodles

2 garlic cloves, peeled

good pinch of salt

2 tablespoons vegetable oil

¼ cup minced raw prawn (shrimp) meat – from
    about 100 g (3 oz) raw prawns (shrimps)
    in their shells – or ¼ cup minced (ground) pork

¼ cup bean sprouts, trimmed

½ tablespoon white sugar

good pinch of ground white pepper

1 tablespoon light soy sauce

½ tablespoon fish sauce

¼ cup chopped spring (green) onions

¼ cup chopped coriander

4 tablespoons tapioca flour

about 12 large fresh spring-roll
    skins – approximately 8 cm (3 in) square

vegetable oil, for deep-frying

a few leaves Chinese lettuce

1 small cucumber, trimmed and sliced

1–2 large sprigs Thai basil

plum dipping sauce (see below), to serve

+ PLUM DIPPING SAUCE

I prefer my plum sauce not to be too spicy,
so I tend towards the lower scale of heat,
but you can increase the chilli if you wish.
In Thailand this sauce is left unrefrigerated,
but if you want to keep it for several days
it would be wise to chill it.

¼–½ long red chilli, to taste

1 teaspoon salt

3 tablespoons white sugar

3 tablespoons white vinegar

¼ cup Chinese plum sauce

Deseed the chilli, then chop it roughly and,
using a pestle and mortar, pound it to a
fine paste with the salt. Transfer to a small
pan, together with the sugar, vinegar, plum
sauce and ¼ cup of water. Simmer, stirring
occasionally, for about 10 minutes or until
the sauce is quite thick and the chilli has
lost its raw heat. Allow to cool then check
the seasoning: the sauce should taste sweet,
plummy, hot, sour and a little salty.

ปอเปี๊ยะทอด

POPIA TORT

DEEP-FRIED SPRING ROLLS

The best spring rolls are small, golden and crunchy – in fact, they are mostly pastry with just a little filling. Try to find chilled rather than frozen spring-roll skins, as the latter colour unevenly and absorb more oil as the rolls deep-fry.

I like prawns in my spring rolls, but on the street minced pork is more common. I have seen one or two versions that add a little shredded yam bean and bamboo to the filling, with delectable results. Thais can buy freshly made glass noodles (also called bean thread noodles), but elsewhere the dried version is readily available in Chinese shops.

Some stalls will serve their spring rolls cut into two or three pieces, making them easier to eat and also showing off the crispness of the skins. Most will offer a few fresh vegetables alongside, to give a contrasting texture and cut through any oiliness.

- First make the filling. Place the shiitake mushrooms in a small pan with a cup of water and the oyster sauce or soy sauce and simmer until tender – about 5 minutes. Allow them to cool in the liquid, if time permits, then remove the stalks and slice the mushroom caps finely; reserve the cooking liquid. Soak the noodles in warm water for about 15 minutes until pliable. Drain, then cut into 4 cm (1½ in) lengths with scissors. Crush the garlic to a somewhat coarse paste with the salt – either by pounding it using a pestle and mortar or finely chopping it with a knife.
- In a small wok or frying pan, heat the oil and fry the garlic paste over a medium heat until golden, then add the minced prawns and cook for a moment before adding the sliced shiitake mushrooms and simmering for a minute. Now, turn up the heat and add the noodles. If the noodles are not quite soft enough, add a tablespoon or two of the mushroom-cooking liquid and simmer until the noodles are soft and the mixture is quite dry again. Add the bean sprouts, then season with the sugar, pepper, soy sauce and fish sauce. Stir through the spring onions and coriander, then remove from the heat and put to one side to cool completely.
- Make a thick slurry by mixing the flour with 2 tablespoons of water. Lay a spring-roll skin on the bench and place a heaped teaspoon of the filling in a line along its centre. Roll the skin tightly around the filling, folding in the sides halfway through to form a parcel, then continue to roll to the end, sealing the edge with the slurry. Repeat until all the filling is used, keeping the finished spring rolls covered with a clean, slightly damp cloth.
- Pour the deep-frying oil into a large, stable wok or a wide, heavy-based pan until it is about two-thirds full. Heat the oil over a medium–high flame until a cooking thermometer registers 180°C (350°F). Alternatively, test the temperature of the oil by dropping in a cube of bread – it will brown in about 15 seconds if the oil is hot enough. Deep-fry the spring rolls, a few at a time, turning constantly so they cook evenly, until the skin is golden and crunchy.
- Serve with lettuce, cucumber and Thai basil on the side and with plum dipping sauce.

300 g (9 oz) pork loin or neck
50 g (2 oz) pork back fat (fatback) – optional

MARINADE
1 teaspoon cleaned and chopped
 coriander roots
pinch of salt
1 teaspoon chopped garlic
½ teaspoon ground white pepper
2 tablespoons shaved palm sugar
dash of dark soy sauce
2 tablespoons fish sauce
2 tablespoons vegetable oil

12–15 bamboo skewers
3 pandanus leaves – optional
about ¼ cup coconut cream

หมูปิ้ง
MUU
BING

GRILLED PORK SKEWERS

I am addicted to these. Along the street there are small grills, often just a large metal bowl with a rack perched on top. I'll stop and look and long for the fruits of their labour – smoky grilled skewers of pork. I'll smuggle some home as if carrying a guilty secret to relish in private. Sometimes, most of the time, I'll break into the cache on the way home.

Grilling is one of the more popular techniques of the streets, where there are many ad hoc pieces of equipment and the grill is one of the most common. They are everywhere, grilling pork, satays, dumplings and squid. Using a charcoal grill imparts a depth of flavour that makes meat such as this grilled pork irresistible. It is important to light the grill 30–60 minutes before using and allow the coals to burn until they glow gently. If you have a charcoal grill you'll know how long it takes to get to the right stage. Grilling over too high a heat will char and burn the pork before it is cooked and smoky.

Very often there will be a small piece of pork fat at the bottom of the skewer. This helps to moisten the pork as it grills.

The Thais use mangrove charcoal from near the mouth of the Chao Phraya River. Not everyone has a charcoal grill, however, and these pork skewers can also be cooked on a chargrill plate (ridged griddle) on the stovetop or under a preheated grill (broiler). While the taste will be less complex, they will still be extremely agreeable.

- Slice the pork into thinnish pieces about 2 cm (1 in) square. Cut the pork fat, if using, into small rectangles, say 2 cm × 5 mm (1 in × ¼ in).
- Next make the marinade. Using a pestle and mortar, pound the coriander root, salt, garlic and pepper into a fine paste. Combine with the sugar, soy sauce, fish sauce and oil. Marinate the pork and fat in this mixture for about 3 hours. The more cautious can refrigerate this but, if doing so, then it is best marinated overnight.
- It's a good idea to soak the bamboo skewers in water for about 30 minutes. This prevents them from scorching and burning as the pork grills. Some cooks like to use a brush made out of pandanus leaves to baste the pork. To make a pandanus brush, fold each pandanus leaf in half then trim to make an even edge. Cut up into the trimmed ends four or five times to make the brush's 'bristles'. Tie the pandanus leaves together with string or an elastic band to make a brush. Of course a regular brush will do too.
- Prepare the grill. Meanwhile, thread a piece of pork fat, if using, onto the skewer first followed by two or three pieces of the marinated pork. Repeat with each skewer. When the embers are glowing, in fact beginning to die, gently grill the skewers, turning quite often to prevent charring and promote even caramelisation and cooking. Dab them with the coconut cream as they grill. This should make the coals smoulder and impart a smoky taste. Grill all the skewers.
- On the streets, they are simply reheated over the grill to warm them through before serving, although this is not entirely necessary as they are delicious warm or cool.

1–3 long red chillies, deseeded and chopped
good pinch of salt
½–1 garlic clove, peeled
½ cup white vinegar
½ cup white sugar
2 tablespoons roasted and ground peanuts

Use a pestle and mortar to pound the chillies with the salt, then add the garlic and pound to a smooth paste. Scrape the paste into a small pan, along with the vinegar and sugar, and simmer until thick. Allow to cool before stirring in the peanuts.

MAKES 4–5 CAKES

BATTER
very small pinch of lime paste
1 cup rice flour
¼ cup coconut cream
1 teaspoon salt

vegetable oil, for deep-frying
3 heaped cups – about 600 g (1¼ lb) – small raw
    prawns (shrimp), rinsed and drained, whiskers
    trimmed or 1 kg (2 lb) raw prawns (shrimp),
    peeled and chopped
1 tablespoon chopped coriander
sweet chilli and peanut sauce (see right), to serve

ก้งฝอยทอด

GUNG FOI TORT

CRUNCHY PRAWN CAKES

A large wok filled with hot oil waiting to be filled with crunchy cakes of prawns is the tell-tale sign of this stall; often the same place sells fish cakes, with piles of both ready and waiting for the customer to come. Small prawns, such as school prawns, are best for this dish, as there is no need to peel them. For the unconvinced, peeled prawns will do – although the cakes will be less crunchy and toothsome. Try to find small prawns or, failing that, chop them.

○ First make the batter. Dissolve the lime paste in just over ⅓ cup of water and wait for about 15 minutes until it has completely precipitated. Drain off and reserve the lime water, discarding the sludgy residue. Knead the flour with ¼ cup of water to form quite a firm dough. Rest for 30 minutes, then combine the coconut cream, ¼ cup of the lime water and the salt and work into the dough. It should now have a thick, pancake-like consistency. If the batter is left to stand for some time, it may be necessary to dilute it with a little extra lime water or coconut cream as the flour swells.

○ Pour the deep-frying oil into a large, stable wok or a wide, heavy-based pan until it is about two-thirds full. Heat the oil over a medium–high flame until a cooking thermometer registers 180ºC (350ºF). Alternatively, test the temperature of the oil by dropping in a cube of bread – it will brown in about 15 seconds if the oil is hot enough.

○ Check the texture and seasoning of the batter by dropping a spoonful of it into the waiting oil. Deep-fry for a moment and then lift out with a spider. Drain and allow to cool slightly, then taste: it shouldn't be too dry or firm and it must be pleasingly salty. Adjust the batter with a little more lime water or salt, as necessary.

○ Mix half the prawns with about half the batter. Using a large spoon, carefully drop spoonfuls of the batter into the hot oil: this amount of batter should make 2 or 3 cakes. Deep-fry the prawn cakes until golden, turning two or three times to ensure even cooking and colour. Lift out with a spider and drain on paper towels. Repeat with the remaining prawns and batter.

○ Sprinkle with the coriander and serve with a bowl of sweet chilli and peanut sauce.

BATTER

¼ cup mung bean flour

2 level tablespoons rice flour

good pinch of salt

vegetable oil, for frying

¼ cup shelled raw mussels – from about
    500 g (1 lb) mussels in their shells

1 tablespoon chopped spring (green) onions

1 egg, lightly beaten

1 garlic clove, finely chopped with a smidgen of salt

1 cup bean sprouts, trimmed

1 tablespoon fish sauce

pinch of white sugar

ground white pepper

good pinch of coriander leaves

small bowl of sauce Siracha, to serve

หอยทอด

HOI MALAENG PUU TORT

CRUNCHY OMELETTE OF MUSSELS

For this to be a success, the mussels must be shelled raw. This can be done with a shucking knife, in the same way as you would open oysters. In fact, oysters were probably the original molluscs used in this dish, which first arrived with Chinese immigrants from Hainan a century or more ago. Oysters are still a popular alternative.

The winning feature of this dish is the contrasting crispness of the batter with the soft rich eggs and the toothsomeness of mussels and bean sprouts.

A flat, heavy-based frying pan or skillet is best to make this omelette. Street vendors use a large cast-iron pan with raised sides that is always hot and ready to go, and they often cook three or four omelettes at once. They also use an astonishing amount of oil – up to half a cup per portion – during the cooking. The omelette is almost shallow-fried, although most of the oil is drained off before serving.

I sometimes think this dish is made for sauce Siracha, as the two complement each other perfectly. Sauce Siracha is a wonderful chilli sauce that is available in all Asian shops. It takes its name from a seaside town on the eastern coast of the Gulf of Thailand, where it was created to accompany the seafood that is so prevalent and so delicious in that region. I recommend you buy a good version from that area. Try a few to see which one you prefer. I like a mildly spiced one, which allows me to eat more of it with this omelette.

I also think this is best cooked a portion at a time, so the recipe is for one only. To make more servings, just multiply the quantities accordingly.

- Make the batter by mixing the flours with the salt and ¼–½ cup of water. Make sure there are no lumps and that the batter is not too thick – it should have a pancake-like consistency.
- Heat a heavy pan until quite hot (a wok will not do). Add 3 tablespoons of oil and swirl it around the pan. Stir the batter well, as it may have separated slightly. Test that the oil is hot enough by adding a drop of batter: if it sizzles, pour in ⅓ cup of the batter and swirl the pan to form a rough semi-circle. Scatter over the mussels and a pinch of the spring onions. Cook over a medium–high heat until the batter begins to colour and crisp at the edges. Shuffle the pan to prevent the batter from sticking and, once it is crisp, use a spatula to break it up into two or three pieces. Add another tablespoon of oil, drizzling it around the rim of the pan to ensure that it is hot by the time it reaches the batter. Pour in the egg – mostly where there is little or no batter, but making sure that a little of it goes onto the pieces of batter.
- As the egg begins to set, use the spatula to break it up and fold everything over and around. Once the egg has cooked, but not overly so, and the batter is coloured and crisp, break up the omelette into three or four pieces before sliding them to one side of the pan. Add yet another tablespoon of oil and, when it is hot, fry the garlic until fragrant and beginning to colour, then add the bean sprouts and, after a moment, the fish sauce, sugar and a pinch of pepper. Mix to incorporate then fold over the omelette.
- Serve sprinkled with the remaining chopped spring onions and another pinch of pepper, accompanied by a bowl of sauce Siracha.

SERVES 2–3

1 tablespoon cleaned and chopped
    coriander roots
1 garlic clove, peeled
pinch of salt
2 tablespoons vegetable oil
1 heaped tablespoon Thai shrimp paste (gapi)
2 cups cooked jasmine rice
1½ tablespoons white vinegar
about 1 tablespoon white sugar, to taste

ACCOMPANIMENTS
2–4 lime wedges
sweet pork (see right)
½ cup dried prawns (shrimp), rinsed – if *too* dried,
    soak for about 3 minutes in warm water to
    soften, then drain
1 cup shredded green mango, from about
    1 small green mango
2–3 red shallots, somewhat coarsely sliced
2 small stalks lemongrass, finely sliced
1 tablespoon coriander leaves
2–4 bird's eye chillies (scuds), finely sliced –
    less for the timid
1–2 salted duck eggs, boiled for 15 minutes,
    shelled and cut in half
cha-om or plain omelette (see right)
raw vegetables, such as sliced cucumber,
    sliced white turmeric, green beans and
    Chinese cabbage

+ SWEET PORK

This pork can be made a few hours in
advance but should be kept warm, to ensure
the meat remains soft.

100 g (3 oz) pork belly
3 tablespoons shaved palm sugar
½ tablespoon fish sauce
1 point star anise – optional
2 red shallots, sliced and deep-fried – optional

Blanch the pork in simmering water until
cooked – about 10–15 minutes – then let it
cool before chopping into 1 cm (½ in) pieces.
Melt the sugar in a small pan, add the pork,
fish sauce and star anise (if using) and simmer
very, very gently, covered, until the pork is dark
golden but still tender. This can take half an
hour or even longer. If the sugar boils, it could
burn and will certainly toughen the meat,
so be sure to cook this over the lowest possible
temperature. If the sugar begins to caramelise
or the pork is not covered by the liquid, then
add a tablespoon of water (this will evaporate
as the pork simmers). Once the pork is ready,
stir in the deep-fried shallots, if using.

+ OMELETTE

Cha-om is a delicate, edible fern with a robust
mineral taste and robust aroma. If it is not
available, make a simple herbless omelette
and shred it finely when it is cool.

1 egg
¼ cup picked cha-om
pinch each of salt, white sugar and
    ground white pepper
1 teaspoon vegetable oil

Mix the egg into the cha-om and season with
salt, sugar and pepper. Heat a small shallow
pan and smear with the oil. Pour in the egg
and cook gently, trying not to let it colour too
much. When the omelette is just set, remove
from the pan and allow to cool before cutting
it into 2 cm (1 in) squares.

ข้าวคลุกกะปิ
KAO KLUT GAPI

RICE SEASONED WITH SHRIMP PASTE

This is a wonderful and easy lunchtime dish. On the streets, it is made several hours in advance, but
I find it is at its best about 30 minutes after being made – just long enough for it to cool down and settle.
If making this ahead of time, keep covered in a warm place to prevent the rice from drying out.

There are many versions of this dish, but this is perhaps one of the most simple and pure. It relies
upon the quality of its ingredients. Shrimp paste or gapi is the soul of Thai cooking. It is at the heart of
many dishes, giving depth and body to any dish in which it is used. Dark and rich, it has an earthy quality
despite being made from fermented prawns. Some commercial pastes are harsh, too salty and acrid
tasting. Try to find a good-quality one, which should be fecund and sweet to taste.

○ Using a pestle and mortar, pound the coriander roots, garlic and salt to a fine paste. In a small pan or wok,
  fry the paste in the oil until fragrant but not coloured. Add the shrimp paste and simmer gently, stirring
  attentively, until all is aromatic. Make sure the shrimp paste is well broken up and not in clumps.
○ Add the rice and stir gently but thoroughly with a wooden spoon to ensure the paste is well combined
  with the rice: the rice grains should remain whole and yet be fragrant and coated by the shrimp paste.
  Be careful not to let too much of the rice catch as it fries – although some always does. Season the rice
  with the vinegar and sugar (because of the salty shrimp paste, it's unlikely to need any salt). It should
  taste rich, pungent and aromatic and slightly salty, but should not be over-seasoned. Allow to cool for
  about half an hour.
○ Serve the rice with its accompaniments. To eat, divide the rice among individual plates. Squeeze over
  some lime juice and mix a little of the sweet pork, dried prawns, green mango, shallots, lemongrass,
  coriander and chillies, salted duck egg and omelette together. Eat with a few raw vegetables.

SPICE BAG

4 cm (1½ in) piece cassia bark

1 star anise

1 teaspoon coriander seeds

½ teaspoon cumin seeds

2 cardamom leaves or dried bay leaves

2 cloves

muslin (cheesecloth), rinsed and wrung out

PASTE

1 tablespoon cleaned and chopped coriander roots

large pinch of salt

3–4 garlic cloves, peeled

1 tablespoon chopped ginger

¼ teaspoon white peppercorns

2 tablespoons vegetable oil or rendered pork fat

300 g (9 oz) pork belly, cut into 2 cm (1 in) pieces

pinch of salt

1 tablespoon shaved palm sugar

1 tablespoon light soy sauce

1 teaspoon dark soy sauce

1 teaspoon five-spice powder

6 cups stock

2 pandanus leaves, knotted

2 hard-boiled eggs, shelled

100 g (3 oz) deep-fried firm bean curd

100 g (3 oz) blood cake – optional

100 g (3 oz) dried guay jap noodles (rice flakes)

1 tablespoon rice flour

100 g (3 oz) roast pork, chopped into small
pieces – optional, but highly desirable

GARNISH

2 tablespoons chopped spring (green) onions

2 tablespoons chopped coriander

2 tablespoons garlic deep-fried in oil or with
pork scratchings (see page 358)

1–2 large pinches of ground white pepper

fish sauce, white sugar, roasted chilli powder and
chilli sauce (see below), to serve

+ CHILLI SAUCE

4 fresh long orange or red chillies

1 bamboo skewer, soaked in water for 30 minutes

1 tablespoon cleaned and chopped coriander roots

salt, to taste – up to ½ teaspoon

2 garlic cloves, peeled

3–4 tablespoons white vinegar

1 teaspoon white sugar

Thread the chillies onto a skewer and grill until charred, then allow to cool. Using a pestle and mortar, pound the coriander roots with the salt and garlic, add the chillies and pound to a very coarse paste, then stir in the vinegar and sugar. Steep the sauce for several hours before serving, to allow the flavours to develop. Keeps for several days refrigerated.

GUAY JAP NAHM KON

ROLLED NOODLES WITH PORK

A very Chinese affair, this was one of the first noodle dishes to make the leap into the Thai repertoire. There are two versions of the soup: one is a clear broth, similar to any noodle soup; the other, the one that follows, is dark, rich and aromatic. Both kinds were served to Chinese workers in markets and factories for breakfast.

It is almost impossible to buy these noodles fresh outside the occasional Thai market – even in Thailand dried ones are most often used, and these are readily available outside of Thailand where they are known as rice flakes. Blood cake is available from most butchers down in Chinatown. It is steamed pork blood, which sounds appalling but is surprisingly pleasant once you are accustomed to it. Sometimes it's referred to as black bean curd.

Pork liver, lung, stomach and intestines usually form a part of the authentic dish. Once cleaned, these are boiled in water with some sliced galangal, coarsely ground white pepper and a few kaffir lime leaves and pandanus leaves until tender. This can take as long as 2 hours. The vendor will always ask what offal is preferred, popping in a few slices, but while it adds to the dish, it is not essential. Indeed, many Thais will decline the pleasure of having some innards added to their bowl of guay jap, as you might too. But few can resist the addition of a little roast pork: although this can be bought at most barbeque shops in Chinatown, I've included a recipe on page 296.

Chopsticks are not necessary to eat these small rolled noodles, and the soup is generally eaten with just a Chinese soup spoon.

- First make the spice bag. Gently toast each spice individually in a dry wok or frying pan until fragrant. Allow to cool then wrap in muslin (cheesecloth), securing the spices in the bag with a knot or a rubber band. Set aside.
- Next make the paste. Use a pestle and mortar to pound all the ingredients to a slightly coarse texture.
- Heat the oil and fry the paste until aromatic but not yet coloured. Add the pork belly and fry gently, turning often, until nicely coloured. Season with the salt, sugar, soy sauces and five-spice powder, and simmer for several more minutes until fragrant. Add the stock, spice bag and one of the pandanus leaves, and continue to simmer, skimming as required, until the pork is almost cooked – about 20 minutes.
- Add the eggs, bean curd and blood cake, if using, and simmer gently for about 20 minutes. Allow to cool before quartering the eggs, cutting the pork belly into fine slices, and the bean curd and the blood cake into small pieces.
- Meanwhile, prepare the noodles. Bring 2 cups of salted water to the boil in a medium pan with the remaining pandanus leaf, add the noodles and simmer for about 5 minutes until they are tender and have curled. Make a slurry by mixing the rice flour with 2 tablespoons of water, then stir this into the noodles and simmer very gently for another 4–5 minutes.
- Ladle the noodles and some of the thickened cooking liquid into each bowl. Cover with the chopped roast pork, eggs, bean curd and blood cake. Ladle over the stock and pork belly then sprinkle with the chopped spring onions and coriander, the deep-fried garlic with pork scratchings and the ground white pepper.
- Serve with bowls of fish sauce, white sugar and roasted chilli powder and the chilli sauce, to season the soup as preferred.

GREEN CURRY PASTE

1 teaspoon coriander seeds

generous ½ teaspoon cumin seeds

4 Thai cardamom pods *or* 2 green cardamom pods

10 white peppercorns

good pinch of grated nutmeg

20–30 small green bird's eye chillies (scuds) –
    about 1 tablespoon

1 long green chilli, deseeded and roughly
    chopped – optional

good pinch of salt

2 tablespoons chopped lemongrass

1 tablespoon chopped galangal

3 tablespoons chopped red shallots

2 tablespoons chopped garlic

1 teaspoon finely grated kaffir lime zest

2 teaspoons chopped turmeric

1 teaspoon cleaned and chopped coriander roots

½ teaspoon Thai shrimp paste (gapi)

2 cups coconut cream, plus 2–3 tablespoons extra

good pinch of salt

250 g (8 oz) beef – flank, brisket or rump –
    cut into 5 mm (¼ in) thick slices
    about 2 cm × 1 cm (1 in × ½ in)

1 stalk lemongrass, bruised

2 red shallots, bruised – optional

2 Thai cardamom pods *or* 1 green cardamom pod,
    roasted – optional

2 cm (1 in) piece cassia bark, roasted – optional

1 Thai cardamom leaf or dried bay leaf,
    roasted – optional

about 3 cups coconut milk or water

2–3 tablespoons fish sauce

3–4 kaffir lime leaves, torn into large pieces

pinch of roasted chilli powder, to taste

10–15 small green bird's eye chillies (scuds),
    to taste

roti (see opposite), to serve

โรตีจิ้มแกงเขียวหวานเนื้อ

ROTI JIM GENG KIAW WARN NEUA

GREEN CURRY OF BEEF WITH ROTI

This way of eating comes from the deep south of Thailand, where the sauce and a few morsels of meat from Muslim-style curries are served with roti. In Malaysia and Singapore, this is called roti chana; the following recipe is a Bangkok adaptation with a rich and spicy green curry. It is usually eaten as a mid-morning snack, rather than with rice at a curry shop.

Simmering the beef in coconut cream until it is soft and tender, leaving just a residue of oil, is an age-old technique, although one that is now somewhat uncommon. It is ideal for tougher cuts of meat – which, frankly, is most meat in Thailand – as it yields a supple, rich finish. Be careful that the coconut cream is not too heavy or oily; if necessary, add some water to lighten it and prevent it from separating. The beef can be braised in advance, but I find that it is best not to chill the cooked meat as it tightens and toughens the fibres. Fortunately, since the beef is effectively preserved in the coconut cream, it can be kept at room temperature for a few hours with little danger – aside from pilfering fingers.

For those who prefer fancy street food, the curry can be served with a plate of sliced cucumbers and sprigs of Thai basil.

- First make the paste. In a dry, heavy-based frying pan, separately roast the coriander, cumin and cardamom, shaking the pan to prevent the spices from scorching, until aromatic. Husk the cardamom, then grind to a powder with the coriander, cumin, peppercorns and nutmeg, using an electric grinder or a pestle and mortar.

- Using a pestle and mortar, pound the chillies with the salt, then add the remaining ingredients in the order they are listed, reducing each one to a fine paste before adding the next. Alternatively, puree the ingredients in an electric blender. It will probably be necessary to add a little water to aid the blending, but try not to add more than necessary, as this will dilute the paste and alter the taste of the curry. Halfway through, turn the machine off and scrape down the sides of the bowl with a spatula, then turn it back on and whiz the paste until it is completely pureed. Finally, stir in the ground spices.

- To braise the beef, simmer 1 cup of the coconut cream with the salt and, when it has thickened slightly and is beginning to separate, add the beef and lemongrass, along with the shallots and spices, if using. Moisten with some of the coconut milk or water and add a tablespoon of the fish sauce. Continue to simmer gently, stirring regularly, until the coconut is absorbed and the beef is tender yet still a little resilient: this should take about 20 minutes or so, but it will be necessary to moisten with more coconut milk or water during this time to prevent the meat becoming too dry. Be careful not to braise the beef until it is falling apart, or it will have a stringy texture. Once the beef is cooked, drain off the excess oil, keeping it for the next stage, and pick out the lemongrass and spices. Cover and set aside. Try to resist eating more than a few delectable slices of the beef – in fact, put it out of reach!

- Next make the curry. Heat a few tablespoons of the reserved oil with 1 cup of coconut cream and fry the paste over a medium heat for 5 minutes, stirring often to prevent it from catching. When it is rich and aromatic and quite oily, add 1–2 tablespoons of fish sauce and simmer for a minute before adding 1 cup of coconut milk or water. Simmer for 2–3 minutes before adding the beef and the kaffir lime leaves, then continue to simmer for another 10 minutes or longer – until the curry is quite thick, rich and creamy. It may be necessary to add some more coconut milk, stock or water. Check the seasoning – the curry should taste rich, hot, spicy and salty. Allow it to sit for 20 minutes or so.

- On the streets this curry would be eaten at room temperature – and it does taste better this way. If you prefer to reheat it, do so gently, adding the extra coconut cream, along with roasted chilli powder and scuds to taste. Serve with roti.

Making roti from scratch is a difficult task to master, and you may wish to buy some ready made – they won't be as good, but at least you won't go insane. When freshly made and cooked these are so good, however, that I feel it is worth risking a spell in the asylum! You could make half this recipe and have just enough to go with the green curry, but given the effort involved, it is worth making more than enough.

Try to find a soft flour (cake or pastry flour), as it will make for a more tender roti. It may be surprising to come across margarine in this context, but the best rotis are made with it – at least in Thailand. Using butter would make the rotis too rich, and they would reek of the dairy.

MAKES ABOUT 10

1 teaspoon salt

500 g (1 lb) cake or pastry flour – about 4 cups

1 large egg, lightly beaten – about 3 tablespoons

40 g (1½ oz) margarine, broken into
    1 cm (½ in) pieces

2 cups oil – ideally flavourless pure coconut oil
    (nahm man bua)

3 tablespoons chopped spring (green) onions

Mix the salt into 1 cup of water. Sieve the flour into a bowl and make a well in the centre. Add the egg, stirring to form a crumbly dough, then gradually work in the salted water. Knead for about 15 minutes until the dough is silken, soft and tender. Transfer to a large bowl rubbed with a smear of the margarine and leave to rest, covered, for an hour.

Roll the dough between cupped hands to make a large oval. Squeeze off small balls about 4 cm (1½ in) in diameter and roll with cupped hands to smooth their surface. There should be about 10 of them.

Return the dough balls to the bowl and cover in the oil dotted with the margarine pieces then leave to steep, covered and in a warm place (but not so warm that the margarine will melt), for at least 3 hours or overnight.

Oil the bench (work surface) and your hands well with some of the oil from the bowl. Take out one of the dough balls and press it against the bench with two or three fingers, spreading the dough to make a disk about 15 cm (6 in) in diameter. Now 'cast' the dough by holding one edge of the disk and, using a throwing motion and the weight of the dough itself, stretch it until it is as thin and film-like as strudel or filo pastry. Those less daring or dexterous can resort to a rolling pin!

Strew with a little of the chopped spring onion, then pick up one edge of the stretched pastry disk with one hand and drape it gently down into the palm of the other hand in a circular motion, twisting and rolling it from the centre of the palm outwards to form a snail-like pastry. Cover with a cloth and repeat the process with the remaining dough balls.

Next, flatten each 'snail' to make a disk about 10 cm (4 in) in diameter and 5 mm (¼ in) thick. Cook by frying in a heavy-based frying pan over a medium heat with a smear of the oil. Shuffle the pan to prevent the roti from sticking. Allow to cook and colour on one side before turning over and frying the other side with a little more oil. Often a small piece of the margarine is added to the pan to give the roti additional flavour. If you use a very large pan, you can cook two or three rotis at a time. Keep in a warm place while you cook the remaining roti, but do not cover lest they lose their crispness.

Once they are all cooked, cut each one into 3 or 4 wedges and serve. Have a piece yourself beforehand – you deserve it.

Overleaf: Green curry of beef with roti

3 garlic cloves, peeled

good pinch of salt

2 tablespoons roasted peanuts, coarsely crushed

2 tablespoons dried prawns, rinsed and drained

2 slices or small wedges of lime – optional

6 cherry tomatoes, quartered

2 snake beans, cut into 1 cm (½ in) lengths

4–6 bird's eye chillies (scuds), to taste

2 cups shredded green papaya, from
    about 1 small papaya

3–4 tablespoons shaved palm sugar, to taste

2–3 tablespoons fish sauce

2–3 tablespoons lime juice

1 tablespoon tamarind water

steamed rice and raw vegetables, to serve

ส้มตำมะละกอ

SOM DTAM MALAKOR

GREEN PAPAYA SALAD

There are many versions of this spicy north-eastern vegetable salad that is traditionally made, crushed and dressed in a wooden pestle and mortar: cucumber, green mango, green beans, pineapple or white guava are some options. The salad can be flavoured with salted land crabs, dried prawns or fermented fish (plaa raa).

The traditional way to shred a papaya, as seen on the streets of Bangkok, is to hold it in one hand while it is cut and shredded vigorously with a large, sharp knife held in the other hand. Every so often the knife is used to pare away the papaya, yielding a somewhat coarse, uneven shred. Many home cooks, however, use a hand-held grater. It is certainly easier and faster but the uniform cut means the papaya loses some of its rustic appeal.

A special pestle and mortar is used for making this salad: the terracotta mortar is deep and conical with tall sides that prevent splattering, and the pestle is made of wood. A more regular granite one will do, but beware of the tomatoes!

Green papaya salad is always eaten with rice: steamed sticky rice or occasionally jasmine rice dressed with coconut cream and sugar. A stall selling grilled pork or sweet pork can usually be found nearby – it is the perfect companion.

- Using a pestle and mortar, pound the garlic with the salt then add the peanuts and dried prawns and pound to a coarse paste. Add the lime (if using), bruising it with the pestle, then add the cherry tomatoes and beans to the mortar and carefully work everything together. Next add the bird's eye chillies, barely crushing them. The more they are pounded, the hotter the dish – and how hot you want it is up to you. Add them earlier if you're after revenge.
- Finally, add the green papaya and lightly bruise with the pestle, while turning and tossing the mixture with a large spoon held in your other hand. Season the salad with palm sugar, fish sauce, lime juice and tamarind water. It should taste sweet, sour, hot and salty.
- Place about 1 cup of steamed rice on each plate. Spoon over the green papaya salad and eat with fresh raw vegetables, such as cabbage, green beans and betel leaves.

SERVES 3–4

300 g (9 oz) beef rump or sirloin
2 tablespoons fish sauce or light soy sauce
pinch of salt
pinch of ground white pepper
pinch of white sugar
1 teaspoon coriander seeds, coarsely
    crushed – optional
vegetable oil, for deep-frying
chilli and tamarind sauce (see right), to serve

+ CHILLI AND TAMARIND SAUCE

5 bamboo skewers
6 dried long red chillies
2–3 dried bird's eye chillies
1 fresh long red chilli
4 red shallots, unpeeled
3 large garlic cloves, unpeeled
3 tablespoons tamarind pulp
2–3 tablespoons fish sauce – ideally maengdtaa
2 coriander roots, cleaned and chopped
pinch of salt
good pinch of white sugar
large pinch of roasted chilli powder

Soak the skewers in water for about 30 minutes. Nip off the stalks of the dried long red chillies then cut along their length and scrape out the seeds. Soak them, along with the dried bird's eye chillies, in water for about 15 minutes.

Meanwhile, heat a charcoal or gas grill, or place a large, heavy-based pan over a moderate heat.

Drain the dried chillies, squeezing to extract as much water as possible, then thread the fresh chilli, two types of dried chillies, red shallots and garlic onto individual skewers. Grill all the skewers: sear and slightly char the chillies; the shallots and garlic, which will take longer, must be soft. Allow to cool, then peel the shallots and garlic and deseed the fresh chilli.

Meanwhile, dissolve the tamarind in the fish sauce, squeezing with your hands to work the flesh away from the seeds and fibre. Strain.

Using a pestle and mortar, pound the coriander roots and salt to a paste. Add the chillies, then the shallots and garlic, pounding each to a fairly fine paste.

Stir in the tamarind-infused fish sauce and add the sugar. Check the seasoning: it may need to be lightened with a few tablespoons of water. Finish with the chilli powder. The sauce should be equally sour, hot and salty.

NEUA KEM TORT JIM JAEW

DEEP-FRIED SALTED BEEF WITH CHILLI AND TAMARIND SAUCE

Slightly salted and dried beef, grilled or deep-fried, was probably the way beef was first introduced into the Thai diet. Strips of salted meat were – are – left out in the sun to dry for a day or so, and the Thai name for salted beef, neua dtat dtiaw, literally means just that. Some cooks will sprinkle a few bruised coriander seeds onto the meat before it is dried.

I think the best cuts for this are rump or sirloin. I like a bit of fat attached, but that's because I like fat. Some might prefer a leaner cut, such as shoulder or blade.

The chilli and tamarind sauce is delectable. It can be served with any deep-fried meat or fish. I like to use maengdtaa fish sauce (made from rice roaches, bugs that scurry through the paddy fields), for its haunting aroma, but any good-quality fish sauce will do.

○ Cut the beef into pieces approximately 5 cm × 2 cm (2 in × 1 in) and about 5 mm (¼ in) thick. Marinate in the fish or soy sauce, salt, pepper and sugar for about 30 minutes only. Add the coriander seeds, if using.

○ Dry the beef in the sun for half a day, or longer if there are no clear skies . . . and in the oven overnight with the pilot light on if in a cold climate.

○ Pour the deep-frying oil into a large, stable wok or a wide, heavy-based pan until it is about two-thirds full. Heat the oil over a medium–high flame until a cooking thermometer registers 180°C (350°F). Alternatively, test the temperature of the oil by dropping in a cube of bread – it will brown in about 15 seconds if the oil is hot enough. Deep-fry the beef over a medium heat for about 4 minutes, turning the pieces to ensure even cooking.

○ Drain on paper towel and allow to cool slightly before slicing. Serve with steamed sticky or jasmine rice and chilli and tamarind sauce.

125 g (4 oz) fresh pat thai noodles *or* 100 g (3 oz)
    dried thin rice noodles (rice sticks)
3 tablespoons shaved palm sugar
2 tablespoons tamarind water
dash of white vinegar – optional
1 tablespoon fish sauce
3 tablespoons vegetable oil
4 red shallots, coarsely chopped with a pinch of salt
2 eggs – some cooks will use duck eggs
30 g (1 oz) yellow bean curd or firm bean curd,
    cut into small rectangles or squares –
    about 2 heaped tablespoons
1 tablespoon dried prawns, rinsed and dried
½ teaspoon shredded salted radish,
    rinsed and dried
1 tablespoon coarsely crushed roasted peanuts
handful of trimmed bean sprouts
handful of Chinese chives, cut into 2 cm
    (1 in) lengths
extra bean sprouts and crushed roasted peanuts,
    lime wedges, roasted chilli powder and raw
    vegetables (such as Asian pennywort, banana
    blossom, cabbage or snake [yard-long] beans),
    to serve

ผัดไท
PAT THAI

PAT THAI

Although widely associated with Thai cooking, this dish is in fact a relatively new addition to the repertoire, emerging during a period of ultra-nationalism in the late 1930s and early 40s, under the military regime of Field Marshal Phibun. He declared that the Thai people should endeavour to incorporate noodles into their eating habits, so competitions were held in schools, government offices and various nationalistic organisations to devise new noodle recipes, including the winning one that included tamarind and palm sugar. It was given the name pat thai, in keeping with the chauvinistic tenor of the times, and to distinguish it from Chinese noodle dishes, even though it has much in common with them – bean sprouts, bean curd, salted radish, Chinese chives and, of course, the noodles themselves.

Since then, pat thai's fame has spread and it is now considered a classic of the Thai kitchen – at least by Westerners, though it is definitely popular among the Thais too.

Thin, flat, quite chewy rice noodles are preferred here: fresh ones make a much better dish, but they are hard to find outside of Thailand. However, the dried version, also known as rice sticks, are readily obtainable.

There is now a gentrified version of pat thai that uses fresh prawns. If you want to stroll along boulevards rather than trawl the alleys, then add six medium-sized cleaned raw prawns as the shallots begin to fry – and omit the dried prawns called for later in the recipe.

- If using dried noodles, soak them in water for about 15 minutes until soft but not overly so. Meanwhile, bring a pan of water to the boil. Drain the noodles well then blanch them in the boiling water for a moment only and drain once again (this prevents the noodles from clumping together when they are stir-fried).
- Mix the palm sugar with the tamarind, vinegar (if using), fish sauce and 1–2 tablespoons of water in a bowl, stirring until the sugar has dissolved.
- Heat the oil in a wok over medium heat and fry the shallots until fragrant and beginning to colour. Crack in the eggs and stir for a few moments until they begin to look omelette-like.
- Turn up the heat, then add the drained noodles and fry for about 30 seconds while breaking up the eggs. Add the tamarind syrup and simmer until it is absorbed. Mix in the bean curd, dried prawns, salted radish and peanuts then simmer, stirring, until almost dry. Add the bean sprouts and Chinese chives and stir-fry for a moment.
- Check the seasoning: pat thai should be salty, sweet and sour. Divide between two plates and sprinkle with the extra bean sprouts and peanuts. Serve with lime wedges, roasted chilli powder and raw vegetables.

POACHING STOCK

about 4 cups chicken stock

½–1 teaspoon salt, to taste

2 tablespoons crushed yellow rock
sugar – optional

1 pandanus leaf, knotted

small piece dried tangerine or orange
peel – optional

2 garlic cloves, unpeeled

a few coriander stalks

2 cm (1 in) piece ginger

2 chicken breasts on the bone –
about 750 g (1½ lb)

good pinch of salt

1 tablespoon white vinegar

RICE

3 cups old jasmine rice or a mixture of jasmine
rice with 1–2 tablespoons white sticky rice

2 coriander roots, cleaned

good pinch of salt

2 garlic cloves, peeled

1 tablespoon sliced ginger

2 tablespoons rendered chicken fat (see below)
or peanut oil

1 pandanus leaf or a few pieces of crispy
chicken skin – optional

SOUP

salt, to taste

pinch of white sugar

200 g (6 oz) green Asian melon or bitter melon,
peeled, deseeded and cut into 2 cm (1 in)
pieces or 100 g (3 oz) pickled mustard greens,
rinsed and sliced

a little light soy sauce, to taste

sliced cucumber, coriander leaves, sliced
spring (green) onions, deep-fried garlic,
ground white pepper and yellow bean sauce
(see above right), to serve

+ RENDERED CHICKEN FAT

3–4 tablespoons chicken fat and skin

good pinch of salt

Rinse the fat and skin, then chop it roughly.
Place in a small pan, add the salt and
cover with water. Simmer until the fat has
rendered – about 10 minutes. When the
skin and fat are golden and the aroma is
rich and nutty, strain the rendered fat into
a metal bowl – you should have about
3 tablespoons. Keep it and the crispy chicken
skin separately.

+ YELLOW BEAN SAUCE

2–3 coriander roots, cleaned

small pinch of salt

3 garlic cloves, peeled

2 cm (1 in) piece ginger, peeled

3 tablespoons yellow bean sauce, rinsed

1 tablespoon white vinegar

pinch of shaved palm sugar

½ long yellow, green or red chilli, quite finely sliced

a little dark soy sauce, to taste

a little light soy sauce, to taste

1 teaspoon yellow bean sauce, unrinsed – optional

Using a pestle and mortar, pound the coriander
roots with the salt, then add the garlic and
ginger and continue pounding to a fine paste.
Stir in the rinsed yellow beans and moisten
with the vinegar. Add the sugar and, once
dissolved, stir in the sliced chilli and soy sauces
to taste. Check the seasoning – it should taste
richly salty, sour, hot and slightly sweet – and
adjust accordingly. If you find you need a little
more yellow bean flavour, add the teaspoon of
unrinsed yellow bean sauce.

KAO MAN GAI

CHICKEN AND RICE

This Hainanese dish arrived in Bangkok in the nineteenth or very early twentieth century with immigrants
from that region of China, and it is still usually sold by their descendants, mostly men. It is actually a suite
of dishes – chicken, rice, soup and a sauce – that are almost always served together.

Old rice is the best rice to use for this dish: it has a deeper flavour than regular jasmine rice, and it can
be found in most Chinese grocers. Rendered chicken fat reinforces the rich flavours in this dish. I really
recommend it; it is simple and you should have enough fatty offcuts to make it. However, I do have to
confess that this is unlikely to be done on the streets of Bangkok, where just plain old oil is used.

○ First make the poaching stock. Bring the chicken stock to the boil in a pan or stockpot and add
the aromatics.

○ Clean and trim the chicken breasts (keeping the fat and any excess skin for rendering, if desired), then
rub with the salt and vinegar – this will help to keep the skin white. Rinse and dry. Skim the simmering
stock, then add the chicken breasts and poach gently for 20 minutes or until cooked, not overly but
completely. Remove the chicken – reserving the stock – and allow to rest while you prepare the rice and
the soup. (Some stalls will plunge the chicken into iced water to arrest the cooking and firm the skin.)

○ Rinse the rice in several changes of water, then leave to drain. (Some cooks like to soak the rice for
about half an hour to leach out more of the starch.) Using a pestle and mortar, pound the coriander
roots to a fine paste with the salt, garlic and ginger. In a saucepan with a tight-fitting lid, fry the paste
in the chicken fat or oil until it is just beginning to colour, then add the drained rice and fry for another
minute or so, turning the rice gently so as not to break the grains. Pour in enough of the warm poaching
stock to reach from the surface of the rice to the first joint of your index finger. Bring to the boil, cover
with the lid, reduce the heat to low and simmer until the rice is cooked. Season the rice with a little
more salt, if necessary. Put to one side, covered, in a warm place for about 20–30 minutes. (Some cooks
like to bury a pandanus leaf in the rice as it sits; others add a few pieces of crispy chicken skin.)

○ To make the soup, bring the remaining poaching stock to the boil and season with salt and sugar. Add
the prepared melon (if using bitter melon, rub the pieces with some salt and leave for about 20 minutes
in a colander to leach out some of the bitterness, then rinse well) and simmer for 10–15 minutes until
completely cooked and truly tender. The soup should be well seasoned: add some more salt, if necessary,
and a little light soy sauce – but not too much as the soup should have a light and clear appearance.

○ Lift the chicken meat from the bone, trying to keep each breast as whole and well-shaped as possible.
I like to leave the skin on, but you might prefer to remove it. Cut the chicken into slices across the
grain on a slight diagonal. Place a mound of rice in each of four bowls, place several slices of chicken
on top and garnish with a slice or two of cucumber. Serve with a bowl of the soup sprinkled with
coriander leaves, sliced spring onions, deep-fried garlic and white pepper, and a small bowl of yellow
bean sauce alongside.

SERVES 2

2–3 garlic cloves, peeled

good pinch of salt

3–4 tablespoons vegetable oil – peanut is
    a good choice

2 eggs – ideally 1 duck and 1 chicken

2 cups cooked rice – freshly cooked and warm
    but not steaming hot

2–3 tablespoons light soy sauce

pinch of white sugar

pinch of ground white pepper

approximately 100 g (3 oz) cooked crabmeat –
    more, if feeling generous

3 spring (green) onions, trimmed and finely
    chopped

coriander leaves, lime wedges and cucumber
    slices, to serve

chillies in fish sauce (see below), to serve

Cooking fresh crab

To cook a live crab, despatch it humanely
by placing it in the freezer for about an hour,
then boil or steam the beast for 6–10 minutes
per kg (3–5 minutes per lb), depending on
the variety. The yield of crabmeat will be in the
region of 40–50 per cent of the weight of
the crab in its shell.

ข้าวผัดปู

KAO PAT BPUU

FRIED RICE WITH CRAB

This is a classic version of fried rice and one of the best. Fried rice made its debut on the streets of Thailand about 80 years ago. In the Chinese community, where fried rice has been eaten for much longer than this, it is traditionally one of the last dishes to be served at a celebratory banquet – say, for a wedding or to mark Chinese New Year – and so it has to be good to entice diners to take some.

Most authorities advocate allowing the cooked rice to cool completely, but I have found that if the rice is too cold it clumps – and forcing the clumps apart during frying breaks the rice grains. I actually prefer rice that is still slightly warm, ideally freshly cooked then left to cool for an hour or two. If it is too hot, the fried rice will be sticky; too cold, and it will be slightly tough and possibly marred by broken grains.

Some cooks say the best fried rice is made with an equal amount of duck and chicken eggs, and here's where the controversy begins: should the egg go in before the rice or afterwards? Each cook will have their own stance, but I believe the egg should go first. If the egg is added after the rice, I find it can make the fried rice gluey, sticky and heavy – especially if using a duck egg or two.

Blue swimmer crab has the sweetest meat so is the perfect choice for fried rice, but naturally almost any crabmeat will do. If you want the freshest most succulent crabmeat then you must cook and shell the crab yourself – it really does make a difference. Almost any other meat can be used, including fresh pork, chicken, prawns, Chinese barbeque pork or duck; if using raw meat or seafood, add them to the wok along with the garlic to ensure both are ready at the same time.

In Thailand, fried rice always comes with a few slices of cucumber and tomato as well as a few wedges of lime to squeeze over the rice. I like the refreshing crunch of the cucumber, and I think the lime is de rigueur, but I am not so convinced about the tomato.

+ CHILLIES IN FISH SAUCE

¼ cup fish sauce

5–10 bird's eye chillies (scuds), finely sliced

1 garlic clove, finely sliced – optional
    but desirable

good squeeze of lime juice – optional

good pinch of chopped coriander

Combine the fish sauce, chillies and garlic in a bowl and set aside. It keeps for some time – in fact it becomes richer and milder as it settles for a day. Make sure it is covered if you are making it in advance – and if the fish sauce evaporates, add an equivalent amount of water to refresh it. Just before serving, stir through the lime juice and coriander.

- Crush the garlic to a somewhat coarse paste with the salt – either by pounding it using a pestle and mortar or finely chopping it with a knife.
- Heat a well-seasoned wok over a low–medium heat and add about 2 tablespoons of the oil, then stir in the garlic paste and fry until it has lost its sharp raw aroma, has become nutty, and is just beginning to colour. Take care not to burn the garlic, as this would taint the fried rice and ruin it. Crack in the eggs and allow them to set slightly before stirring and scrambling, trying to keep them in quite large, soft curds. Be careful not to overcook the egg and so make it dry.
- Add the rice, turn down the heat to low and mix and toss the rice, frying it gently and ensuring that all the grains are lightly coated with egg and oil. If it seems too dry, dribble a little extra oil down the side of the wok, but don't overdo it – the oil should just coat the rice, not swamp it.
- Season with the soy sauce, sugar and pepper and continue to fry until the soy sauce is absorbed. Taste the rice: it should be gently seasoned, nicely but not overly salty and pleasingly rounded in flavour. Under-seasoning the rice will make it taste spare and hollow – add a little more soy sauce, if necessary. Now stir through most of the crabmeat and spring onions but reserve a little of both to sprinkle over the fried rice when serving.
- Divide the rice between two plates and sprinkle with the reserved crabmeat and spring onions. Serve with coriander leaves, some slices of cucumber and a wedge or two of lime, and accompany with a small bowl of chillies in fish sauce.

PASTE

2 coriander roots, cleaned and chopped

1 tablespoon chopped ginger

1 tablespoon chopped garlic

½ tablespoon chopped turmeric

good pinch of salt

2 heaped tablespoons curry powder for chicken
(see page 356) or other mild curry powder

2 tablespoons fish sauce

pinch of white sugar

about ½ cup yoghurt or sour milk

salt

3 chicken legs and thighs, each cut
into 3 or 4 pieces

vegetable oil or ghee, for deep-frying

½ cup sliced red shallots – about 8–10 red shallots

2–3 tablespoons ghee

2 cardamom leaves or dried bay leaves

3 cm (1¼ in) piece cassia bark, lightly roasted

2 Thai cardamom pods *or* 1 green cardamom pod,
lightly roasted

1 large tomato, cut in half, deseeded then
coarsely chopped

1 cup mint leaves, chopped

1 cup coriander leaves, chopped,
plus 1 tablespoon extra

3 cups old jasmine rice, rinsed and drained

4 cups chicken stock

good pinch of saffron, steeped in 3 tablespoons
warm water for a few minutes

1 pandanus leaf, knotted

cucumber slices and sweet chilli sauce (see above
right) or mint sauce (see below), to serve

+ MINT SAUCE

2–4 coriander roots, cleaned

pinch of salt

1–2 green bird's eye chillies (scuds)

2 slices ginger

1 slice galangal

2 cups coriander leaves, coarsely chopped

2 cups mint leaves, coarsely chopped

1–3 teaspoons white sugar, to taste

3–4 tablespoons white vinegar, to taste

Using a pestle and mortar, pound the
coriander roots with the salt and chillies.
Add the chopped coriander and mint and
continue to pound until smooth. Season to
taste with the sugar and vinegar. The sauce
should taste of the herbs, sweet and slightly
sour but not very hot at all.

+ SWEET CHILLI SAUCE

2 long red chillies, deseeded and roughly chopped

1–2 bird's eye chillies (scuds) – optional

good pinch of salt

2 small coriander roots, cleaned

1 large garlic clove, peeled

⅓ cup white sugar

⅓ cup white vinegar

Using a pestle and mortar, pound the chillies
to a paste with the salt, coriander roots and
garlic. Transfer to a small saucepan, add the
sugar, vinegar and ⅓ cup of water, then simmer
to make quite a thick syrup – this should take
about 5 minutes. If it threatens to become too
thick, add a few extra tablespoons of water.
Allow to cool before serving. The sauce should
taste sweet, sour and a little hot.

KAO MOK GAI

CHICKEN BRAISED IN RICE
WITH TURMERIC AND SPICES

This is a Thai version of a biryani, with its origins in the Moghul courts of northern India. It was bought
to South-East Asia by Muslim Indian merchants and became an important dish during times of feasting,
after festivals and Friday prayers.

Old rice is simply rice from last year's harvest. Almost all rice available in shops is of the current
vintage. It is fresh, sweet and soft in texture once cooked. However, there is usually some left over from
the previous harvest, and this old rice is slightly desiccated, is stronger in taste and has a slightly
different, less obvious aroma. It is also more resilient, and so is able to withstand the frying, boiling and
stirring entailed in this dish. Old rice is readily available from Chinese grocers – just ask for it. If you
can't find it, be extra careful when frying and cooking the rice so as not to break the grains.

This dish is always served sprinkled with deep-fried shallots and a bowl of sweet chilli or mint
sauce. On more formal occasions, it is accompanied by an oxtail soup.

- First, make the paste. Using a pestle and mortar, gradually pound the coriander roots, ginger, garlic
and turmeric with the salt to quite a fine paste. Stir in the curry powder. In a large bowl, mix half of the
paste with the fish sauce, the sugar, half of the yoghurt or sour milk and a pinch of salt. Add the chicken
and leave to marinate in the refrigerator for a few hours. Reserve the other half of the paste for later.

- Pour the deep-frying oil or ghee into a large, stable wok or a wide, heavy-based pan until it is about
two-thirds full. Heat the oil over a medium–high flame until a cooking thermometer registers 180°C
(350°F). Alternatively, test the temperature of the oil by dropping in a cube of bread – it will brown in
about 15 seconds if the oil is hot enough. Deep-fry the shallots until golden. Remove and drain, then
add the marinated chicken and deep-fry over medium heat until golden and aromatic. Drain.

- Heat the ghee in a heavy-based pan and briefly fry the remaining half of the paste with the cardamom
leaves or bay leaves, cassia bark and cardamom until fragrant. Add the tomato, mint and coriander and
fry for several more minutes until the tomato has broken down, but be careful not to let the paste catch
and burn. Add the chicken and the rice and fry for a moment, then pour in the stock. Add the saffron
water, pandanus leaf, half of the deep-fried shallots, the remaining yoghurt or sour milk and a pinch of
salt, stirring to scrape the bottom of the pan, but being careful not to break up the rice. Bring to the boil
then cover the pan, turn down the heat to very low and cook for about 20–25 minutes. When the rice
is cooked, so too should the chicken be. Very gently lift and turn the rice to incorporate anything
caught on the bottom of the pan – these caramelised bits have the richest taste as long as they are not
truly burnt black. Allow to rest, covered, for at least 30 minutes or even longer; it improves decidedly
with time. Taste the rice – it may need a little salt.

- Sprinkle with the remaining deep-fried shallots and the extra coriander. Serve with sliced cucumber
and a bowl of sweet chilli sauce or mint sauce.

PASTE

12 dried long red chillies, deseeded, soaked in
water for 15 minutes then drained

large pinch of salt

1 tablespoon cleaned and chopped coriander roots

1 tablespoon chopped galangal

2 tablespoons sliced red shallots

1 garlic clove, peeled – optional, but I like the
richer taste it brings

5 small crabs *or* 1–2 blue swimmer crabs (blue
crabs) – about 600 g (1¼ lb) in total

100 g (3 oz) dried thin rice noodles (rice sticks)

4–5 tablespoons vegetable oil

2–3 tablespoons fresh crab tomalley, from cleaning
the crabs – a desirable but optional addition

2 stalks lemongrass, cleaned and bruised

½ cup shaved palm sugar

2–3 tablespoons tamarind water

2–3 tablespoons fish sauce, to taste

good pinch of ground white pepper

¼ bunch Chinese chives, cleaned and
cut into 2 cm (1 in) lengths – about ½ cup

1 cup bean sprouts, washed and trimmed

wedges of lime, to serve

ACCOMPANIMENTS

betel leaves

Asian pennywort, trimmed

cucumbers, cut into elegant pieces

banana blossoms, peeled down to white leaves
then cut into quarters or sixths and steeped in
salted water soured with lime juice or
white vinegar

SEN CHAN PAT PBUU

CRAB NOODLES FROM CHANTHABURI

Chanthaburi is a large market town and minor port on the east coast of the Gulf of Thailand. It has been settled by Malays, Chinese, Vietnamese, Cham and of course Thais, all of whom have left their mark, making the food of this province quite distinct.

There are three or four stalls in the main market in town that specialise in this rich and wonderful dish, and they have large platters piled high with the prepared noodles dotted with crabs. They use very small crabs, only about 2 cm (1 in) across, which are simmered whole in the sauce. But even in Chanthaburi these crabs can be hard to find, so segmented blue swimmer crabs or small prawns are used as alternatives.

Crab tomalley is effectively the liver and pancreas of the crab – which is mostly found tucked inside the edge of the carapace. Despite its unpromising beginnings, it is delicious when cooked, imparting a rich and strong flavour. In most crabs it is either green or yellow, and it is the yellow colour that gives it its alternative name, crab mustard. Roe is comprised of the bright red or occasionally orange eggs of the crab, and it also lies beneath the carapace, running down the centre of the back. Naturally then, female crabs only contain roe at certain times of the year. And the girls are said to always have the sweetest meat too, so I am told.

These noodles are often served with bitter leaves, as their astringency counters the sweetness of the sauce.

- First make the paste. Using a pestle and mortar, pound the ingredients in the order they are listed, reducing each one to a fine paste before adding the next.
- Now clean the crab. In the unlikely event that you can find fresh small crabs from Chanthaburi, simply wash them. For the rest, use blue swimmers. Wash them. Remove the tail and discard, then take off the head cap and scrape out the tomalley and roe, if any. Chop the crab in half down the centre of its body and then cut each half into 3 or 4, depending on its size.
- Place the noodles in a bowl of water and leave to soak for 15 minutes until softened. Bring a large pan of water to the boil.
- Meanwhile, heat the oil in a wok or pan then fry the paste for 3–4 minutes or until quite fragrant. Add the tomalley and, after a moment, the chopped crab. Fry over a medium heat for 3–4 minutes before adding the lemongrass, palm sugar, tamarind water, fish sauce and pepper. Simmer for a few minutes, stirring regularly, until the crab is cooked and the sauce is thickened. It should taste sweet, hot and sour. Put to one side but keep warm.
- Drain the noodles well, then blanch them in the boiling water for a moment only and drain once again (this prevents the noodles from clumping together as they are cooked). Add the noodles to the hot sauce and simmer, stirring often, until the sauce is evenly distributed and almost absorbed, then add the Chinese chives and bean sprouts.
- Serve with some or all of the accompaniments and wedges of lime.

200 g (6 oz) fresh wide rice noodles

½–1 teaspoon dark soy sauce – optional

2–3 tablespoons vegetable oil

2 garlic cloves, peeled

pinch of salt

100 g (3 oz) chicken breast fillet,
    cut into about 10 slices

1 tablespoon yellow bean sauce

ground white pepper

1½ cups chicken stock

1 teaspoon white sugar

100 g (3 oz) young Chinese broccoli,
    cut into approximately 3 cm (1¼ in)
    lengths – about 1 cup

1 tablespoon tapioca flour, mixed to a slurry
    with 2 tablespoons water

1 teaspoon light soy sauce, to taste

1 teaspoon fish sauce, to taste

extra fish sauce, white sugar, roasted chilli powder
    and chillies steeped in vinegar (see page 355),
    to serve

RAAT NAR GAI

CHARRED RICE NOODLES AND CHICKEN WITH THICKENED 'GRAVY'

Flat, wide rice noodles are most commonly used for this dish. In Chinatown these noodles are made fresh every morning before being sent to the markets. Freshly made, they are wonderful. Old or dry ones are not quite as good. These – and even fresh ones that have been refrigerated or are a little dry – should be steamed for a moment until they are soft and tender then allowed to cool before use. The noodles need to be charred in a wok over a medium heat to give them the smoky taste that is a desired characteristic. A well-seasoned wok (see page 253) is essential for this. Some cooks will rub a little soy sauce onto the noodles beforehand to accentuate the taste. If the noodles are very fresh, this is not really necessary, but if they have been steamed to rejuvenate them, it is wise to do so as the already softened noodles can break up if fried too much. Do not add any oil at this stage but only once they begin to colour, otherwise the noodles will knot and gnarl.

The sauce is thickened with tapioca flour, which gives it a decidedly thick and toothsome texture. It should not be too highly seasoned, as the seasoning should be finished by each person to their taste.

- Spread and tease the noodles. If they have been steamed, rub them with the dark soy sauce. Heat the wok and spread the noodles over its surface, allowing them to char and crisp before lifting and turning. Try not to break up the noodles. Once they are charred, add a drop of oil if the wok seems too dry. The noodles should be dark and aromatic, almost burnt in parts. Divide between two bowls and keep warm.
- Crush the garlic to a somewhat coarse paste with the salt – either by pounding it using a pestle and mortar or finely chopping it with a knife. In a small pan – or the cleaned wok – heat the oil, add the garlic paste and fry until it is beginning to colour. Add the chicken and continue frying until the garlic is golden and the chicken is sealed. Add the yellow bean sauce and fry for a minute or so. Sprinkle in a pinch of pepper and fry for a moment before adding the stock. Bring to the boil and add the sugar and broccoli. Simmer until the broccoli is wilted and quite tender – it must not be too crispy – then pour in the tapioca slurry. Simmer, stirring constantly, as the sauce thickens and swells slightly: it should be really quite thick, almost translucent and pleasingly glutinous. Season with the light soy and fish sauces: it should taste salty, sweet and smoky.
- Pour the sauce over the noodles and sprinkle with white pepper. Serve with fish sauce, white sugar, roasted chilli powder and sliced chillies steeped in vinegar.

300 g (9 oz) dried glass (bean thread) noodles

1 teaspoon cleaned and chopped coriander roots

pinch of salt

1 slice ginger

2 large garlic cloves, peeled

pinch of ground white pepper

3 tablespoons vegetable oil

5 straw or oyster mushrooms,
    cleaned and cut into quarters

4–6 small fresh shiitake mushrooms,
    stems removed

2–3 tablespoons fermented bean curd

pinch of white sugar

2 tablespoons light soy sauce

1 cup light vegetable stock or water

2 tablespoons pickled garlic syrup

1 tablespoon Chinese rice wine – optional,
    but a welcome addition

1 cup chopped Chinese cabbage *or*
    2 cups picked baby spinach leaves

2 tablespoons sliced pickled garlic

1–2 long red chillies, sliced – optional

3 tablespoons Asian celery
    cut into 2 cm (1 in) lengths

2 tablespoons spring (green) onions
    cut into 2 cm (1 in) lengths

2 tablespoons coriander leaves

good pinch of ground white pepper

Light vegetable stock

A simple vegetable stock can be made by simmering some of the Chinese cabbage and mushroom offcuts with a little onion (both regular and green), garlic, ginger and coriander for about 30 minutes. Strain and use in place of water for a greater depth of flavour.

WUN SEN PAT DTAO HUU YII

GLASS NOODLES STIR-FRIED WITH MUSHROOMS AND FERMENTED BEAN CURD

This is a wonderful vegetarian dish – a rarity on the streets of Bangkok. Fermented bean curd is a rich, nutty preparation of small cakes of bean curd cured in wine and spices that is sold in cans or jars at most Asian supermarkets. There are two varieties: one red and more pungent, the other creamy coloured and more mellow. I prefer the latter for its rich, toasty flavour and agreeable mustiness. As it is always quite salty, tread carefully with the level of saltiness in this dish. Jars of pickled garlic are also available in Asian shops.

- Place the noodles in a large bowl, cover with warm water and leave to soften for about 20 minutes. Meanwhile, using a pestle and mortar, pound the coriander roots, salt, ginger and garlic into a somewhat coarse paste. Drain the noodles and cut into roughly 10 cm (4 in) lengths.
- Heat the oil in a wok, add the paste and fry until it is beginning to colour. Add the straw or oyster mushrooms and the shiitake mushrooms and stir-fry for a minute or so. Add the fermented bean curd and fry until it has slightly separated before adding the sugar, soy sauce, stock or water, pickled garlic syrup and Chinese rice wine. Bring to the boil and add the cabbage, if using, then simmer for a minute before adding the noodles. However, if using baby spinach leaves, add them at the same time as the noodles. Simmer for another moment to ensure the noodles are cooked, but be careful not to overcook them or they will clump together and be disagreeably sticky. Stir in the pickled garlic, Asian celery and spring onions.
- Serve sprinkled with the coriander leaves and white pepper.

¼ cup black sticky rice
¼ cup white sticky rice

PANDANUS NOODLES
½ cup rice flour
1 tablespoon tapioca flour
good pinch of lime paste
15–20 pandanus leaves
3 cups ice

1 cup shaved palm sugar
¾ cup coconut cream

Thai dessert-noodle presses
In Thailand these noodles are made using
what looks like a large canister sieve with
a handle on one side, 2 mm (⅛ in) holes in its
base and a plunger to push pastes through
them. Such contraptions may be found in
Thai specialty shops or online; I recommend
you pick one up if you ever travel to Thailand.
Otherwise, a colander and the back of
a large spoon should work.

ลอดช่องข้าวเหนียวดำ

LORD CHONG KAO NIAW DAM

PANDANUS NOODLES WITH BLACK STICKY RICE

Thais love desserts chilled with ice. Such desserts were once the province of the rich or regal but now they are firmly entrenched on the streets. They quench the thirst, cool and refresh in the torpid heat of the tropical day. They are also very welcome after a spicy dish or two.

Black sticky rice gets its characteristic aubergine (eggplant) colour from the bran. As it soaks overnight, it loses some of this intensity, staining the soaking water a dark burgundy, which helps to dye the white sticky rice. You need to use both types of rice, for despite its name black rice is not sticky when it is cooked – the bran layer prevents this – so it is the white rice that makes the rice cohere.

The noodles should be soft, silken and intensely green. Most stalls will use green food colouring to ensure this, but pandanus is the original, the best and the most natural way. These delicate noodles are made over a bowl of water, so they drop straight into it without being touched. Once made, they should be kept in iced water, which helps to make the tender little things just that bit more resilient. I like to use large pieces of ice, as these chill the dessert but melt slowly and so don't overly dilute the coconut cream. Others prefer small cubes or even shaved ice, which they chew. The choice is yours.

- Rinse both types of rice carefully to remove any excess starch without breaking the grains, then soak them together in plenty of water overnight.
- The next day, drain the rice, rinse and place in a steamer; normally the raw grains of rice cling together, so they rarely fall through the holes, but if you're feeling cautious line it with some rinsed muslin (cheesecloth). Make sure the rice is not piled too high in the centre, nor too widely spread, so that it cooks evenly, and keep the water level below the steamer high to ensure there is plenty of steam. Steam the rice until tender (test some grains from the area where the mound of rice is deepest) – this should take 25–35 minutes. Place the cooked rice in a glass or ceramic bowl, cover and set aside to cool.
- To make the noodles, mix the rice and tapioca flours together in a bowl. Work in 1–2 tablespoons of warm water and knead for a minute or so to make a stiff yet slightly crumbly paste. Now gradually add about ¼ cup of warm water until you have a putty-like dough. Leave to rest in the bowl, covered with plastic film, for no less than 30 minutes or as long as 2 hours.
- Next make the lime water and the pandanus water. Dissolve the lime paste in 1½ cups of water and wait for about 15 minutes until it has completely precipitated. Meanwhile, for the pandanus water, roughly chop the pandanus leaves then place in a blender with ½ cup of water and blend for a minute or so until the leaves are completely pureed. Strain the pulp through a fine sieve into a bowl, pressing manically to obtain as much of the vivid green water as possible, then set aside.
- Drain off and reserve the clear lime water, discarding the sludgy residue. Add the lime water to the rested dough, stirring well to make a batter. Pass through a fine sieve into a small brass wok or shallow saucepan – the batter should have the consistency of milk. Place over a low–medium heat and stir slowly, constantly and completely, taking in all the corners of the pan. The batter will become momentarily lumpy at first, but an untraditional whisk fixes this problem and, as it cooks, it should turn into a smooth thick paste. When it is ready, after about 5 minutes, the paste should come away slightly from the pan. Add the pandanus water and continue to simmer and stir for a few moments until it smells cooked and enticing with pandanus. The colour should be an alluring green.
- Pour the hot paste into a colander (or Thai dessert-noodle contraption, if you have one) straight from the pan. Position it over a bowl containing at least 4 cups of cold water. Push the paste through with the back of a large spoon (or press the plunger of the contraption) in short, sharp and decisive presses to form noodles 2–3 cm (1–1¼ in) in length. The noodles should be thicker at the beginning with a slightly thinner tail. Once all the noodles are made, drain off the murky warm water in the bowl and replace it with plenty of cold water, pouring it down the side of the bowl or over your hand to protect the fragile noodles. Top with several ice cubes – even though the ice will melt, the noodles can now be kept like this for a few hours.
- To serve, stir the palm sugar into the coconut cream until dissolved. Divide the rice among six bowls, then use a slotted spoon to add a spoonful of drained noodles (don't worry if there is a little water). Top with some sweetened coconut cream, add some ice and serve immediately.

ROTI

¼ teaspoon salt

125 g (4 oz) cake or pastry flour – about 1 cup

½ egg, lightly beaten – about 1½ tablespoons

1 tablespoon margarine, broken
    into 1 cm (½ in) pieces

½ cup oil – ideally flavourless pure
    coconut oil (nahm man bua)

vegetable oil, for frying

1 banana

a few tablespoons condensed milk –
    as much as you dare

1–2 teaspoons white sugar

โรตีกล้วย

ROTI GLUAY

SWEET BANANA ROTI

Lines form around these stalls as people wait patiently for their rotis. They are made one at a time, the pastry stretched and thrown, the banana sliced and the roti folded and cooked in front of the growing crowd. It is patently worth the wait, because people come back time and again. Make one and find out why. The stalls tend to be quite large, to accommodate the vast, round and slightly concave and beautifully seasoned hotplate on which the roti can be slid around. The gentle heat is always on, as there is always a roti on order.

Margarine seems such an improbable ingredient here, but it is what is used. Thai cooks believe it enriches the dish without making it 'smelly', as butter would. So margarine it is, for the sake of unlikely authenticity.

Some stalls offer variations: banana with egg, roti alone or with coconut jam. I think just sliced banana is best, but for me the pièce de résistance is the addition of condensed milk and sugar – perfection!

- To make the roti, mix the salt into ¼ cup of water. Sieve the flour into a bowl and make a well in the centre. Add the egg, stirring to form a crumbly dough, then gradually work in the salted water. Knead for about 15 minutes until the dough is silken, soft and tender. Transfer to a bowl rubbed with a smear of the margarine and leave to rest, covered, for an hour.
- Roll the dough between cupped hands to make a large oval. Squeeze into two balls about 4 cm (1½ in) in diameter and roll with cupped hands to smooth their surface.
- Return the dough balls to the bowl and cover in the oil dotted with the margarine pieces. Steep, covered and in a warm place (but not so warm that the margarine will melt), for at least 3 hours or overnight.
- Place a large, heavy, well-seasoned pan over a very low heat.
- Oil the bench (work surface) and your hands well with some of the oil from the bowl. Take out one of the dough balls and press it against the bench with two or three fingers, spreading it to make a disk about 15 cm (6 in) in diameter. Now 'cast' the dough by holding one edge of the disk and, using a throwing motion and the weight of the dough itself, stretch it until it is as thin and film-like as strudel or filo pastry. Those less daring or dexterous can resort to a rolling pin! Fold in the outer edges to even the roti and make a large square.
- Spoon a few tablespoons of the oil from the bowl into the pan. Allow it to heat then carefully lift the roti into the pan. Shuffle the pan and, once the roti has begun to cook, move it about with a spatula. Quickly peel the banana and cut into 5 mm (¼ in) slices, then cast them into the centre of the roti. When the roti has partly cooked, fold two opposite sides over the banana then bring over the other two sides to form a sealed, square parcel. Add a piece of the margarine from the bowl and shake the pan as it melts and sizzles, cooking and burnishing the roti. Carefully turn the roti over with the spatula, adding a little more oil if necessary and shuffling the pan to prevent the roti from sticking. As this side cooks, add another piece of the margarine. Once the second side is golden and cooked, turn the roti two or three times quite quickly, then remove to a plate. Make the other roti.
- Leave the rotis to cool slightly before cutting into bite-sized pieces. Drizzle with the condensed milk and sprinkle with the sugar.

¼ cup arrowroot flour

1½ cups tapioca flour

½ cup sticky rice flour

1¾ cups coconut cream

4–5 pandanus leaves

1½ cups white sugar

1½ cups jasmine water or water
  perfumed with a few drops rose
  or orange flower water

KANOM CHAN

PANDANUS LAYER CAKE

This is a very unusual dessert – sticky and stodgy yet truly addictive. It demands a level of commitment: not only is it an acquired taste, but it also takes some time to prepare. Do try it, though – I think it is really worth it.

The various types of flour can be bought in most Asian shops. The combination used here ensures a gooey and malleable texture. Jasmine water is made by steeping Thai jasmine flowers in water overnight (see page 358). Asian stores sometimes sell jasmine essence but it can be coarse and harsh, so use only a few drops. Alternatively, add a few drops of good-quality rose or orange flower water to plain water – both of these flower waters can be found in Middle Eastern shops and some supermarkets.

The mould used for this cake in Thailand is a small aluminium or stainless-steel tin about 10 cm (4 in) square and 5 cm (2 in) deep, but any heatproof square or rectangular container will do. The best steamer to use is a simple Chinese metal one: they are cheap and reliable if none too sturdy. Just make sure it has a tight-fitting lid.

There are usually two alternating layers: one opaque white, made with coconut cream; and the other green, coloured and flavoured with pandanus leaves. Each layer must be completely cooked before the next layer is added; in total, the cake will take about 2½ hours to steam, and then it must be allowed to cool. Pandanus layer cake should really be eaten on the day it is made, since it toughens as it ages – and, while it could be kept covered overnight, it will not be at its best.

- In a large bowl, combine the flours, then pour in the coconut cream and knead to a soft dough. Cover and leave to rest for about an hour.
- Meanwhile, finely chop the pandanus leaves, then blend until pureed. Gradually add ½ cup of water, in two or three stages, to obtain the proper intensity and texture: the pandanus water should be a vivid green and as thick as cream. Pass through a fine sieve, pressing manically to extract as much flavour and colour as possible. Set aside.
- In a small pan, combine the white sugar and jasmine water to make a syrup, and simmer for about 5–7 minutes until it has reached 112°C (235°F), known as soft-ball stage – that is, when a little of the syrup dropped into cold water forms a soft ball. When cooled to room temperature, it should be as thick as honey.
- Mix the jasmine syrup into the dough to make a pancake-like batter, then strain it through a fine sieve.
- Divide the batter into two halves, then stir all except 3 tablespoons of the pandanus water into one half.
- Pour boiling water into the base of the steamer. Throughout the prolonged steaming, the water level must be no less than 1 cm (½ in) from the base of the perforated segment of the steamer. Make sure the water is regularly replenished to keep it at this level, and use boiling water to maintain the temperature. It is also essential that the inside of the steamer is kept as dry as possible. Each and every time the steamer is opened, the lid should be wiped dry, to avoid condensation dripping onto the cake.
- Heat the mould in the steamer until very hot, about 20 minutes. Remove and wipe dry. To make the first layer, pour the plain batter into the mould to a depth of 5 mm (¼ in). Steam for 20 minutes. Lift off the lid of the steamer, dry it, and then pour in a 5 mm (¼ in) layer of the pandanus batter and steam for 20 minutes. Repeat, making alternate layers of the two batters, drying the lid each time and steaming each layer for 20 minutes. Do at least four layers of each batter, eight in all, then finish with the remaining pandanus batter enriched with the reserved 3 tablespoons of pandanus water. In total it should take about 2½ hours to steam and when complete the layered cake should be about 4 cm (1½ in) high.
- Allow to cool completely before cutting into 4 cm (1½ in) squares.

ร้านข้าวแกง
CURRY SHOP
RAAN KAO GENG

A curry shop is easy to spot. The stall generally extends onto the street. Trays, bowls, dishes and pots filled with an array of curries line the shelves and vie for attention. There usually seems to be a crowd milling around, lured by the shop's wares, chatting, considering and choosing. Thais are always interested in food and will peruse what's on offer with intense curiosity, whether hungry or not.

The first curry shops or stands selling prepared foods were only really established in the late nineteenth century. Faded sepia photographs show some stalls – actually little more than two or three baskets – clustered together under the shade of some trees wherever people and their hunger were liable to gather: at markets and crossroads; on bridges, piers and riverbanks; near government offices, temples, schools and the like. Initially the meals were served on wooden trays: a curry or two with rice and some basic accompaniments, such as cucumber relish, dried fish, boiled salted eggs or deep-fried salted beef. Later, to attract more customers, new dishes were added to the menu: soups, fried eggs, grilled or deep-fried fish, a nahm prik relish or two, and maybe even fish braised with palm sugar. Each region will serve some of its own specialties but even in the outlying provinces, it seems central plains curries – among the most well known of the Thai canon, including red and green curries, as well as the quintessential sour orange curry – are always at the ready. Bangkok curries are usually milder, catering to more urban, gentrified tastes. Most places sell no less than ten dishes and some offer as many as forty.

The preparation starts with a dawn visit to a local market, when all the provisions necessary for making the day's curries are bought. Then the dishes are prepared in a small kitchen at the back of the shop – or, if the stall is small, at home, and then transported. Usually family members assist, or a few friends and neighbours may help with the cooking.

To be honest, few stalls make their own curry pastes. Mostly, they are purchased ready-made from a stall specialising in them – each marketplace has one or two. They are generic but they are fresh. As few readers will be able to pop down to the corner shop for a fresh batch, I have included specific recipes for each curry paste. Fresh coconut cream is also made at Thai markets, but sadly there are no supermarkets I know of that will grate and squeeze coconuts while you wait. Making your own curry paste and coconut cream makes a dramatic difference to the finished dish, and I firmly believe it is worth the time and effort. You may not, however. It's undoubtedly faster and more convenient to use ready-made stuff, but it will be at the cost of the lip-tingling vitality and vibrancy that so defines good Thai food. Finally, while Thai cooks might make a simple and light stock with a few bones of chicken or pork simmered with a few aromatics, if there is no stock to hand, they will not blanch at using plain water.

The shop opens quite early, about 10 a.m., and remains open until everything is sold, usually around mid-afternoon. Some shops close later – in the early evening – to capture a different customer. Once the food has been sold, the stall closes. And sufficient food is prepared to have just enough for the day with none left over, so that all is spankingly fresh and made daily. This rhythm is in harmony with the markets and their customers' needs and habits. Even if a shop prospers, it still usually keeps these hours and practices.

Since the food is prepared in advance, it is fast and convenient. Once the items are selected, they can be served in a few ways. For a single serving, a ladleful of one or sometimes two dishes is poured over rice. If a few people are sharing, then the curries – usually two or three – are served in separate bowls, along with plates of rice. And there is invariably a bowl of chopped chillies in fish sauce on the table. Or there's always takeaway (sai tung), where the curries are poured into plastic bags and taken home to eat.

SOUR ORANGE CURRY PASTE

6 dried long red chillies

3–4 dried bird's eye chillies

good pinch of salt

a few bird's eye chillies (scuds) – optional

2 tablespoons chopped red shallots

1 teaspoon Thai shrimp paste (gapi)

2–3 tablespoons poached fish
   (see recipe introduction)

3 cups stock or water

good pinch of salt

5 red shallots, peeled

pinch of white sugar

2 tablespoons fish sauce

3 tablespoons tamarind water

200 g (6 oz) fish fillet, cut into 3 cm (1¼ in) pieces

handful of Asian greens, such as Siamese
   watercress (water spinach), choy sum or
   Chinese cabbage, cut into 3 cm (1¼ in) lengths

pinch of roasted chilli powder

3 dried long red chillies, dry-roasted
   in a wok or frying pan – optional

GENG SOM PLAA

SOUR ORANGE CURRY OF FISH

A sour orange curry is one of the most popular curries in Thailand, being simple to make and straight-forward in taste, yet richly satisfying. In every market in every town and village, there will be at least one or two local varieties of this thin, tart curry on sale, waiting in deep bowls filled with vegetables and pieces of fish.

Each region has its own favourite fish for this: the meaty white flesh of the serpent-head fish, the formidable catfish, the rich and fatty carp or crunchy featherbacks. On the coast, barramundi, sea bass and kingfish are preferred, but prawns and mussels are happily thrown into the pot too. So there is ample scope to use perch, pike or zander. (If using freshwater fish, add a tablespoon of chopped galangal or grachai to the curry paste.) And from the sea try snapper, red emperor, bream, mussels or clams.

Thais happily eat fish cooked whole or in large pieces, unperturbed by the prospect of bones. They believe that fish tastes better so cooked – and they're right. However, you may prefer fillets. If possible, have the fishmonger fillet the fish for you, so you can have the bones to make a stock. Otherwise use chicken stock or, as many Thais do, plain water. If you are making stock, scrape any flesh from the bones and add it to the curry paste. If you are using a fillet, poach a little of the fish in some stock or water and add that to the paste.

The vegetables used range widely as well: daikon (mooli), fresh or pickled mustard greens, water mimosa (as in the photo opposite), torn betel leaves, baby corn, bamboo shoot, coarsely shredded semi-ripe papaya, heart of coconut or tart green pineapple. Often three or four are used together.

- First make the curry paste. Nip off the stalks of the dried long red chillies, then cut along their length and scrape out the seeds. Soak the chillies in water for about 15 minutes until soft. Rinse the dried bird's eye chillies to remove any dust. Drain the chillies, squeezing to extract as much water as possible, then chop them quite finely. Using a pestle and mortar, pound the chillies to a paste with the salt, then add the remaining ingredients in the order they are listed, reducing each one to a fine paste before adding the next. Alternatively, puree the ingredients in an electric blender. You will probably need to add a little water to aid the blending, but try not to add more than necessary, as this will dilute the paste and alter the taste of the curry. Halfway through, turn the machine off and scrape down the sides of the bowl with a spatula, then turn it back on and whiz the paste until it is completely pureed.
- Bring the stock or water to the boil with the salt. Add the curry paste, rinsing out the mortar or blender to make sure all the paste is used, and simmer for a minute before adding the whole shallots. Simmer for 3–4 minutes, then season with sugar, fish sauce and most of the tamarind water. Add the fish and the greens and continue to simmer until everything is cooked.
- This thin curry should taste sour, salty and a little hot – adjust accordingly with fish sauce, tamarind water and chilli powder. Finish with the roasted chillies, if desired, and serve with steamed rice.

RED CURRY PASTE

7 dried long red chillies

1 tablespoon coriander seeds

1 teaspoon cumin seeds

10 white peppercorns

a little mace or, at a pinch, nutmeg

1 heaped teaspoon dried bird's eye chillies –
  about 5–8

good pinch of salt

3 bird's eye chillies (scuds)

2 teaspoons chopped galangal

2 tablespoons chopped lemongrass

1 teaspoon finely grated kaffir lime zest

2 tablespoons chopped grachai (wild ginger)

2½ tablespoons chopped red shallots

1 tablespoon chopped garlic

1 teaspoon Thai shrimp paste (gapi)

1 × 350 g (10½ oz) catfish
  or about 200g (6 oz) fish fillet

2 cups coconut cream

good pinch of shaved palm sugar

2 tablespoons fish sauce

1 cup coconut milk

3 kaffir lime leaves, torn

½–1 cup fish stock – see method – or water

½ cup shredded grachai (wild ginger) – washed
  in salted water, rinsed and squeezed dry

4 long red or green chillies, cut in half

2–3 bird's eye chillies (scuds), bruised

2 handfuls of holy basil or Thai basil leaves

GENG DAENG PLAA DUK

RED CATFISH CURRY

This is a very fine curry: rich, aromatic and quite thick, with only a slight dappling of coconut oil. It comes from the mid-central plains, where catfish abound. They are a resilient fish, both in life and in death. Kept in large tubs at the market, they are usually despatched to order – this can often be a messy business. This muscular fish can sustain prolonged cooking too. Some recipes I have come across propose to cook the fish for as long as 30–40 minutes, yet it still retains a toothsome texture. While the 10 or so minutes of cooking will present no problem to a catfish, it might result in overcooking of an alternative fish, such as cobbler, pike, zander, perch, or even a very large brook trout like a char. Take this into account when you cook the fish you have chosen.

- First make the curry paste. Nip off the stalks of the dried long red chillies, then cut along their length and scrape out the seeds. Soak the chillies in water for about 15 minutes until soft.
- While the chillies are soaking, roast the coriander and cumin seeds separately in a dry, heavy-based frying pan until they are aromatic, shaking the pan often to prevent the spices from scorching. Grind to a powder with the peppercorns and mace or nutmeg, using an electric grinder or a pestle and mortar.
- Drain the soaked chillies, squeezing to extract as much water as possible, then roughly chop them. Rinse the dried bird's eye chillies to remove any dust. Using a pestle and mortar, pound the chillies with the salt, then add the remaining ingredients in the order they are listed, reducing each one to a fine paste before adding the next. Alternatively, puree the ingredients in an electric blender. It will probably be necessary to add a little water to aid the blending, but try not to add more than necessary, as this will dilute the paste and alter the taste of the curry. Halfway through, turn the machine off and scrape down the sides of the bowl with a spatula, then turn it back on and whiz the paste until it is completely pureed. Finally, stir in the ground spices.
- If using a whole fish, clean and fillet it, but leave the skin on – this should yield approximately 200 g (6 oz) of flesh. Cut the fish fillet into 3 cm × 2 cm (1¼ in × 1 in) pieces. If desired, make a stock from the fish bones and some of the offcuts from the curry paste by simmering them together in water for about 30 minutes.
- Simmer the coconut cream with the curry paste over a medium heat for 5 minutes or until fragrant and slightly oily, stirring regularly to prevent it catching. Season it with the palm sugar and then the fish sauce. Add the prepared fish and simmer for a few minutes. Add the coconut milk, kaffir lime leaves and some stock or water and simmer for another few minutes, then add the grachai, chillies and basil.
- Check the seasoning: the curry should taste hot, salty and rich. It should be creamy from the coconut, redolent of the cumin and mace, and aromatic from the basil and grachai. Leave for 10 minutes to allow the flavours to develop, then serve with steamed rice.

GENG GARI PASTE

7 dried long red chillies

1 tablespoon coriander seeds

1 teaspoon cumin seeds

½ teaspoon fennel seeds

1 teaspoon white peppercorns

pinch of mace

pinch of salt

3 tablespoons chopped red shallots

3 tablespoons chopped garlic

1 tablespoon chopped galangal

2 tablespoons chopped lemongrass

2 coriander roots, cleaned and chopped

1 teaspoon chopped turmeric

12 large raw prawns (shrimp) in their shells

2 cups coconut cream

1 tablespoon shaved palm sugar –
    more or less, to taste

2–3 tablespoons fish sauce, to taste

2–3 cups coconut milk or stock

15 small cherry tomatoes

½ white onion, cut into 6 segments – try to leave
    a little of the root or core attached, as this will
    help to keep the slices together as they cook

2 potatoes, boiled and cut into 2 cm (1 in) pieces

pinch of roasted chilli powder, to taste

handful of deep-fried shallots – optional

cucumber relish (see below), to serve

+ CUCUMBER RELISH

It really is essential to serve some cucumber relish with this curry. The sweet tartness of the syrup cuts through the oil of the curry and reveals its spices, while the cucumber and shallots add a crisp textural contrast to the soft curry. The syrup can be made well in advance and will last indefinitely refrigerated.

¼ cup white vinegar

¼ cup white sugar

½ teaspoon salt – more or less, to taste

1 coriander root, cleaned

1 small cucumber, quartered and sliced –
    some would peel it too

3 red shallots, somewhat coarsely sliced

1 tablespoon shredded ginger

¼ long red chilli, chopped

1 tablespoon chopped coriander

Simmer the vinegar with the sugar, salt, coriander root and a few tablespoons of water. When cold, remove the coriander root then stir in the cucumber, shallots, ginger, chilli and chopped coriander.

GENG GARI GUNG

AROMATIC PRAWN CURRY

This style of curry is one of the most popular on the streets and among Westerners. Large pots of the light yet rich and creamy curry are ready to go, its enticing layer of glistening oil beckoning customers to come and taste. Occasionally a few pandanus leaves or a quill or two of toasted cassia bark are added to the finished curry to keep it sweet as it waits to be sold and to enhance its perfume, which wafts seductively through the air. While the most common version is made with large pieces of chicken, there are many variations, large prawns being one, but pieces of duck, beef and even deep-fried fish may also be found in the pot.

Some cooks will happily use a standard red curry paste supplemented with a few teaspoons of curry powder when making this curry, while others will head down to the market to purchase a specific curry paste – but you can make your own!

- First make the curry paste. Nip off the stalks of the chillies, then cut along their length and scrape out the seeds. Soak the chillies in water for about 15 minutes until soft.
- While the chillies are soaking, roast the coriander, cumin and fennel seeds separately in a dry, heavy-based frying pan until they are aromatic, shaking the pan to prevent the spices from scorching. Grind to a powder with the peppercorns and mace, using an electric grinder or a pestle and mortar.
- Drain the soaked chillies, squeezing to extract as much water as possible, then roughly chop them. Using a pestle and mortar, pound the chillies with the salt, then add the remaining ingredients in the order they are listed, reducing each one to a fine paste before adding the next. Alternatively, puree the ingredients in an electric blender. You will probably need to add a little water to aid the blending, but try not to add more than necessary, as this will dilute the paste and alter the taste of the curry. Halfway through, turn the machine off and scrape down the sides of the bowl with a spatula, then turn it back on and whiz the paste until it is completely pureed. Finally, stir in the ground spices.
- Clean and peel the prawns, but leave their tails intact; the heads can also be left intact for a more pleasing presentation, but it makes for trickier eating later. Remove the dark veins running down their backs.
- Simmer the coconut cream with the curry paste for about 5 minutes, stirring regularly to prevent it catching, until it is fragrant and slightly oily. Season with the palm sugar then the fish sauce. Add the coconut milk or stock and bring quickly to the boil. Add the tomatoes and onion, then turn down the heat and simmer for a few minutes or so until tender. Near the end add the prepared potatoes and prawns and simmer until the potatoes are heated through and the prawns are just cooked. The curry should taste spicy, salty and very slightly sweet and tart – I find it is often improved with the addition of some roasted chilli powder and a little extra fish sauce.
- Sprinkle with deep-fried shallots, if using, and serve with cucumber relish and steamed rice.

RED CURRY PASTE

6–10 dried long red chillies

large pinch of salt

1 tablespoon chopped galangal

2 tablespoons chopped lemongrass

1 teaspoon finely grated kaffir lime zest

1 teaspoon cleaned and chopped coriander roots

2 tablespoons chopped red shallots

3 tablespoons chopped garlic

1 teaspoon Thai shrimp paste (gapi)

150 g (5 oz) white fish fillets, such as sea bass,
    snapper, John Dory or whiting, cut into fine slices

½ cup thick coconut cream

1 small egg, lightly beaten

pinch of white sugar

5–8 kaffir lime leaves, finely shredded

good dash of fish sauce

1 small roll of banana leaves –
    about 300 g (9 oz) – optional

about 12 small toothpicks – optional

handful of Thai basil leaves

1 tablespoon thick coconut cream

¼ long red chilli, deseeded and cut into fine strips

a few coriander leaves

ห่อหมกปลา

HOR MOK PLAA

STEAMED FISH CURRY

Although steamed curries might be less familiar than Thai red and green curries, they are commonly eaten throughout the country. At the back of most curry stalls there is a huge metal steamer where steamed fish curry is cooked and kept warm, waiting to be sold. Saltwater and freshwater fish are most often found in such a curry but prawns, scallops and mussels can also find their way into the spicy mousse. In the north, I have seen parcels filled with chicken, cured pork, wild mushrooms or shredded boiled bamboo treated in this way.

Hor mok literally means something wrapped in a parcel – and in Thailand, that means wrapped with banana leaves. The Thais have created a variety of ways to fold these durable leaves into containers. If banana leaves are unavailable or the intricacies of banana-leaf origami escape you, a less confounding method is simply to steam the prepared mousse in a shallow ceramic bowl. This curry is best served warm, even hot – just lifted from the steamer, garnished and served.

- First make the curry paste. Nip off the stalks of the chillies then cut along their length and scrape out the seeds. Soak the chillies in water for about 15 minutes until soft. Drain the chillies, squeezing to extract as much water as possible, then roughly chop them. Using a pestle and mortar, pound the chillies with the salt, then add the remaining ingredients in the order they are listed, reducing each one to a fine paste before adding the next. Alternatively, puree the ingredients in an electric blender. You will probably need to add a little water to aid the blending, but try not to add more than necessary, as this will dilute the paste and alter the taste of the curry. Halfway through, turn the machine off and scrape down the sides of the bowl with a spatula, then turn it back on and whiz the paste until it is completely pureed.

- Place the fish slices in a glass or ceramic bowl, then gradually and cautiously stir in the coconut cream; like a mayonnaise, it must not separate – if it does, add a little ice-cold water and stir to incorporate. If the coconut cream is beaten in too quickly, the curry will curdle as it steams.

- Fold in the curry paste then stir in the egg, the sugar and most of the shredded lime leaves, reserving a few for garnish. Check the seasoning: smear just a little of the curry on your finger and taste – it should be salty, sweet and redolent with coconut cream. It will probably be necessary to add some fish sauce to achieve the correct balance.

- Cut the banana leaves, if using, into circles about 12 cm (5 in) in diameter. Wipe them with a clean damp cloth then place one circle shiny-side down on the bench (work surface) and place another circle on top, shiny-side up, with the grain of the leaves running at right angles to the first circle. At four evenly spaced intervals crimp the leaves to form a basket, securing with small toothpicks. Flatten the bottom, line with Thai basil leaves and add the curry. (Or, more simply, line a large ceramic bowl with the basil leaves and spoon in the curry.)

- Steam in a metal or bamboo steamer over a moderately high heat for 20–40 minutes, until the curry has set (this will depend on the size of the steaming receptacle). To test, insert a metal skewer or small knife into the curry – it should come out clean and hot to the touch. Remove carefully and finish with the thick coconut cream, chilli and coriander and the reserved shredded lime leaves.

- Leave to settle for 5 minutes before serving with steamed rice.

CURRY PASTE

5 bamboo skewers

9 dried long red chillies

3 Thai cardamom pods *or* 1–2 green
    cardamom pods

1 tablespoon coriander seeds

1½ teaspoons cumin seeds

3 cloves

¼ star anise

½ nutmeg, grated

a few dried bird's eye chillies

4 garlic cloves, unpeeled

4–5 slices turmeric

5 slices ginger

good pinch of salt

½ medium-sized chicken *or* 3 chicken legs
    and thighs – approximately 400–500 g
    (12 oz–1 lb) in total

2 cups coconut cream

1 cup coconut milk

7–8 assam (som kaek), rinsed
    or 4 tablespoons tamarind pulp

3 tablespoons fish sauce

3 tablespoons shaved palm sugar

2 cardamom leaves or dried bay leaves

2 cm (1 in) piece cassia bark

3–4 Thai cardamom pods *or* 2 green
    cardamom pods

1–2 cups additional coconut milk, stock or water

7–8 banana chillies

1–2 tablespoons tamarind water – optional

pinch of roasted chilli powder – optional

GENG KAEK GAI

CHICKEN AND BANANA
CHILLI CURRY WITH ASSAM

This is a southern-style Muslim curry recipe from Penjaa Gaetnakorn, a vendor from Satun province, way down south on the Malay border. It is aromatic and tart rather than infernally hot, as so many dishes from this region are. This curry mellows and deepens if allowed to rest for a while after cooking.

Som kaek is the Thai name for dried Asian woodruff, which is often sold in slices in Asian stores as assam. It is very sour. If it can't be found, use tamarind pulp in its place. Simply remove as much fibre and seeds from the pulp as you can before reshaping the pulp into small disks. Most likely it will have dissolved by the time the chicken has cooked but it will have achieved its point: to imbue the curry with a deep and pleasing tartness.

Thai cardamom leaves are also known as salam leaves, and may be found in some Asian grocery shops – they look like large, thin bay leaves, but are more brittle. Their taste is also quite similar to dried bay leaves, which can be used as a substitute here.

- First make the curry paste. Soak the skewers in water for about 30 minutes. Nip off the stalks of the chillies then cut along their length and scrape out the seeds. Soak the chillies in water for about 15 minutes until soft.
- In a dry, heavy-based frying pan, separately roast the cardamom, coriander and cumin, then the cloves and star anise together, until aromatic, shaking the pan to prevent the spices from scorching. Husk the cardamom then grind to a powder with the coriander, cumin, cloves, star anise and nutmeg, using an electric grinder or a pestle and mortar.
- Drain the soaked chillies, squeezing to extract as much water as possible. Rinse the dried bird's eye chillies to remove any dust. Thread the two types of chilli, garlic, turmeric and ginger onto individual skewers. Grill (broil) or chargrill all the skewers until the chillies are dry, crisp and slightly smoky, the garlic is charred and tender, and the turmeric and ginger are slightly dried and coloured. Allow to cool, then peel the garlic and chop the chillies, turmeric and ginger.
- Using a pestle and mortar, pound the chillies with the salt, then add the grilled garlic, turmeric and ginger, reducing each one to a fine paste before adding the next. Alternatively, puree the ingredients in an electric blender. It will probably be necessary to add a little water to aid the blending, but try not to add more than necessary, as this will dilute the paste and alter the taste of the curry. Halfway through, turn the machine off and scrape down the sides of the bowl with a spatula, then turn it back on and whiz the paste until it is completely pureed. Finally, stir in the ground spices.
- Cut the chicken or chicken legs into roughly 4 cm (1½ in) pieces. Rinse and pat dry with a paper towel.
- Simmer the coconut cream and milk with the curry paste in a large pan over a medium heat for 5–10 minutes or until fragrant, stirring regularly to prevent it catching – it will still be quite wet. Add the prepared chicken and the assam or tamarind pulp, then season with the fish sauce and palm sugar and continue to simmer. While the curry is gently simmering, roast the cardamom or bay leaves, cassia and cardamom pods in a heavy-based pan until they are aromatic; the leaves won't take long, so keep an eye on them. Add the roasted spices to the curry, together with some of the additional coconut milk, stock or water if it is becoming too dry (it should have a similar consistency to cream). Continue to simmer until the chicken is just about cooked and the curry has become tart yet slightly sweet, then add the banana chillies, cover the pan and simmer until they are tender – about 10 minutes.
- By now the chicken and the chillies will be tender and there should be a nice film of oil on the surface. Check the seasoning: the curry should taste spicy, salty and a little sour and sweet. Adjust, if necessary, with a little extra fish sauce, tamarind water, palm sugar and roasted chilli powder.
- Serve with steamed rice.

JUNGLE CURRY PASTE

1–2 dried long red chillies

4–5 tablespoons dried prik gariang chillies
    or dried bird's eye chillies – about 30 g (1 oz)

a few fresh bird's eye chillies (scuds) –
    ideally red ones

good pinch of salt

1 tablespoon chopped galangal

3 tablespoons chopped lemongrass

2 teaspoons finely grated kaffir lime zest

2 heaped tablespoons chopped garlic

2 teaspoons Thai shrimp paste (gapi)

4 medium-sized quail, about 500 g (1 lb)
    in total *or* 200 g (6 oz) minced chicken or rabbit

pinch of salt

4–5 yellow or green apple eggplants –
    about 150 g (5 oz)

1–2 teaspoons vegetable oil

1 tablespoon fish sauce

pinch of shaved palm sugar – optional

1–1½ cups quail stock – see method – or water

1 cup holy basil leaves

GENG BPAA NOK SAP

JUNGLE CURRY OF MINCED QUAIL

This curry is from Phetchaburi, an old trading city to the south-west of Bangkok with a wonderful market that sprawls along several streets. Be warned – it is spicy, damned spicy! Traditionally, this curry uses a special type of chilli grown by the Karen hill tribe who live in this region. Called prik gariang, they are shorter and plumper than bird's eye chillies; surprisingly, they are sometimes available in Asian shops, masquerading under the Thai sobriquet. Otherwise, bird's eye chillies are a fine alternative.

Quail is quite a popular meat in the countryside. Every market sells a few birds, plucked but not gutted, as some like the innards in their curries. Chicken or any game bird would be a logical substitute. And, although unimaginable at a street stall, I think that rabbit could happily jump into the pot too.

- First make the curry paste. Deseed the dried long red chillies by cutting along their length and scraping out the seeds. Soak the chillies in water for about 15 minutes until soft, then drain, squeezing to extract as much water as possible, and roughly chop them. Rinse the dried bird's eye chillies to remove any dust. Using a pestle and mortar, pound the chillies with the salt, then add the remaining ingredients in the order they are listed, reducing each one to a paste before adding the next. Include any seeds, flowers or buds you find when cleaning the basil in the paste as well. Alternatively, puree the ingredients in an electric blender. It will probably be necessary to add a little water to aid the blending, but try not to add more than necessary, as this will dilute the paste and alter the taste of the curry. Halfway through, turn the machine off and scrape down the sides of the bowl with a spatula, then turn it back on and whiz the paste until it is completely pureed.

- Take the quail meat off the bones, then mince it somewhat coarsely with the salt – if you like, you could also include the heart and liver. If desired, make a light stock from the bones by giving them a quick rinse before putting them in a pan with about 3–4 cups of water and a few offcuts from the lemongrass, garlic and galangal used to make the curry paste. Simmer for about half an hour, skimming as needed, then strain.

- Trim the apple eggplants and cut into six wedges. If using yellow eggplants, scrape out the seeds (which are bitter and can cause a slight allergic reaction), then rinse well; if using the green variety, there is no need to do this as its seeds are not irritating. Place the eggplant wedges in a bowl of salted water and set aside.

- Heat the oil and cook the paste over a medium heat until fragrant, stirring furiously to prevent it catching. This should take about 2–3 minutes, but be careful – it will become sneeze-inducingly aromatic. Add the minced quail, and simmer gently until cooked – about 4 minutes. Season the curry with the fish sauce and palm sugar, if using, then pour in 1 cup of the stock or water. Bring to the boil and add the drained eggplant wedges. Simmer until the eggplant is cooked (about 3 minutes), then add the holy basil leaves.

- This curry should be a little thick, but not too dry – it may be necessary to lighten it with a little additional stock or water. It should taste hot, damned hot, and should also be salty and aromatic from the basil with a tinge of bitterness from the eggplants. Leave to cool slightly to deepen its flavour and soften its spicy bite before serving with steamed rice.

1 small black-skinned chicken, about 400–500 g
    (12 oz–1 lb) *or* the equivalent amount of regular
    chicken, guinea fowl, partridge or rabbit

GENG JIN SOM CURRY PASTE
6–10 dried long red chillies
a few dried bird's eye chillies
good pinch of salt
1 tablespoon chopped galangal
2 tablespoons chopped lemongrass
4 tablespoons chopped red shallots
2 tablespoons chopped garlic
1 tablespoon fermented fish (plaa raa)
    or ½ tablespoon Thai shrimp paste (gapi)
2 tablespoons maquem or, at a stretch,
    Sichuan peppercorns, ground

1–2 tablespoons vegetable oil
1–2 teaspoons shaved palm sugar, to taste
2–3 tablespoons fish sauce, to taste
2–3 cups chicken stock – see method – or water
100 g (3 oz) green Asian melon,
    cut into 2 cm (1 in) cubes
1 tablespoon chopped spring (green) onion
1 tablespoon coriander leaves
a little shredded long-leaf coriander (pak chii
    farang) – optional, but desirable
1–2 tablespoons chopped Vietnamese mint
    or laksa leaf (pak bai) – optional
pinch or more of roasted chilli powder

GENG JIN SOM GAI DAM

BLACK CHICKEN AND GREEN MELON CURRY

This is a peppery curry from the north of Thailand, around Chiang Mai. It has a pleasingly suave note from the fermented fish (plaa raa), in surprising contrast to the pungency of the condiment when it stands alone – which is really quite a relief. Plaa raa is made by curing freshwater fish for several months in a brine with roasted rice, and the best one to use here is made from plaa gradii (which should be written somewhere on the label), a gourami-like fish that lives in the rivers of the north and north-east of Thailand. It is readily available in jars in Asian stores. Be prepared for a shock when you open the jar, but do try it in the curry paste – it really brings a depth and richness that no other ingredient can. For those who cannot find it, or for those who have found it but can't quite bring themselves to use it, Thai shrimp paste is a paler alternative.

Macquem is a northern Thai spice that is sharp with a lingering aroma of mandarin peel. It is akin to Sichuan pepper and Japanese sansho pepper, either of which can be substituted here.

Black-skinned chicken is considered to be medicinal but apart from its slightly sinister and scrawny appearance, it tastes like a mild guinea fowl or partridge. Naturally then, these birds could be used in its place. I have also seen rabbit used in this curry in the wilder areas of the mountains to the north of Chiang Mai.

Green Asian melon is available in some variety from most Chinese grocers. Otherwise chayote, the redoubtable choko, can be used in its place.

- If using a whole chicken, clean the bird and remove the backbone and wing tips. Chop it into 2 cm (1 in) pieces. Rinse and pat dry with a paper towel, then cover and set aside. Make a stock from the backbone, wing tips and any other bones. Rinse well and then cover with about 4 cups of cold water. You can add a few offcuts from the curry paste ingredients, such as the shallots, garlic, galangal and lemongrass – not too much, or the flavour will be overpowering. Simmer the stock, skimming as needed, for about 30 minutes, then strain.

- Now make the curry paste. Nip off the stalks of the dried long red chillies then cut along their length and scrape out the seeds. Soak the chillies in water for about 15 minutes until soft. Drain the chillies, squeezing to extract as much water as possible, then roughly chop them. Rinse the dried bird's eye chillies to remove any dust. Using a pestle and mortar, pound the chillies with the salt, then add the remaining ingredients in the order they are listed, reducing each one to a fine paste before adding the next. Alternatively, puree the ingredients in an electric blender. You will probably need to add a little water to aid the blending, but try not to add more than necessary, as this will dilute the paste and alter the taste of the curry. Halfway through, turn the machine off and scrape down the sides of the bowl with a spatula, then turn it back on and whiz the paste until it is completely pureed.

- Heat a little oil, add the paste and fry over a medium heat for 4 minutes or so until fragrant, stirring regularly to prevent it from catching. Season with about half of the sugar and fish sauce, then add the chicken and simmer for several minutes. Cover with the stock or water and add the green melon. Simmer until the chicken and melon are cooked, around 20 minutes, adding a little more stock or water as necessary – the curry should be quite wet. Taste the curry and add more fish sauce if it needs a little more salt, but do not over-season at this stage.

- Finish with the spring onion and coriander, and the long-leaf coriander and Vietnamese mint, if using. Check the seasoning: the curry should taste slightly salty and aromatic. Adjust accordingly with the remaining fish sauce, palm sugar and chilli powder. Serve with steamed rice.

GENG GATI CURRY PASTE

13 dried bird's eye chillies – about 1 tablespoon

10 fresh bird's eye chillies (scuds)

good pinch of salt

1 heaped tablespoon chopped galangal

2 tablespoons chopped lemongrass

2 teaspoons chopped garlic

1 teaspoon chopped turmeric

1 tablespoon chopped grachai (wild ginger)

1 tablespoon Thai shrimp paste (gapi)

1 cup coconut milk

good pinch of salt

1–2 lemongrass stalks, bruised

5 kaffir lime leaves or kalamansi lime leaves,
   each torn into 3 or 4 pieces

200 g (6 oz) sea bass or barramundi fillet –
   leave the skin on, if attractive

pinch of shaved palm sugar

2 tablespoons fish sauce

a few tablespoons stock or water

1 cup coconut cream

a few bird's eye chilies (scuds), lightly bruised

squeeze of lime or kalamansi lime juice – optional

แกงกะทิปลากะพง

GENG GATI PLAA GRAPONG

SOUTHERN SEA BASS CURRY

This is a very thick, very spicy curry from the south of Thailand along the slender peninsula down from Chumporn. The original recipe uses a small shark, which is popular in this region. However, easy alternatives can be found, like barramundi, sea bass, kingfish, barracuda, red emperor, red mullet, even prawns or scallops. Kalamansi lime is a small orange–green citrus fruit with a haunting tangerine-like aroma that is popular in the south of Thailand. It is not too common, but a combination of kaffir lime leaves and regular lime juice can take its place.

This rich curry improves, and the sharp edge of the chillies is reduced, if it sits and settles in a warm place for about half an hour. In climates colder than Thailand it might then be necessary to reheat it slightly: if so, warm it over a low heat, adding a little water to ensure that the curry does not begin to separate and become oily.

- First make the curry paste. Rinse the dried chillies to remove any dust. Using a pestle and mortar, pound the ingredients in the order they are listed, reducing each one to a fine paste before adding the next. Alternatively, puree the ingredients in an electric blender. You will probably need to add a little water to aid the blending, but try not to add more than necessary, as this will dilute the paste and alter the taste of the curry. Halfway through, turn the machine off and scrape down the sides of the bowl with a spatula, then turn it back on and whiz the paste until it is completely pureed.

- Place the coconut milk, salt, lemongrass and about half of the torn lime leaves in a pan and bring to the boil. Add the fish and simmer gently until cooked. In fact, overcook it, pressing the fish with the back of a spoon to break it up a little. Work in the curry paste and simmer until it has lost its rawness and become fragrant – about 3–4 minutes. The curry should be quite thick and dry, with the coconut milk threatening to split and showing just a hint of oil. Season with the sugar and fish sauce, moisten with the stock or water, then stir in the coconut cream. Finish with the scud chillies, the remaining lime leaves and a squeeze of juice, if using.

- Leave for 5–10 minutes to allow the flavours to develop. The curry should taste hot, hot, hot, yet rich and creamy, salty, aromatic and slightly sweet. Serve with steamed rice.

500 g (1 lb) small mackerel, gutted and scaled

3 stalks lemongrass, trimmed

2 stalks sugar cane, peeled and cut into
    5 cm (2 in) lengths then quartered
    lengthwise – optional but desirable

7 slices galangal

7 slices ginger

3–4 coriander roots, cleaned

8 whole red shallots, peeled

3 dried long red chillies, deseeded, soaked
    in water for 15 minutes then drained

½ teaspoon white peppercorns, coarsely crushed

BRAISING STOCK

150 g (5 oz) best-quality palm sugar

½ teaspoon salt

2 tablespoons fish sauce

2 tablespoons dark soy sauce

¼ cup tamarind pulp, broken into 2 or 3 pieces

1–2 bird's eye chillies (scuds), chopped

3–4 red shallots, sliced

pinch of ground white pepper

DTOM KEM PLAA TUU

BRAISED MACKEREL WITH PALM SUGAR AND SHALLOTS

This dish takes a long time to prepare but is very undemanding in its method – a simplicity born of its ancient and rustic origins. All that is required is a large, heavy-based pan, a gentle flame and some patience. It takes about two days for the braised mackerel to become infused with the sweetness of the palm sugar, imbued with an oaky flavour from the wood fire it's traditionally cooked over, and to take on a rich and glistening mahogany sheen; the slow braising also helps to remove the fishy odour from the oily fish. In every market there are large pots of this dish gently simmering away – it is sold at or near to curry stalls so diners can include it in their meal. Little frigate mackerel are the most popular fish to cook in this way, but carp is also a favourite. Often a freshly cleaned length of sugar cane is laid in the base of the pot to give a rich yet slightly bitter edge.

- Wash the mackerel, removing as many of the bloodlines in the cavity as possible. Drain.
- Using a mortar and pestle, lightly bruise the lemongrass, sugar cane (if using), galangal, ginger, coriander roots, whole shallots, soaked chillies and peppercorns. Arrange half of them evenly over the bottom of a large, heavy-based pan or stockpot. Lay the mackerel on top and cover with the other half of the aromatics.
- To make the braising stock, dissolve the sugar in 4–5 cups of cold water then pour this over the fish, covering them completely. If there is not enough liquid, simply add some more water, followed by the salt, fish sauce, dark soy sauce and tamarind pulp. Bring to the boil, then simmer gently for about 2 hours, skimming often and replenishing the stock with water as needed. At all times throughout the prolonged braising the fish must be completely immersed in the liquid, otherwise it will spoil. Thai cooks use two pieces of sugar cane braced against the sides of the pot to form a cross to hold the fish down. An appropriately sized, heatproof plate should also do the trick. Allow the fish to cool overnight in the liquid. In Thailand, cooks will leave it unrefrigerated. I've done this without incident, but you may wish to resort to the safety of refrigeration.
- The next morning, add some more water to ensure the fish is completely submerged and return to the boil. Simmer for a few hours and allow to cool (there is no need to refrigerate – the sugar that will have infused the fish acts a natural preservative). Repeat this process three or four times during the day, simmering, reducing, replenishing and intensifying this remarkable dish. The fish must remain in the pan throughout, otherwise it will break up. By the end the fish should be firm yet tender (often the bones will have melted away) and the stock should be dark, rich and laden with flavours – sweet, salty and sour.
- Cautiously lift out the fish with a wide spatula. Strain over the stock and sprinkle with the chillies, sliced shallots and pepper. Serve with steamed rice.

1 × 400 g (12 oz) catfish, trout or other
    freshwater fish, scaled and gutted

2–3 tablespoons light soy sauce

½ cup shaved palm sugar

2–3 tablespoons fish sauce

3 tablespoons tamarind water

1 large bamboo skewer

100 g (3 oz) neem (sadtao) or witlof
    (chicory or Belgian endive), trimmed

handful each of deep-fried shallots and
    deep-fried garlic

a few dried long red chillies or dried bird's eye
    chillies, grilled

1 tablespoon chopped coriander

ปลาย่างน้ำปลาหวาน

PLAA YANG NAHM PLAA WARN

GRILLED FISH WITH SWEET FISH SAUCE

Catfish is the best fish to use for this dish. Its flesh is rich and fatty and as it grills over the charcoal, it caramelises and becomes dark and smoky. If catfish can't be found then a large trout would be my second choice – it will not have the same depth of flavour, but it will still be very good indeed.

If you can grill over charcoal then do so, as it will impart the rich smokiness and complex taste that plays such an important role in the success of this dish. Prepare the grill half an hour to an hour in advance. The embers should have lost their fierce charring flames and glow with a kind and gentle heat suited to a long slow grilling. On the streets, cooks will grill this fish for an astoundingly long time – as long as an hour, even two, over the lowest possible heat. Thus cooked, the fish is impregnated with a smoky redolence.

The palm sugar, fish sauce and tamarind create a honey-like sauce that marries perfectly with the fish. Deep-fried shallots and garlic bring a nutty taste and texture and the chillies . . . well, they bring a character all of their own. The final taste is a cleansing bitterness from the neem (sadtao). The shoots of this medicinal evergreen tree bear tough, slender, serrated leaves. They are starkly bitter and must be blanched two or three times in water and then left to steep in fresh water – and this is how neem is sold in Thai markets. It is unlikely you will come across it outside Thailand, but blanched witlof has a similarly intense, earthy bitterness.

- Clean the fish, then place it in a glass or ceramic dish with the soy sauce and marinate for a few hours in the fridge, covered.
- Melt the palm sugar with 1–2 tablespoons of water in a small pan over a medium heat. Add the fish sauce and simmer for a few minutes, then add the tamarind water and continue to simmer for another minute or so, skimming as needed, until thick. Strain the sweet fish sauce then allow to cool. Check the seasoning: the balance should be equally salty, sweet and sour.
- Remove the fish from the marinade, pat dry with a paper towel (to stop it sticking to the grill) and impale the fish on the bamboo skewer (this helps to hold the fish together and make it easier to turn – there is no need to soak the skewer, as much of it will be inside the fish and so will not scorch). Chargrill the fish for as long as it takes, turning it occasionally to ensure even cooking.
- Meanwhile, prepare the vegetable. If it is neem, trim its shoots and cut off the tough ends then blanch it two or three times, starting in cold water each time. Rinse and steep in cold water until ready to serve, then drain well and bundle the leaves and tender thin stalks together. Refresh under cold running water. If using witlof, trim the root and bottom of the bulb, then simmer for about 10–15 minutes until tender. Allow to cool before serving.
- Mix the sweet fish sauce with the deep-fried shallots and garlic, chillies and coriander and serve in a bowl to accompany the fish, with the neem or witlof on the side.

ของว่างและขนมหวาน
SNACKS AND SWEETS
KORNG WANG LAE KANOM WARN

As the day wears on, a new team comes into play. This new street-food brigade assembles around offices, schools, bus and train stations – wherever there are people yearning for a snack after the day's work – and there's a lot on offer. The aroma of satay skewers gently grilling over embers lures customers. For those staving off a more substantial hunger, a few cheeky sausages with chillies and coriander should do the trick; sliced madtarbark, a Muslim pastry filled with minced (ground) spiced meat and served with a sweet and sour cucumber relish, can help too. Others will head towards a noodle shop, where they can order a bowl of noodle soup: roast duck or crab and barbeque pork tempt many Thais from their path home.

But the afternoon is the time when the Thai palate begins to head towards the sweet, and this is catered to by the carts and stands that sell trays of such desired treats. The Thai appetite for them is simply astounding: they will eat two or three delights without a thought and without it affecting their meal to come. Among what is available there will certainly be kanom beuang, beguiling little wafers filled with meringue, candied fruit and simmered strands of golden duck egg (foi tong), a classic of the Thai repertoire. Often the same stand will sell a savoury version with coconut and prawns but, given the time of day and the Thai proclivity, even that will be quite sweet.

A word of warning: it's advisable to be on guard when passing schools around the time their charges are released. Girls' schools are the most dangerous, as normally polite young things turn into forceful and menacing St Trinian's alumnae as they surge forth towards the snacks and sweets that will sate their hunger. The younger they are, the more fiendish they are! The older ones are more restrained, perhaps secure in the knowledge that there will always be another cart around the corner and another meal to come.

○ All's A-OK. This stallholder's just about done and ready to go home.

SERVES 2

2 santols

salt

2 tablespoons peanuts

1 teaspoon dried bird's eye chillies –
    about 5–6 – rinsed

2 tablespoons dried prawns

1 tablespoon shaved palm sugar

1 tablespoon fish sauce

3–4 fresh bird's eye chillies (scuds)

 GRATHORN SONG KREAUNG

SANTOLS WITH PEANUTS AND CHILLIES

This dish is a favourite of many Thai women, who relish the sweet, sour and spicy tastes it encompasses. It excites a flagging palate during the heat of the afternoon. Santols are quite a large fruit with a tough honey-gold skin, which must be peeled away to reveal a firm bone-coloured, quince-flavoured flesh. Beneath this, at the heart of the fruit, is a layer of slightly translucent white, soft-textured flesh not unlike that of a mangosteen, with three black seeds at its core. The fruit must be steeped in salted water before being eaten, not only to delay browning but also to leach out some of its astringency.

Santols are not very common, only seeing the light of day in a few South-East Asian specialty shops. However you are might find them pickled in large clear jars. Alternatively you can use rose apples or green mangoes – there is no need to soak them in salted water.

- Peel the santols with a paring knife, immersing them in salted water as they are done to prevent discoloration. Take out one santol and score it from top to bottom at 2 mm (1/16 in) intervals, cutting to a depth of about 5 mm (1/4 in). Return to the salted water and repeat with the other santol. Allow to steep for at least 10 minutes, to help leach out the astringency of the fruit.
- Roast the peanuts in a heavy-based frying pan over a low heat, tossing and turning them to ensure an even colour. Once they are golden and aromatic, pour into a pestle and mortar and grind coarsely. Set the peanuts aside and wipe out the mortar.
- Roast the dried bird's eye chillies in the same pan over a low heat, stirring regularly to prevent scorching, until they have changed colour. Cool, then grind to a coarse powder in the pestle and mortar and set aside. Wipe out the mortar again.
- Place the dried prawns in the mortar and pound several times with the pestle until they are also coarsely ground.
- Dissolve the sugar in the fish sauce over a low heat, then stir in 2 tablespoons of the ground dried prawns. Simmer for a moment until quite thick, then add some or all of the roasted chilli powder, to taste.
- Rinse the santols in plenty of water. Drain and squeeze quite firmly to extract excess water. Arrange on a plate then spoon over the sauce. Sprinkle with the remainder of the dried prawns and the peanuts, then garnish with the scuds.

¼ teaspoon salt

125 g (4 oz) cake or pastry flour – about 1 cup

½ egg, lightly beaten – about 1½ tablespoons

15 g (½ oz) margarine, broken into 1 cm
(½ in) pieces

½ cup oil – ideally flavourless pure coconut oil
(nahm man bua)

FILLING

2 tablespoons chopped red shallots

good pinch of salt

1 tablespoon chopped garlic

1 tablespoon chopped ginger

1 heaped tablespoon curry powder

100 g (3 oz) minced (ground) beef – ideally from
flank, rib or rump

2 tablespoons fish sauce – more or less, to taste

pinch of white sugar

1 small white onion, quite finely sliced

3 tablespoons chopped spring (green) onions

2 tablespoons coarsely chopped coriander

1 egg, lightly beaten

cucumber relish (see below), to serve

MADTARBARK NEUA

MADTARBARK WITH BEEF

This is a delicious, almost hearty Muslim snack that can be made with beef, chicken, goat or mutton. The filling can be made a few hours in advance. I think it is better to use a fatty, slightly coarse cut of beef, like flank, rib or top end of rump, as it gives a decided texture and a rich taste to the dish. Most Thai cooks and certainly all vendors will buy their curry powder from a nearby market or spice shop, so feel free to do the same – just make sure it is fresh and aromatic. Otherwise, it's easy enough to make a batch that you can keep in the refrigerator (see page 356).

Although madtarbark is often sold ready to go, some stalls will make it to order – and this is when it is at its best.

- Mix the salt into ¼ cup of water. Sieve the flour into a bowl and make a well in the centre. Add the egg, stirring to form a crumbly dough, then gradually work in the salted water. Knead for about 15 minutes until the dough is silken, soft and tender. Transfer to a large bowl rubbed with a smear of the margarine and leave to rest, covered, for an hour.
- Roll the dough between cupped hands to make a large oval. Divide into 3 balls and roll with cupped hands to smooth their surface. Return the dough balls to the bowl and cover in the oil dotted with the margarine pieces then leave to steep, covered and in a warm place, for at least 3 hours or overnight.
- Meanwhile, make the filling. Using a pestle and mortar, pound the shallots with the salt then add the garlic and ginger and pound all to a fine paste. Stir in the curry powder. Take 2 tablespoons of oil from the dough bowl and heat it in a small wok or frying pan. Fry the paste in the hot oil until fragrant, then add the minced beef and cook for 4 minutes or so, stirring to prevent it from clumping. If it does, add a tablespoon or two of water to help break it up, simmering until the mixture is quite dry again (if it is too wet, the pastry will become soggy). Season the filling with the fish sauce and sugar: it should be salty and warmly aromatic from the curry powder. Allow to cool then stir in the white and green onions, coriander and egg.
- Oil the bench (work surface) and your hands well with some of the oil. Take out one of the dough balls and press it against the bench with two or three fingers, spreading the dough to make a disk about 15 cm (6 in) in diameter. Now 'cast' the dough by holding one edge of the disk and, using a throwing motion and the weight of the dough itself, stretch it until it is a thin, elongated disk. Continue to throw and stretch the dough until it is very thin, almost transparent, then fold in the outer edges to make a large uneven square, about 20 cm (8 in). Those less daring or dexterous can resort to a rolling pin!
- Heat a large, heavy-based frying pan over a low–medium heat and melt a smear of the oil in it, then carefully lay the pastry in the pan. Let it cook for a moment then place a third of the filling in the centre, pressing down to flatten and spread it, and cook for a moment longer. Fold opposite sides of the pastry into the centre, then repeat with the remaining two flaps, making sure that each flap overlaps one beneath it to create a secure package. Continue to cook for a minute until the first side is golden brown. Add a piece of the margarine and shuffle the pan, then flip the madtarbark over, again shaking the pan to prevent it from sticking. Allow to cook for a minute or so then turn it over once again. When it is golden and cooked, remove. Repeat with the remaining dough and filling.
- Allow to cool slightly and then cut into squarish 2 cm (1 in) pieces. Serve while still warm, with cucumber relish.

+ CUCUMBER RELISH

¼ cup white vinegar

¼ cup white sugar

½ teaspoon salt – more or less, to taste

1 coriander root, cleaned

1 small cucumber, quartered and sliced –
some would peel it too

3 red shallots, somewhat coarsely sliced

½ long red chilli, chopped

1 tablespoon chopped coriander

Simmer the vinegar, sugar, salt and coriander root with a few tablespoons of water until the sugar has dissolved. Take off the heat and allow to cool. (This syrup can be made in advance – it keeps indefinitely refrigerated.) Just before serving, remove the coriander root and stir in the cucumber, shallots, chilli and chopped coriander.

MARINADE

1 tablespoon coriander seeds

1 teaspoon cumin seeds

3 tablespoons finely chopped lemongrass

1 teaspoon salt

1 tablespoon chopped galangal

1½ teaspoons turmeric powder – ideally
  homemade (see page 361)

pinch of roasted chilli powder

½ cup coconut cream

2 tablespoons coconut or vegetable oil

1 tablespoon shaved palm sugar

400 g (12 oz) pork neck or loin

about 30 bamboo skewers

½ cup coconut cream

pinch of salt

lemongrass and pandanus brush
  (see right) – optional

satay sauce and cucumber relish (see opposite),
  to serve

**+ LEMONGRASS AND
PANDANUS BRUSH**

2 small stalks lemongrass, trimmed

2 pandanus leaves

Starting at the thicker ends, make three or four cuts in each of the lemongrass stalks along three-quarters of their length. Fold each pandanus leaf in half and trim to make an even edge, then make four or five cuts in the trimmed ends. Tie the uncut ends of the lemongrass and pandanus with string or an elastic band to make a brush.

MUU SATAY

PORK SATAY

In every market, along every street there'll be a satay stand, its aromatic smoke luring customers to come and buy. The source of this smoke, the grills, are quite primitive – sometimes just a metal bowl holding a few embers and with a wire trellis perched across it. More often, a long, slender metal box of glowing charcoal will be topped with three or four long metal rods. Either way, it is the charcoal that gives the satays their distinctive taste. If you can't fire up some charcoal, then use a heavy chargrill pan (ridged griddle), heating it slowly over a medium heat. It won't imbue the satay with the same complexity, but you'll still have people lining up.

I like to use a fatty cut of pork, such as neck, but you might prefer a leaner cut, like loin. It is a matter of taste, but a fattier cut means the satay remains moist. Brushing the satay with coconut cream also keeps the meat moist, as well as helping to give the satays an inviting caramel colour. Some cooks will use a brush made with lemongrass and pandanus to baste the satay as it cooks. It is easy to make and imparts a subtle perfume, though naturally a regular brush can be used in its stead.

Chicken often finds its way into satay. Beef is no stranger either. If you want to use either of these meats, you'll need to alter the amount of dried spices: less for the chicken and more for the beef.

Finally, you can lighten the load of your preparation by making the satay sauce and the syrup for the cucumber relish well in advance and leaving the pork to marinate overnight. You can even grill the satays some time ahead – like many a canny satay cook in Thailand – then quickly reheat them to satisfy the waiting people.

○ First make the marinade. In a dry, heavy-based frying pan, separately roast the coriander and cumin seeds, shaking the pan, until aromatic. Using a pestle and mortar, grind the spices to a powder before adding the lemongrass, salt and galangal. Pound to a fine paste, then stir in the turmeric and chilli powders. Add the coconut cream, oil and sugar and stir until dissolved. Pour into a bowl.

○ Cut the pork into thin slices about 4 cm × 1 cm (1½ in × ½ in), add to the bowl and leave to marinate in the refrigerator for at least an hour, or as long as overnight.

○ Soak the skewers in water for about 30 minutes, then thread 3 slices of marinated pork onto each skewer. The satays can then be returned to the marinade for a few minutes or a few hours.

○ If cooking over charcoal, light the grill about half an hour before you intend to grill the satays. Stoke the charcoal, letting its fierce heat peter out to a gentle heat so that the pork will gently cook and smoke rather than charring.

○ Place the coconut cream in a wide, shallow bowl and stir in the pinch of salt. Take each satay out of the marinade and give it a cursory dip into the coconut cream before placing it on the grill. Grill the satays over the prepared charcoal or in a chargrill pan over a medium heat, cooking three or four at a time, or more if you can manage it. Baste with the salted coconut cream, using the lemongrass and pandanus brush if you like. Turn the satays often, taking care not to let them colour too much.

○ Meanwhile, gently warm the sauce, if desired. Serve the satays with the sauce and cucumber relish.

+ SATAY SAUCE

4 dried long red chillies
1 tablespoon coriander seeds
1 tablespoon cumin seeds
pinch of salt
1 tablespoon chopped lemongrass
½ tablespoon chopped galangal
½ teaspoon finely grated kaffir lime zest
1 tablespoon chopped red shallots
2 tablespoons chopped garlic
½ tablespoon cleaned and chopped coriander roots
1½ cups coconut cream
2 tablespoons shaved palm sugar
½ cup finely ground peanuts
½ cup stock, water or coconut milk
1 pandanus leaf, knotted – optional
1 tablespoon fish sauce – more or less, to taste
pinch of roasted chilli powder

Nip off the stalks of the chillies then cut along their length and scrape out the seeds. Soak the chillies in water for about 15 minutes until soft. While the chillies are soaking, toast the coriander and cumin seeds separately in a dry, heavy-based frying pan until they are aromatic, shaking the pan often to prevent the spices from scorching. Grind to a powder using an electric grinder or a pestle and mortar then set aside.

Drain the soaked chillies, squeezing to extract as much water as possible, then roughly chop them. Using a pestle and mortar, pound the chillies with a pinch of salt, then add the lemongrass, galangal, kaffir lime zest, shallots, garlic and coriander roots one ingredient at a time, reducing each to a fine paste before adding the next. Alternatively, puree the ingredients in an electric blender. You will probably need to add a little water to aid the blending, but try not to add more than necessary. Halfway through, turn the machine off and scrape down the sides of the bowl with a spatula, then turn it back on and whiz the paste until it is completely pureed. Finally, stir in the ground spices.

Heat 1 cup of the coconut cream in a small pan and simmer for a minute or two before adding the paste and frying it gently for 4–5 minutes until fragrant and oily, stirring regularly. Season with the palm sugar then moisten with the remaining coconut cream. Simmer for 2–3 minutes, then stir in the peanuts and simmer for 5 minutes. Moisten with the stock or coconut milk, add the pandanus leaf, if using, and simmer for another 5 minutes. Season with the fish sauce, chilli powder and a pinch of salt. It should be quite oily, rich, dark, sweet, nutty and spicy. Remove from the heat and let the sauce sit for about an hour – it will improve happily. Serve warm or at room temperature.

Overleaf: Pork satay

+ CUCUMBER RELISH

¼ cup white sugar
¼ cup white vinegar
pinch of salt
1 small cucumber, quartered and sliced
4 red shallots, sliced
¼ long red chilli, chopped
2 tablespoons chopped coriander

Simmer the sugar with the vinegar, salt and ¼ cup of water. When the sugar has dissolved, take off the heat and allow to cool.

Add the remaining ingredients just before serving.

PASTRY

1 cup rice flour

¼ cup tapioca flour, plus a few tablespoons
    for dusting

2 tablespoons sticky rice flour

large pinch of salt

3 tablespoons vegetable oil

FILLING

400 g (12 oz) fresh bamboo shoot *or* 125 g
    (4 oz) canned shredded bamboo, drained

4 tablespoons best-quality dried prawns

2 tablespoons deep-fried garlic

good pinch of salt

good pinch of white sugar

2–3 tablespoons light soy sauce

1 banana leaf – optional

vegetable oil, for frying

soy and chilli sauce (see opposite), to serve

ขนมกุยช่ายไส้หน่อไม้

KANOM GUI CHAI SAI NOR MAI

BAMBOO AND DRIED PRAWN CAKES

Finding fresh bamboo can be difficult and, even if you do find it, often it really isn't that fresh. I have included instructions for preparing it below, but if you have to resort to a can of good-quality shredded bamboo, rinse it well in a few changes of water before blanching it from a cold start in salted water, to help remove any metallic taint.

Some stalls make smaller cakes about 2 cm (1 in) in diameter. Usually these daintier ones are steamed before being sprinkled with a little minced deep-fried garlic, while the larger versions are usually fried.

- First make the pastry. Mix the flours together with the salt. Work in the oil, then add 1½ cups of water and work to form a thick but quite wet dough. Put the pastry in a pan or brass wok and stir constantly over quite a low heat. You may need to resort to a whisk if the flour begins to clump. Do not let it catch. When the pastry is half-cooked – it will start to become very sticky and take on an opaque sheen – remove from the heat and allow to cool for a few minutes.

- Cast a few tablespoons of tapioca flour on a board and work into the warm pastry for about 5 minutes until it is comparatively firm and clean to the touch. Be careful not to use too much flour as it will make the finished pastry heavy. Roll into nine or ten balls, each approximately 4 cm (1½ in) in diameter, cover with a clean damp cloth and leave to rest for at least 10 minutes.

- Next prepare the bamboo. If using fresh bamboo, score down its length with a small, sharp knife then peel off the hard, dark and fibrous outer leaves to reveal the softer, ivory-coloured layers beneath. Be careful of the dark hairs on the leaves as they can irritate the skin. Trim off the coarse base of the shoot and cut down its sides to smooth the surface. Rinse thoroughly, then steep in salted water. When ready to cook, cut the shoot in half lengthways and then into 5 mm (¼ in) slices crossways. Turn these slices on their side and cut into thin shreds. Place in a pan and cover with plenty of salted water. Bring to the boil and simmer for a minute. Drain carefully, then cover with salted water and bring back to the boil. Simmer for a minute. Carefully lift out a piece and taste it. It should be nutty and pleasingly bitter. If it is unpalatably so, then blanch once again and let it cool in the water. If using canned shredded bamboo, rinse it thoroughly then blanch it from a cold start in salted water.

- Once it is blanched and shredded, you should have about 1½ cups bamboo – 125 g (4 oz) – and it will keep refrigerated for several days.

- For the filling, rinse the dried prawns and soak in water for a few minutes until soft, then drain well. Mix with the bamboo, deep-fried garlic, salt, sugar and soy sauce. Make sure the filling is well-seasoned but not too salty.

- Lightly knead each pastry ball between the fingers, then press out on a board or plate, one at a time, into a thin disc that is very slightly thinner at the edges and about 10 cm (4 in) in diameter. Place a pastry disc on the palm of one hand and spoon 2 heaped tablespoons of the filling into the centre, making sure there is no excess liquid. Lift the edges of the pastry up and over then fold and crimp together, working your way around and pushing the pinched edges up into the centre – there should be about ten folds. Pinch the edges together into the centre, twist them together, then press down and seal. Each cake should be about 5 cm (2 in) in diameter. Keep covered with a damp cloth. Repeat with the remaining pastry balls and filling.

- Steam the cakes on a banana leaf or baking (parchment) paper in a metal or bamboo steamer for 15 minutes – it could take a little longer, depending on your steamer and the heat under it. Remove and smear with a dash of oil, then return to the steamer for another minute or so. Lift out, smear with oil once again then allow to cool for a moment before serving.

- Often, however, the cakes are reheated by shallow-frying them in some oil until golden, as pictured in overleaf. If doing so, let the cakes cool almost completely beforehand – this will help to stop them from sticking as they fry. Heat a heavy frying pan until quite hot, then pour in 2–3 tablespoons of oil. Add the cakes and shallow-fry over a low–medium heat, shaking the pan and gently shuffling the cakes to prevent them from sticking. Allow the cakes to colour lightly before turning with a spatula. Turn them two or three times until they are lightly coloured on all sides, making sure they do not get too brown. Remove and drain on paper towels.

- Serve with soy and chilli sauce.

1 yam bean, about 10 cm (4 in) in diameter

1–2 teaspoons salt

good pinch of white sugar

2 tablespoons light soy sauce

2 tablespoons small dried prawns – optional

ขนมกุยช่ายไส้มันแกว

KANOM GUI CHAI SAI MANG GAEW

YAM BEAN CAKES

+ SOY AND CHILLI SAUCE

4 tablespoons dark soy sauce

1 tablespoon light soy sauce

a drizzle of sesame oil – optional

1 tablespoon white vinegar

1 long orange or red chilli, chopped

Combine all the ingredients with 1–2 tablespoons of water – it should taste dark, rich and salty.

Overleaf: Bamboo and dried prawn cakes (left), Yam bean cakes (right).

These and bamboo and dried prawn cakes (see opposite) are sometimes sold at the same stalls as Chinese chive cakes (see page 56), and all of them can be eaten at any time of the day. If you can't decide, you could always make a little of all three fillings.

Available in Asian markets, where it is sometimes called sweet turnip or jicama, yam bean has a silvery brown skin and white, crisp, succulent and slightly sweet flesh. The tubers vary greatly in size, but the larger ones tend to be drier, starchier and less flavoursome.

○ Peel the yam bean. Cut it in half lengthways, and then into 5 mm (¼ in) slices crossways. Turn these slices on their side and cut into thin shreds – you should have about 2 cups. Rub the salt into the shredded yam bean and leave to drain in a colander. After 10 minutes rinse and drain once again, then wrap in a clean tea towel and squeeze to extract as much water as possible. Mix with the sugar, soy sauce and dried prawns, if using. Make sure the filling is well seasoned but not too salty.

○ Make, fill and cook the cakes in the same way as for the bamboo and dried prawn cakes (see opposite).

○ Serve with soy and chilli sauce.

1 cup self-raising (self-rising) flour

good pinch of salt

FILLING

125 g (4 oz) pork shoulder or leg

1 heaped teaspoon five-spice powder

2 tablespoons light soy sauce

1 tablespoon dark soy sauce

1–2 tablespoons white sugar

100 g (3 oz) firm bean curd

1 egg

drizzle of vegetable oil

3–4 cm (1¼–1½ in) Chinese sausage,
    steamed (see below)

4 cm (1½ in) piece of cucumber

¼ cup bean sprouts

¼ cup fresh crabmeat

SAUCE

2 garlic cloves, peeled

pinch of salt

1 bird's eye chilli (scud) *or* 2 cm (1 in)
    deseeded long red chilli

2 tablespoons roasted unsalted peanuts

½ cup tamarind water

¼ cup white sugar

2 tablespoons light soy sauce

½ teaspoon cornflour (cornstarch)

sprigs of coriander and chillies steeped in
    vinegar (see page 355), to serve

Chinese sausage

Good air-dried Chinese sausage is a
wonderful thing. There are two types and
both are available in Chinese shops. One is
lighter in colour and is made from pork, fat,
brown sugar and five spice, while the other
is slightly darker as it includes duck liver in
the mix. I prefer the former, and this is the
one needed here. The sausage needs to be
steamed for about 15 minutes before using.
This can be done over water, but if you have
a small bamboo steamer that will fit over the
small pan, you can steam it over the braising
pork to enhance the flavours.

ปอเปี๊ยะสด

POPIA SOT

FRESH SPRING ROLLS WITH PORK, CHINESE SAUSAGE AND CRAB

These wonderful spring rolls are quite different from the more familiar deep-fried ones. The contrast of flavours and textures between the tender anise-flavoured braised pork, the crisp rich Chinese sausage and the sweet fresh crabmeat makes for a memorable pleasure from the streets. Every element can be prepared in advance, making the final assembling quick and easy. However, the spring-roll wrappers are a little tricky to make until you get the hang of them. The method below is how it is done on the streets – where it is done on a large flat grillplate (griddle) – but if you find the prospect of making the wrappers daunting, there are a few alternatives. These wrappers are very much like crêpes, so if you have a foolproof recipe for those, you might prefer to use it – just make sure they are paper-thin. You may be lucky enough to find freshly made wrappers. And of course you can resort to dried wrappers, but you'll need to follow the instructions on the package.

- First make the wrappers. Mix the flour with the salt in a large bowl. Form a well, then gradually work in ½ cup of water and knead for about 5 minutes to form a smooth, sticky dough. Leave to rest, covered, for about an hour.

- While the dough rests, braise the pork and bean curd for the filling. Cut the pork into thin rectangles about 1.5 cm × 5 mm (¾ in × ¼ in), rinse, then place in a small pan and cover with 2 cups of water. Add the five-spice powder, soy sauces, sugar and bean curd, then simmer gently for about an hour, skimming often, until the meat is tender. The stock should taste rich and pleasingly salty. Make sure there is at least ½ cup of stock in the pan for later use – add more water, if necessary – then leave to the side, covered.

- To cook the wrappers, season a 15 cm (6 in) heavy-based frying pan by covering the base with a layer of salt and placing over a medium heat for about 20 minutes, then leaving it to cool. Wipe away the salt, but do not wash the pan. Reheat and keep the pan on a low heat. (If the pan is too hot, the wrappers will be too thick; too cold and they will be too thin.) Gather the dough, working it into a small, loose ball and holding it in one hand. Press or smear the warm pan with the dough ball, lifting it off quickly. There should be a film of dough remaining on the pan. Leave for a few moments then lift it off with a small bamboo skewer or a spatula and place on a plate. (If the dough doesn't stick to the pan, you may need to work an extra tablespoon of water into the dough. Knead well and let it rest for a further 10 minutes before trying again.) Repeat, making at least six wrappers and keeping the finished wrappers covered.

- Next make the sauce. Using a pestle and mortar, pound the garlic with the salt and chilli, then add the peanuts and continue pounding to a fine paste. Heat the tamarind water (taste it first – if it is very salty, you'll need to add less soy sauce) with the sugar and soy sauce in a small pan, then stir in the paste. Simmer gently for 3–4 minutes, stirring regularly to ensure that the peanuts do not clump – if they do, break them up with the back of the spoon. Pour in ¼ cup of the pork stock and simmer for another 3 minutes or so, stirring often. Some cooks will strain the sauce at this stage, but it is not really necessary unless the peanuts have proved to be tough little nuts. Make a slurry by mixing 2 tablespoons of stock or water into the cornflour then stir it into the sauce and simmer, stirring, for another 4 minutes or until the flour has cooked. The sauce should be thick enough to coat the back of a spoon, sour, sweet, salty and nutty with just a fillip of spice. Set aside to cool.

- Meanwhile, prepare the rest of the filling. Crack and lightly whisk the egg. Heat a non-stick frying pan or a well-seasoned frying pan with a drizzle of oil, then pour in the egg to make a thin omelette. Cook over a low heat, making sure it does not colour too much. Flip and continue to cook for a moment. Remove and allow to cool before rolling up like a cigar then finely shredding. Cut the Chinese sausage into slices on the diagonal, then slice once again to make thin batons about the same size as the pieces of braised pork. Do the same with the cucumber. Lift out the braised bean curd and cut it into a similar size. Rinse and trim the bean sprouts, then rinse again before leaving to drain.

- To assemble the spring rolls, lay out the wrappers on the bench (work surface) and place a line of filling – braised pork, sliced bean curd, sausage, cucumber and bean sprouts – down the centre. Divide about half the crabmeat and omelette among the wrappers, then roll up each wrapper quite tightly to form an open-ended cigar-like roll about 2–3 cm (1–1¼ in) in diameter.

- Stir the sauce to break the skin that forms on standing, and add a little extra water if it seems too thick. Cut each roll into two or three on the diagonal, arrange on a plate and spoon over the sauce. Sprinkle with the remaining crabmeat and omelette. Serve with sprigs of coriander and a small bowl of chillies steeped in vinegar.

about 40 g (1½ oz) sausage casing

salt

1 tablespoon white vinegar

100 g (3 oz) jasmine rice

½ cup peeled garlic cloves – about 50 g (2 oz)

500 g (1 lb) skinned fatty pork belly, minced (ground)
    using a medium grate of about 5 mm (¼ in)

vegetable oil, for frying

bird's eye chillies (scuds), sliced ginger, wedges of
    raw cabbage and sprigs of coriander, to serve

ไส้กรอกเปรี้ยวอุดร

SAI GROP BRIO UDON

SOUR PORK SAUSAGES FROM UDON

These sausages have to be some of the best in the world. They can be formed into long links or into cute little nuggets then grilled or deep-fried. It is important to use fatty minced pork from, say, a pork belly. Some stalls sell freshly made sausages but I prefer the ones that have been slightly fermented – overnight in Thailand or longer elsewhere. They have so much more character.

I had always thought that the only rice to use when making these sausages was sticky rice, but in Ubon Ratchathani I had some of the best I have ever tasted. The only secret I could wrestle from the old woman who was selling them was that she used jasmine rice. Since her version was so good, I tried her way – the one that follows. Of course you could use some steamed sticky rice in place of the jasmine rice. You can mince the pork yourself or, if you have a friendly butcher, ask him or her to do it for you. It needs to be done using a medium grate: too fine and the sausage will be a little mushy, too coarse and it will be crumbly and tough.

Try to find natural sausage casings made from intestine. I know that sounds repugnant, but they do make the best sausages; synthetic casings will rupture and shrink as they grill. Natural sausage casings can be ordered from your friendly butcher or online (where they might have to be ordered in a large quantity – but once cleaned they keep very well indeed and can even be frozen).

Once made, the sausages are left to ferment before being grilled or deep-fried. They should always be eaten with chillies, sliced ginger and cabbage, all of which help to cut the fattiness of the sausage, sharpening your appreciation of this marvel.

○ Clean the sausage casing by rubbing with salt and vinegar. Rinse well, then slip one end of the casing onto the tap and run water through it (if this reveals any holes, discard the offending length of casing). Set the clean casing aside to dry.

○ Meanwhile, cook the rice and allow it to cool. Rinse the rice in several changes of water to remove excess starch.

○ Using a pestle and mortar, pound the garlic to a paste with a teaspoon of salt. Add the rice and pound to reduce to a mushy paste. Combine the paste with the pork mince.

○ Fry a little of the mixture to check the seasoning and adjust accordingly: it should be under-salted at this stage, since it will lose up to 15 per cent of its weight in water as it ferments and so the relative proportion of salt will increase.

○ If you have a special sausage-stuffing attachment for your mincer or mixer, now is the time to use it. Otherwise, fit a wide nozzle to a piping bag and wipe the nozzle with a little oil. Slip one end of the casing onto the nozzle and tie a knot in the other end. Fill the piping bag with the pork mixture and slowly squeeze it into the casing. Link the casing to make small dumpling-shaped sausages or larger 4 cm (1½ in) lengths, as you prefer. To do this, simply twist and turn the sausage to separate the parcels. When you have a chain of small sausages, knot the other end of the casing.

○ Hang the sausages to ferment in a warm airy place for 1–2 days, placing a tray underneath as they may weep. Test after a day by either frying or grilling one: it should taste lip-smackingly good – rich, slightly sour and a little salty. The length of time you need to leave them depends on the ambient temperature and on how sour and pungent you want them to be. They can be fermented for as long as 4 days – but no longer, or they will spoil.

○ When ready, the sausages are best cooked and eaten straightaway, but will keep for several days refrigerated. To cook them, pierce the skin a few times with a skewer to help prevent the casings from splitting. Deep-fry the sausages in a wok over medium heat for about 5 minutes until they are cooked. Alternatively, they can be shallow-fried or grilled (ideally over charcoal) on medium–low heat for around 5–10 minutes. Allow to cool slightly before eating with scud chillies, coriander, slices of ginger and pieces of cabbage.

pinch of lime paste

¾ cup rice flour

scant ½ cup mung bean flour

¼ cup plain (all-purpose) flour

pinch of salt

1 egg yolk

2 tablespoons shaved palm sugar

FILLING

1 egg white

pinch of salt

good pinch of cream of tartar

3 tablespoons icing (confectioners') sugar

TOPPINGS

candied watermelon rind (see opposite)

   or 1 dried persimmon, finely sliced

¼ cup golden strands (see opposite)

   or freshly grated coconut

½ teaspoon sesame seeds, toasted

ขนมเบื้อง
KANOM BEUANG

THAI WAFERS

These thin biscuit-like confections are especially popular in the afternoon. On the streets, they are cooked on a gleamingly smooth grillplate (griddle) that is always well seasoned so no oil is used. At home a large non-stick frying pan is ideal.

The wafers are filled with meringue and served with sweet and savoury toppings, often both together. Thais see nothing strange in the combination of sweet and salty tastes, which can come as a surprise to the unsuspecting, but is a satisfying pleasure to those so accustomed.

The sweet topping has many variations, the most common one being golden strands of egg and candied watermelon rind. However, freshly grated coconut is also quite common, and sliced dried persimmon can be used in place of the melon. Dried persimmons are readily available in Chinese grocery shops: look for flat, dark maroon fruits coated with a white powder.

There is an alternative, equally popular filling made with prawns and coconut, which is very similar to the prawn topping for sticky rice parcels (see page 50), except that no kaffir lime leaves are used. Make one or both – either is a delightful addition to an afternoon's fare.

- Dissolve the lime paste in ⅓ cup of water and wait for about 15 minutes until it has completely precipitated. Drain off and reserve the lime water, discarding the sludgy residue.
- Combine the flours with the salt in a large bowl. Work in the egg yolk and sugar to form a crumbly dough, then gradually add about ¼ cup of the lime water to make a thick pancake-like batter. Leave to rest for about 30 minutes. (It can be kept for a day or so refrigerated, but bring it to room temperature before using.) The batter will thicken as the flour swells, so it will probably be necessary to dilute it with a few tablespoons of the remaining lime water.
- To make the filling, whisk the egg white with the salt and cream of tartar in an electric mixer until it is beginning to form peaks. Gradually add the icing sugar and continue whisking until it forms stiff peaks – just like meringue. Once made, it will last for hours.
- Heat a non-stick or impeccably seasoned frying pan over a low–medium heat. Add a teaspoon of the batter then use the back of a spoon to spread it into a thin disk 4–5 cm (1½–2 in) in diameter. Repeat to make another two or three wafers, depending on the size of your pan. When the wafers begin to colour around the edges and smell cooked, spoon a teaspoon or so of the filling onto each wafer and smear it almost to the edges of the wafer. Fold one half of each wafer up and over with a wide spatula to form a half-moon-shaped shell. Repeat until all the batter and 'meringue' are used.
- Carefully lift the wafers out of the pan and sprinkle with a few slices of the candied watermelon or dried persimmon, and a pinch of each of the golden strands or grated coconut and sesame seeds.

These strands have made their way from Siamese palaces to the Thai streets. Many stalls sell them, although few vendors will actually make them – they prefer to purchase them ready-made. Look around: you may be lucky enough to find some in a Thai specialty shop. For those without that option, here is a recipe for these delicious rich strands.

Normally this sweetmeat is made with duck eggs, which impart a richness of taste, lustre and colour that chicken eggs cannot. Although not authentic, I like to add a pinch of saffron to the syrup to enhance the flavour, especially if using chicken eggs.

2 duck eggs *or* 3 chicken eggs
1 cup castor (superfine) sugar
1½ cups jasmine water (see page 358)
　　or water perfumed with a few drops of
　　rose or orange flower water
pinch of saffron, steeped in 1 tablespoon
　　water – optional
handful of Thai jasmine flowers – optional

Separate the eggs, saving the shells. Strain the yolks through a fine sieve or damp muslin (cheesecloth), then stir in the thick egg white that remains attached to the shells and rest this mixture for a few hours.

In a separate bowl, mix about a tablespoon of the egg white with a few crushed eggshells.

Combine the sugar and perfumed water in a brass wok or a wide shallow saucepan. Simmer over a low heat, stirring occasionally, until the sugar has completely dissolved. Let the syrup boil for a further minute before adding 2 table-spoons of cold water to arrest the boiling.

Add the reserved egg white and crushed eggshells, then bring back to the boil. The egg white and eggshells will trap any impurities in the syrup, clarifying it, before forming a raft and rising to the surface. Lift away the resulting foam with a slotted spoon. Simmer for another few minutes, skimming the syrup regularly with a clean, hot spoon: ensure there is a bowl of hot water nearby to keep the spoon clean and hot, so as not to reintroduce impurities. Add the saffron, if using. When the syrup is totally clean and clear, strain through a fine sieve.

Return the syrup to the boil. Have a small bowl of cold water nearby, ready to sprinkle into the simmering syrup to keep it at a reasonably constant sugar density: the strands will be brittle if the syrup is too heavy, but the required filaments will not form if it is too thin. Pour the yolks into an icing bag fitted with the finest nozzle. Stream the equivalent of a few table-spoons of the mixture in a circular motion about 10 cm (4 in) above the hottest part of the syrup, where it is bubbling, then turn the heat down to medium. Allow to cook for 1 minute, then turn the heat to very low and drag a long chopstick or skewer through the syrup to collect the strands. (Lowering the heat before removing the strands allows the egg strands to relax and the syrup to settle, making it easier to collect and 'comb' the strands.) Drag the chopstick backwards and forwards, collecting all the strands, teasing and unknotting them. Lay on a plate, folding the strands into thirds. Add 2 tablespoons of cold water to the syrup, return it to the boil, skim the surface, then stream in more yolk mixture.

Once cooked, the strands are often moistened with a little syrup to give them an alluring gleam. They can also be perfumed in a covered bowl with several jasmine flowers for a few hours.

pinch of lime paste
50 g (2 oz) watermelon rind – about ½ cup
¼ cup white sugar

Dissolve the lime paste in 1 cup of water and wait for about 15 minutes until it has completely precipitated. Drain off and reserve the lime water, discarding the sludgy residue.

Peel off the watermelon rind's green skin, leaving just the firm white pith. Cut the pith into large wedges about 7–9 cm (3–3½ in) in length. Steep in the lime water for about 20 minutes, then drain and rinse thoroughly in fresh water. Make a syrup by simmering the sugar with ¼ cup of water (ideally, perfumed with jasmine – see page 358) in a saucepan over a low heat. Add the watermelon rind and simmer gently for up to an hour, until it is glistening and translucent. Leave to cool.

Store the candied rind in the syrup, covered – it lasts a few days at room temperature, much longer refrigerated. Before using, cut into small slices about 2 cm × 2 mm (1 in × ⅛ in).

Overleaf: Thai wafers

SERVES 3–6

1 cup flattened rice
¼ cup shaved palm sugar
½ teaspoon maltose or corn syrup
½ cup grated coconut
5–6 sugar bananas

BATTER
½ cup rice flour
1 small egg, lightly beaten
1–2 tablespoons coconut cream
pinch of lime paste

vegetable oil, for deep-frying

ข้าวเม่าทอด
KAO MAO TORT

BANANA FRITTERS

This is an afternoon treat that traces its origins to the cool arcades of Siamese palaces but has now found its way onto the infernal streets of Thailand.

Maltose or corn syrup is liquid sugar based on starch or corn. Here it prevents the sugar from crystallising and helps to keep the finished paste malleable. Flattened rice is simply flattened flakes of rice, also known as beaten rice or rice flakes. It is readily available in some health-food shops, as well as in Asian and Indian shops, where it is called poha rice – try to find the unbleached variety. The best bananas to use are the short plump ones known as Ducasse or sugar bananas.

- Toast the flattened rice in a dry wok or frying pan over a low heat, tossing regularly, until it is an even light-golden colour. Allow to cool.
- In a small bowl, work the palm sugar and maltose or corn syrup into the grated coconut. Transfer to a small pan, place over a low heat and simmer gently until it is quite sticky, stirring constantly and taking care not to let it catch and scorch. It may be necessary to add a few tablespoons of water so that it cooks evenly, but make sure that all the water evaporates.
- Stir in the toasted flattened rice thoroughly and continue to cook over a gentle heat, stirring and turning, until it forms quite a thick paste – this should take about 2–3 minutes. Allow to cool.
- Peel the bananas and then press, wrap and enclose the bananas in the paste. This can be done a few hours in advance – because they are fully enclosed, the bananas will not become overly discoloured.
- To make the batter, combine the rice flour, egg and coconut cream in a large bowl, kneading for several minutes to form a smooth, silken dough. Wrap in plastic film and leave to rest for at least 30 minutes. Meanwhile, dissolve the lime paste in ½ cup of water and wait for about 15 minutes until it has completely precipitated. Drain off and reserve the lime water, discarding the sludgy residue. Work the lime water into the rested dough to produce a batter with a thick, pancake-like consistency. Let it rest for another 20 minutes or so.
- Pour the deep-frying oil into a large, stable wok or a wide, heavy-based pan until it is about two-thirds full. Heat the oil over a medium–high flame until a cooking thermometer registers 180°C (350°F). Alternatively, test the temperature of the oil by dropping in a cube of bread – it will brown in about 15 seconds if the oil is hot enough. Dip the bananas into the batter, coating them generously. Deep-fry in batches over a moderate heat, turning constantly with tongs, a small spider or long chopsticks, until golden. Drain on paper towels. When all the banana fritters are cooked, pour the remaining batter into the hot oil and cook until golden, then drain.
- Serve the banana fritters warm or at room temperature, sprinkled with the additional crunchy batter.

20–30 Thai jasmine flowers *or* 3–4 pandanus
leaves, cut into 5 cm (2 in) lengths

COCONUT CANDIES

½ cup shaved palm sugar

1 tablespoon maltose or glucose

1 cup grated coconut

DUMPLING DOUGH

⅓ cup sticky rice flour

pinch of salt

THICKENED COCONUT CREAM

½ cup rice flour

1 tablespoon arrowroot flour

1 cup coconut cream

1 teaspoon salt

+ WRAPPING IN BANANA LEAVES

1 roll of banana leaves – about 2 metres (6 feet)

15–20 wooden toothpicks

Cut the banana leaves into strips
approximately 25 cm × 5 cm (10 in × 2 in).
You will need about 36 banana-leaf strips,
allowing for a few trials and some errors. From
the remaining banana leaves, cut 15–20 ties,
each about 30 cm × 5 mm (12 in × ¼ in).

Trim the end of each strip into an
elongated oval point and wipe both sides
with a damp cloth. Now place one strip on
the bench (work surface), with its shiny side
facing down, and place another directly on
top, with its shiny side facing upwards.

Place a small matchbox or similar-sized
wooden block in the centre of the two banana
leaf strips. Bring each end up to make a crease.
Remove the block and place a dumpling in
the centre of the creased leaves. Cover with
a tablespoon or two of the thickened coconut
topping, then fold up each end to form
a package. Wrap with a tie and then secure
with a toothpick.

Repeat with the remaining banana leaves
and dumplings.

KANOM SAI SAI

STEAMED COCONUT CANDIES
IN THICKENED COCONUT CREAM

This is a fantastic sweet – it's rich, luscious and nutty. Each small, chewy nugget of caramelised coconut is rolled in rice-flour dough, covered in a soft, thick and luscious coconut cream and then wrapped
in a banana leaf and steamed. It is a difficult recipe, but one that's well worth the effort, I assure you.

Perfumed water gives this dessert its distinctive flavour. If you can find Thai jasmine flowers,
infuse the water with them overnight (see page 358). Otherwise, perfume the water with pandanus
leaves or use water perfumed with a few drops of rose or orange flower water.

These candies are traditionally wrapped in banana leaves before being steamed but, perhaps
to your relief, you can also steam them in mini muffin tins. They won't look as impressive, but they'll
taste just as good.

- First make the perfumed water: either steep the jasmine flowers overnight in 2 cups of water then strain,
or simmer the pandanus leaves in 2 cups of water for a few minutes before cooling and straining.
- For the coconut candies, melt the palm sugar and maltose or glucose in a brass wok or small non-
reactive pan. Add the grated coconut and ½ cup of perfumed water and stir over a low heat until all the
sugar has been absorbed by the coconut. Allow to cool. Roll the candy into balls about 1 cm (½ in)
in diameter – there should be about 15 of them.
- To make the dumpling dough, sieve the flour with a pinch of salt. Gradually pour in about 3 tablespoons of warm perfumed water, gathering and kneading to form a smooth, putty-like dough.
(It is difficult to give an accurate measurement for the water, as it depends on the quality of the flour:
if the dough seems too dry or firm, add a little more water; if too wet, incorporate more flour.) Roll into
a log about 2 cm (1 in) in diameter, and leave to rest for a few minutes.
- Cut the log of dough into 5 mm (¼ in) slices then press and wrap each slice around a coconut candy
ball, rolling it into a seamless dumpling. Repeat until all the candy and pastry are used.
- For the thickened coconut cream, mix together the rice flour, arrowroot flour and ⅓ cup of perfumed
water. Knead well then leave to rest for at least 30 minutes. Transfer to a brass wok or non-reactive pan,
add another ¾ cup of perfumed water and stir over a low heat until smooth. Simmer, stirring regularly,
until it has thickened slightly and lost its raw aroma – about 5 minutes. Add half the coconut cream
with the salt and continue to cook until thick. Add the remaining coconut cream and when the mixture
is thick, suave and silken, remove from the heat.
- Either wrap the dumplings in banana leaves (see left) or place in lightly oiled mini muffin tins, adding
a tablespoon or two of the thickened coconut cream to each one.
- Steam for about 15 minutes. Serve at room temperature – Thai room temperature – never cold.

SERVES 4–6

4–6 ripe plump small plantains or ripe
    sugar bananas, unpeeled

GLUAY BING

GRILLED BANANAS

These are simplicity itself. The bananas the Thai use for this dish are ripe, plump, small plantains called gluay hakmuk. Sugar bananas (gluay nahm wai) are an alternative, but they must be over-ripe so that their starchy sugar content holds them together as they cook. If they are under-ripe, the starches will make for a chewy, potato-like texture and taste.

Of course these bananas can be grilled on a cast-iron grillplate (griddle) and they'll be good, but they won't have the lingering smokiness that grilling over charcoal imparts.

There is another version on the streets, where sugar bananas are peeled and threaded onto bamboo skewers then grilled very slowly for about 30 minutes. Either version is best eaten slightly warm, since the bananas become slightly starchy when they cool.

o Prepare a grill and let the flames die down so that the embers are not too hot.
o Place the bananas on the grill and cook at this lower temperature for 10–15 minutes, turning them often to ensure they cook evenly.
o As the bananas cook, they will swell. When this happens, carefully cut along the length of each banana so it won't burst. Continue to grill – without turning – until the bananas are soft.

ก๋วยเตี๋ยวแห้งและน้ำ
NOODLES AND NOODLE SOUPS
GUAY TIO HAENG LAE NAHM

The noodle is the premier food of the street. On every corner, down every alley, in markets virtually anywhere where there are Thais, there is bound to be a stall selling noodles. They are a great levelling institution as all Thais, no matter what their class or wealth, will happily sit, precariously stooped, on wobbly plastic stools, to enjoy this favoured type of food.

Noodles are made throughout Thailand and some towns or provinces are renowned for their manufacture. For instance, Chanthaburi, on the east coast of the Gulf of Thailand, produces a dried thin rice noodle that is sold throughout the country. Up in the north-east, the cities of Korat and Pimai are also known for good thin rice noodles.

The basic distinction with noodle dishes is between wet and dry. For wet noodle dishes the broth is at the heart of good noodles. It must always be served boiling – and kept simmering and regularly replenished with water, always ready to go. There are as many variations of stock as there are noodles. The most popular stock is based on pork, but chicken, beef and occasionally fish are also used.

The best bones for noodle soup stock, whether pork or beef, are from the hip, knuckle and leg, which make a sweet, savoury and rich stock. The bones should be cracked to expose the marrow. Some like to soak their bones in water for at least 30 minutes before cracking them, to keep the stock clear and clean. I like to blanch the bones from a cold-water start before rinsing them well.

Daikon makes the stock sweet and gives it a rounded flavour. Garlic, often unpeeled, adds richness and weight. Some stalls will add spring onions, ginger, Chinese cabbage, coriander roots and stalks, old galangal and Asian celery to their stocks. Yellow rock sugar is used not only to sweeten the stock but also to give it a glistening sheen – not a terribly common trait on the streets.

White pepper is a common ingredient, often wrapped in muslin to mute its sharpness. Depending on the style of noodle dish and the meat, fish, bean curd or vegetables used, lightly roasted star anise, black and Sichuan peppercorns, cassia, and coriander and cumin seeds may also be added to the spice bag. Some stocks, called kom, contain soy sauce, both light and dark, which makes the soup somewhat dark and mottled. Another version, nahm dtok, includes some blood. The last style is called sai, and is a clear, rather light stock.

On the counter where the noodles are blanched and dressed, there is normally a clutter of bowls and dishes containing various seasonings.

Naturally, there are fish and soy sauces. There is ground white pepper and garlic deep-fried in oil or occasionally in pork fat, as well as preserved Chinese vegetable (dtang chai). Chopped spring onions, coriander and Asian celery leaves – one, two or all three – are used to garnish the noodles, depending on the dish.

Most stalls specialise in fish and seafood, roast duck and pork or beef, but they will sell a variety of noodle dishes based on these. Usually wet and dry noodles are sold from the same stand, which will often have a glass display cabinet and a sign above, saying what's for sale and for how much. At the front of the shop, there will be a large table with a central well that contains boiling stock and water. The well will have an insert to divide it into three sections, so the noodles can be blanched then rinsed. The second segment contains the stock, and the third is a back-up.

When an order for wet noodles (noodle soup) is received, a clean bowl is washed out with some hot water. The selected noodles are placed in a perforated ladle then plunged into the boiling water. If they are rice noodles, they only need to be heated through before being drained and placed in the bowl. If egg noodles are used, then the process is a little more involved. The noodles are teased apart, blanched while held in the ladle, then refreshed in warm water before being blanched again. This removes as much starch as possible while retaining the texture of the noodles.

Once the noodles are blanched, they are drained well before being placed in their bowls. Some stalls might dress them with a little deep-fried garlic, sugar and pepper, but most don't. Then the meat, fish or seafood is blanched, and dumplings are reheated; some cooks leave their dumplings in one of the segments of their central well, especially if it is a busy stall, so they can be drained and added to the noodle soup as required. The meat is added and the broth ladled over. If the meat is already cooked, such as roast duck or pork or braised meat, then it is laid on top of the noodles after the broth has been added. All noodle soups contain a small amount of vegetables: Chinese broccoli or choy sum, or even a handful of bean sprouts.

If the noodles are to be served dry, they are dressed and seasoned with deep-fried garlic and oil, preserved Chinese vegetable (dtang chai), fish sauce, white pepper and sugar. Most stalls now also use MSG to enhance the flavour and, regrettably, most Thais have come to prefer it. However, the noodles can of course be ordered without – say 'mai sai pong chuu rot'.

○ Noodles are blanched amid clouds of steam, ready to be served dry or in soups.

Ordering noodles is pretty straightforward – at least it is if you speak Thai. At most stalls, you simply walk up to the cook and tell them what you want to eat. In larger noodle shops, you make your request to the food server. Both have extraordinarily well-developed short-term memories and can hold many orders in their head. State the type of noodles first: rice noodles (sen) or egg noodles (ba mii), then whether you want them wet (nahm) or dry (haeng). Next you say what you would like with them: pork (muu), beef (neua), fish (plaa), duck (bpet), dumpling (luk chin) – whatever is for sale can be ordered. Putting it all together, you might ask for 'Guay tio, nahm, sen yai, luk chin plaa' (noodles, with broth, wide rice noodles, fish dumplings). Some Thais occasionally order the broth with its ingredients but with no noodles, 'gao lao', if they are not very hungry or if they are eating a second bowl and therefore don't want to eat too much. Others will order the 'wiset' portion – that is, with extra meat or dumplings in the dish. If no Thai can be spoken, then hungry gesticulation will often succeed, since most of the ingredients are at hand.

The cook prepares the noodles with rapt concentration. Many I've seen are masters of elegant and efficient movement, fast and focused. The dish is cooked in moments and brought to the table. If several dishes are ordered, then they are prepared one at a time and sent to the rickety table as they are ready. There is no ceremony on the streets – everything comes quickly.

The dish will normally be only lightly seasoned. This is done with the expectation that it will always be finished at the table, each to their own preference. On the table there is usually a cluster of condiments (kreuang brung): the jars will generally contain roasted chilli powder, chillies steeped in vinegar, fish sauce, white sugar and, depending on the stall and the dishes served, crushed roasted peanuts.

Noodle soups are eaten with chopsticks and a Chinese soup spoon; dry noodles are eaten with either spoon and fork or chopsticks. Customers will taste the noodles first, as every cook will cook the dish slightly differently, then they will add anywhere from a dash to a tablespoon of each seasoning before mixing them in. Then they eat . . . and maybe order another bowl.

The last two noodle dishes in this chapter are quite different to those served in clear broths from the steaming stalls. Although they are also soups based on blanched noodles, their broths are rich, creamy and curry-like. They are served from different stalls and have a different origin.

Chiang Mai curried noodles (kao soi) and laksa are cousins, distantly related to noodle dishes brought to Asia by Indian and Persian merchants, caravans, traders and ships. Over time these evolved into the northern Thai dish of kao soi, which uses egg noodles, and a southern Thai version of laksa, which uses rice noodles. The noodles are prepared with the same attention, and the garnishes play an integral role in completing the seasoning and giving these dishes some memorably polished tastes.

○ Noodle magic being woven.

PORK SOUP STOCK

200 g (6 oz) pork bones

1 small daikon (mooli), peeled and sliced

2–3 coriander roots, cleaned

5 garlic cloves, bruised but unpeeled

5 slices ginger

offcuts from the spring (green) onions – see below

1 teaspoon crushed white pepper

1 point star anise

1½ teaspoons salt

1 tablespoon light soy sauce

1–2 tablespoons crushed yellow rock sugar,
    to taste

CRAB WONTONS

75 g (2½ oz) fatty minced (ground) pork

30 g (1 oz) cooked crabmeat

pinch of salt

pinch of white sugar

1 generous teaspoon oyster sauce

pinch of ground white pepper

½ teaspoon very finely chopped ginger

good pinch of chopped coriander

good pinch of chopped spring (green) onions

16–20 wonton skins

1 cup choy sum trimmed and cut into
    3 cm (1¼ in) lengths

20 slices barbeque pork – about 125 g (4 oz)

30 g (1 oz) cooked crabmeat – optional

3 tablespoons garlic deep-fried in oil or with pork
    scratchings (see page 358), if desired

1 tablespoon preserved Chinese vegetable
    (dtang chai), rinsed and drained

3 tablespoons chopped spring (green) onions –
    keep the offcuts for the stock

2 tablespoons chopped coriander

ground white pepper

fish sauce, roasted chilli powder, white sugar
    and chillies steeped in vinegar (see page 355),
    to serve

Cooking fresh crab

To cook a live crab, despatch it humanely by placing it in the freezer for about an hour, then boil or steam the beast for 6–10 minutes per kg (3–5 minutes per lb), depending on the variety. The yield of crabmeat will be in the region of 40–50 per cent of the weight of the crab in its shell.

Storing stock

I really do believe that stock is best used on the day it is made, but that is not always possible. If keeping stock, allow it to cool then cover and refrigerate. It will keep for 2 or 3 days chilled, longer frozen. When reheating, add a slice or two of ginger to rejuvenate it.

GIO NAHM MUU DAENG

CRAB WONTON AND BARBEQUE PORK SOUP

This is a lovely noodle dish. The pork stock gives a sweet, soft body to the noodles; however, those with dietary restrictions will find chicken stock more acceptable and almost as satisfactory. Most stalls use a plain, lightly seasoned stock but the one used here gives the soup true merit and depth.

To make life easier, the barbeque pork can be purchased in Chinatown, but for those who want to make their own, I have included a recipe on page 302. Alternatively, pork loin can be used, simply poached in the stock until completely cooked then finely sliced. Blue swimmer crab is the best crab to use as its meat is sweeter, but naturally any other crab will do.

- First make the stock. Wash the bones and place in a stockpot or large pan. Cover with cold water and bring to the boil. Drain, then rinse the bones well. Return the bones to the pan, along with the vegetables and spices. Cover with about 3 litres (3 quarts) of cold water and bring to the boil, skimming as needed. Add the salt, soy sauce and sugar, then simmer gently for a few hours. This should make about 2 litres (2 quarts) of stock.
- Next make the wontons. Mix together all the ingredients except the wonton skins and leave the filling to marinate for 30 minutes. Have a bowl of water and a chopstick or teaspoon at the ready. Place a wonton skin in the palm of one hand, holding it with one of the corners pointing toward your fingertips. Using the chopstick or spoon, place about ½ teaspoon of the filling in the centre. Dampen the top and bottom corners of the wonton skin, then fold the bottom half over the filling to make a loose triangle and press to seal. Bring the left-hand corner across the centre, then bring the right-hand corner across. Now dampen the top of the wonton and fold down the top corner, pinching and crimping to form the wonton. Repeat with the remaining wonton skins and stuffing. Keep the finished wontons covered with a slightly damp cloth to prevent them from drying out.
- Bring the pork stock to the boil – it must be at a rolling boil when it is ladled over the wontons.
- Bring another large pan of salted water to the boil. Blanch the wontons in this, then scoop them out and refresh under cold running water to rinse off any excess starch. Return the wontons to the pan of boiling water, along with the choy sum, and simmer for a moment. Take out and drain.
- Place four wontons and some choy sum in each bowl and ladle over about a cup of the boiling pork stock. Top with the sliced barbeque pork, extra crabmeat (if using), deep-fried garlic, preserved Chinese vegetable, spring onions and coriander. Sprinkle with the pepper.
- Serve accompanied by fish sauce, roasted chilli powder, white sugar and chillies steeped in vinegar.

DUCK STOCK

bones from the roast duck – about 400 g (12 oz)

3 litres (3 quarts) light chicken or pork stock
   or water

½ small daikon (mooli), peeled and sliced –
   use the other half to make the chicken
   or pork stock, if desired

offcuts from cleaning the spring (green) onions –
   see below

4–5 garlic cloves, bruised but unpeeled

2 large coriander roots, cleaned and bruised

pinch of cracked white pepper

pinch of cracked Sichuan pepper – optional

¼ star anise

2 tablespoons oyster sauce

1 teaspoon crushed yellow rock sugar

pinch of salt

1–2 tablespoons fish sauce, to taste

pinch of white sugar

1 cup coarsely chopped or torn Chinese lettuce

200 g (6 oz) fresh egg noodles
   or 150 g (5 oz) dried egg noodles

3 tablespoons garlic deep-fried in oil
   or with pork scratchings (see page 358)

pinch of ground white pepper

1 teaspoon fish sauce

1 tablespoon preserved Chinese vegetable
   (dtang chai), rinsed and drained

1 cup choy sum trimmed and cut into
   approximately 3 cm (1¼ in) lengths

¼–½ Chinese roast duck, meat removed from
   bones and sliced – about 150 g (5 oz)

3 tablespoons chopped spring (green) onions –
   keep offcuts for stock

2 tablespoons chopped coriander

large pinch of ground white pepper

fish sauce, roasted chilli powder, white sugar
   and chillies steeped in vinegar (see page 355),
   to serve

BA MII NAHM BPET YANG

ROAST DUCK AND EGG NOODLE SOUP

This is one of my favourite noodle dishes. I find it hard to walk past a stall selling this type of soup, with its arresting ducks and rich broth. Roasting duck in the Chinese way takes years to master, but fortunately Chinese roast duck can be bought from any barbeque shop in Chinatown. Barbeque pork, poached chicken or prawns are more than acceptable alternatives.

○ First make the duck stock. Simmer the duck bones in the stock or water with the daikon, spring onion offcuts, garlic, coriander roots, white and Sichuan pepper and star anise for 20 minutes, skimming regularly. Add the oyster sauce and yellow rock sugar then simmer for about 2 hours, skimming as needed. Strain the stock, discarding the solids, then return to the heat and keep simmering. Season the stock with the salt, fish sauce and sugar.

○ Line four bowls with the Chinese lettuce.

○ To blanch the noodles, tease them apart then drop them into a pan of boiling salted water. Simmer for a moment or two, then drain and rinse with hot water and drain once again. Some cooks will quickly blanch and rinse the noodles twice in order to leach out as much starch as possible. Either way, drain the noodles well and place them in a large bowl. Add 2 tablespoons of the deep-fried garlic, the pepper, fish sauce and preserved Chinese vegetable and mix, stirring with chopsticks to coat well, then divide the noodles among the bowls.

○ Blanch the choy sum in a pan of boiling water for a few moments, just until it becomes vivid green, then drain and place in the bowls. Ladle over the hot duck stock and place the sliced duck on top. Sprinkle with the spring onions and coriander. Spoon over the remaining deep-fried garlic and sprinkle with white pepper before serving.

○ Accompany with bowls of fish sauce, roasted chilli powder, white sugar and chillies steeped in vinegar.

about 1 cup light chicken or pork stock or water

salt

100 g (3 oz) pork loin or shoulder, trimmed

6–8 clams or mussels, cleaned and debearded

4 medium-sized raw prawns (shrimp), peeled
    and deveined but with tails left intact

50 g (2 oz) squid or cuttlefish, cleaned,
    scored and cut into 4 pieces

100 g (3 oz) fresh egg noodles
    or 75 g (2½ oz) dried egg noodles

1 tablespoon fish sauce – more or less, to taste

pinch of white sugar

good pinch of ground white pepper

3 tablespoons deep-fried garlic in oil
    or with pork scratchings (see page 358)

good pinch of preserved Chinese vegetable
    (dtang chai), rinsed and drained

1 cup coarsely chopped or torn Chinese lettuce

pinch of chopped coriander and wedges of lime,
    to serve

บะหมี่แห้งทะเล

BA MII HAENG TARLAE

MIXED SEAFOOD AND PORK EGG NOODLES

Prawns, crab, squid or mussels can each or all find themselves in this happy medley. Chicken or barbeque duck or pork can also mingle successfully. It is important to blanch the noodles then rinse them well to remove as much starch as possible and make them less glutinous. Possibly as crucial, since there is no soup to augment their flavour, the noodles must be well seasoned with fish sauce, garlic deep-fried with oil or pork scratchings, sugar and pepper.

○ Pour the stock or water into a small pan with a pinch of salt and bring to the boil. Add the pork and poach gently for 10–15 minutes until cooked. Take out and allow to cool before slicing finely. Keep the stock to cook the seafood.

○ Bring the stock back to the boil. Add the clams and, when they begin to open, stir in the prawns and squid. When all the seafood is cooked – no more than a minute altogether – remove and leave to cool slightly while you blanch the noodles.

○ Bring a large pan of salted water to the boil. Tease the noodles apart then drop them into the boiling water. Simmer until tender (fresh noodles will be ready in a moment or two, but dried noodles will take a little longer), then drain and rinse with hot water and drain once again. Place the noodles in a large bowl and dress with the fish sauce, sugar, pepper, deep-fried garlic and preserved Chinese vegetable, mixing well with chopsticks. Add the cooked seafood and sliced pork, then stir in the Chinese lettuce.

○ Divide between two bowls and serve with coriander and wedges of lime.

SAUCE

1 tablespoon cleaned and chopped coriander roots

pinch of salt

3 garlic cloves, peeled

1–2 slices galangal

1½ teaspoons chopped ginger

2 tablespoons yellow bean sauce, rinsed

3 tablespoons white vinegar

pinch of ground white pepper

good pinch of white sugar – more or less, to taste

¼ long red chilli, sliced

4 cups pork soup stock (see page 204)
   or chicken stock

1 pandanus leaf, knotted

1–2 slices ginger

250 g (8 oz) sea bass or barramundi fillets

1 cup chopped Chinese lettuce

300 g (9 oz) fresh rice noodles – wide or thin,
   as preferred

2–3 tablespoons garlic deep-fried in oil
   or with pork scratchings (see page 358)

ground white pepper

2 tablespoons preserved Chinese vegetable
   (dtang chai), rinsed and drained

good pinch of galangal powder – optional

1 cup bean sprouts, trimmed, rinsed and drained

2 tablespoons chopped Asian celery

2 tablespoons chopped spring (green) onions

2 tablespoons chopped coriander

roasted chilli powder, white sugar and chillies
   steeped in vinegar (see page 355), to serve

GUAY TIO NAHM PLAA

FISH AND RICE NOODLE SOUP

Pork stock is the most common base for Asian noodle dishes, and it provides a suave and supple backdrop to this soup. If dietary restrictions preclude it, then chicken stock can successfully be used.

This recipe calls for fish alone, and the best type of fish is white, clean and meaty, making sea bass, barramundi, John Dory or kingfish prime choices. A little crabmeat or a handful of small peeled prawns could also be tossed into the mix, and in Thailand wontons, fish dumplings (as in the photo opposite) and sausages may also make an appearance in the soup, which can be as complex or as simple as you like.

Make the sauce several hours before it is needed – it improves with keeping and will last as long as a week refrigerated in an airtight container.

- First make the sauce. Using a pestle and mortar, pound the coriander roots to a paste with the salt, then add the garlic, galangal and ginger and pound well. Add the yellow bean sauce and bruise – some cooks like to pound the yellow beans to a paste but I like to keep some of their texture. Moisten with the vinegar then stir in the pepper, sugar and chilli. The sauce should taste sour, sharp and salty.
- For the soup, bring the stock to the boil and add the pandanus leaf and ginger. Simmer gently, skimming as required, while everything else is assembled and prepared – a matter of minutes. The stock should be well seasoned but don't let it reduce too much, otherwise it will become disagreeably heavy, salty and oily. Replenish with water if too much evaporates.
- Cut the fish into elegant lozenges about 3 cm × 1 cm (1¼ in × ½ in). Line four bowls with the Chinese lettuce and bring a pan of salted water to the boil. Pull apart the rice noodle strands and add them to the boiling water. Simmer for a moment or two then lift out the noodles, drain them well and place in bowls. Spoon over a little of the deep-fried garlic, a good pinch of white pepper, the preserved Chinese vegetable and the galangal powder, if using.
- Plunge the fish into the pan of boiling water and simmer for a minute or so until just cooked. Lift out, drain well and place on top of the noodles. Briefly blanch the bean sprouts, then drain and place alongside the fish. Ladle over the simmering seasoned stock.
- Sprinkle the soup with the chopped Asian celery, spring onions, coriander, the remainder of the deep-fried garlic and a pinch of white pepper. Serve with roasted chilli powder, white sugar, chillies steeped in vinegar and a small bowl of the sauce.

KAO SOI PASTE

3 bamboo skewers

4 dried long red chillies

1½ teaspoons coriander seeds

½ black or brown cardamom, husked – optional

4 medium-sized red shallots, unpeeled

3–4 large garlic cloves, unpeeled

1 tablespoon sliced turmeric

2 tablespoons sliced ginger

good pinch of salt

3 coriander roots, cleaned and chopped

2 cups coconut cream

2 chicken legs and thighs, chopped into
　　2 cm (1 in) pieces

about 1 teaspoon shaved palm sugar –
　　more or less, to taste

2 tablespoons light soy sauce or fish sauce

3 teaspoons dark soy sauce

2 cups stock, water or coconut milk

1–2 pandanus leaves, knotted

roasted chilli powder, to taste

250 g (8 oz) fresh egg noodles *or*
　　200 g (6 oz) dried egg noodles

1–2 tablespoons vegetable oil

GARNISH

about 25 g (1 oz) egg noodles, deep-fried

3 tablespoons chopped spring (green) onions

3 tablespoons chopped coriander

10–15 dried bird's eye chillies, deep-fried

ACCOMPANIMENTS

1 cup sliced red shallots

2 limes, cut into wedges

1 cup pickled mustard greens, rinsed,
　　drained and shredded

a small bowl of dried chillies in oil
　　(see above right)

+ DRIED CHILLIES IN OIL

3 bamboo skewers

1 cup (about 15) dried long red chillies

2 cloves garlic, peeled

good pinch of salt

4 tablespoons vegetable oil

large pinch of roasted chilli powder

Soak the skewers in water for about 30 minutes. Nip off the stalks of the chillies, then cut along their length and scrape out the seeds. Soak the chillies in water for about 15 minutes until soft.

Drain the chillies, squeezing to extract as much water as possible. Thread the chillies onto the skewers and grill until golden. When cool, grind to a powder using an electric grinder or a pestle and mortar.

Crush the garlic to a coarse paste with the salt – either by pounding it using a pestle and mortar or finely chopping it with a knife. Heat the oil in a small wok or pan, add the paste and cook until it is lightly golden. Add the chilli powder and simmer for a minute until it is fragrant, then cool.

KAO SOI GAI

CHIANG MAI CURRIED NOODLES AND CHICKEN

Most places in the north of Thailand have a version of this noodle dish, which is believed to have travelled from the south of China with Muslim traders. This version comes from Chiang Mai, the capital of the north. The soup can be made well in advance and left to simmer gently until needed. It should not be too thick and should be dappled with an alluring film of oil – rendered from simmering the coconut cream and cooking the chicken. It is important to have this layer of oil as it will coat the noodles, making them taste rich and luscious. The best noodles to use are flat egg noodles about 5 mm (¼ in) wide. Deep-fry a few of them in very hot, clean oil to use as a garnish, along with a small handful of dried bird's eye chillies, but be careful – the noodles splatter as they expand and become crisp.

Black or brown cardamom is a musty, dark, ridged seed with a smoky, slightly tart flavour. Some cooks add a little star anise and cassia bark to the paste in addition to or in lieu of this spice.

- First make the paste. Soak the skewers in water for 30 minutes. Nip off the stalks of the chillies, then cut along their length and scrape out the seeds. Soak the chillies in water for about 15 minutes until soft.
- Meanwhile, separately roast the coriander seeds and cardamom in a dry, heavy-based frying pan, shaking the pan, until aromatic. Grind to a powder using an electric grinder or pestle and mortar.
- Drain the chillies, squeezing to extract as much water as possible, then thread the chillies, shallots, garlic, turmeric and ginger onto individual skewers. Grill all the skewers: the chillies, turmeric and ginger need only be coloured, but the shallots and garlic must be charred and the flesh soft. Allow to cool, then peel the shallots and garlic.
- Using a pestle and mortar, pound the grilled chillies with the salt, then add the shallots, garlic, turmeric, ginger and coriander roots, reducing each ingredient to a fine paste before adding the next. Alternatively, puree the ingredients in an electric blender. You will probably need to add a little water to aid the blending, but try not to add more than necessary, as this will dilute the paste and alter the taste of the dish. Halfway through, turn the machine off and scrape down the sides of the bowl with a spatula, then turn it back on and whiz the paste until it is completely pureed. Finally, stir in the ground spices.
- Simmer 1 cup of the coconut cream until it is thick, slightly oily and just beginning to separate or 'crack'. Fry the kao soi paste in the coconut cream until it is fragrant and quite oily – about 5 minutes. Add the chicken pieces, turn down the heat and simmer for a few minutes. Season with palm sugar, then add the light soy or fish sauce and 2 teaspoons of the dark soy sauce. Moisten with stock, water or coconut milk and continue to simmer until the chicken is cooked – about 20 minutes. Add the remaining cup of coconut cream and pandanus leaves, then let it sit for about 30 minutes to allow the flavours to settle and ripen. Check the seasoning: the soup should taste salty, aromatic from the spices and slightly sweet from the coconut cream. It will probably be necessary to add a little roasted chilli powder.
- Bring a large pan of salted water to the boil. Tease the noodles apart then drop them into the boiling water. Simmer until tender (fresh noodles will be ready in a moment or two, but dried noodles will take a little longer), then lift out the noodles. Drain them, rinse with hot water and drain again. Blanch the noodles a second time to remove as much starch as possible, then drain well and mix with the remaining teaspoon of dark soy sauce and the vegetable oil.
- Divide the noodles among five bowls and pour the curried chicken soup over them. Garnish with deep-fried noodles, spring onions, coriander and deep-fried chillies and serve with the accompaniments.

LAKSA PASTE

2 bamboo skewers

5 dried long red chillies

1 tablespoon coriander seeds

1 teaspoon cumin seeds

2–3 cloves

5 slices ginger

4 garlic cloves, unpeeled

4–5 dried bird's eye chillies

pinch of salt

2 tablespoons chopped lemongrass

1 tablespoon chopped galangal

2 tablespoons chopped red shallots

1 teaspoon Thai shrimp paste (gapi)

2 teaspoons curry powder for beef
    (see page 356)

pinch of grated nutmeg

400 g (12 oz) beef flank, cheek, shin (shank)
    or brisket

2 cups coconut milk

3 cups stock or water

2¼ cups coconut cream

good pinch of salt

3 cardamom leaves or dried bay leaves

2 Thai or green cardamom pods

3 cm (1¼ in) piece cassia bark

2 pandanus leaves, knotted

2–3 tablespoons fish sauce, to taste

pinch of white sugar

¼–½ teaspoon roasted chilli powder, to taste

½ cup sliced red shallots

vegetable oil, for deep-frying

5–10 dried bird's eye chillies

150 g (5 oz) firm bean curd

250 g (8 oz) fresh rice vermicelli
    or 200 g (6 oz) dried rice vermicelli,
    soaked for about 20 minutes and drained

3 cups bean sprouts, trimmed

¼ cup dried prawns, coarsely ground

2 tablespoons preserved Chinese vegetable
    (dtang chai), rinsed and drained

3 eggs, hard-boiled, shelled and cut into quarters

¼ cup roasted peanuts, coarsely ground

2 tablespoons chopped spring (green) onions

2 tablespoons chopped coriander

wedges of lime and roasted chilli powder,
    to serve

Storing pastes

A paste made using a pestle and mortar can be made a few days in advance. It will keep well in the refrigerator – stored in an airtight container, with some plastic wrap pressed against the surface of the paste. However, a paste made in a blender with water added to it does not store well – a day at the most – before it deteriorates.

ก๋วยเตี๋ยวแขก

GUAY TIO KAEK

LAKSA WITH BEEF AND DRIED PRAWNS

Laksa has a chequered past, arriving in Siam with the Chinese and Malays, whose traditions and food crossed not only cultures but borders too. The most common laksa in Thailand is one made with beef and dried prawns, a variation not often found farther south; however, fresh prawns, chicken, clams and fish dumplings are also occasionally seen floating in this classic Asian noodle soup.

The variety of spices confirm the Muslim origin of this dish. The paste is complex to make but the resulting taste is worth it, and it can be made at least a day in advance and kept refrigerated in an airtight container. While I cannot advocate the practice, some cooks in Bangkok will cheat and simply use a red curry paste, adding a tablespoon of curry powder.

- First make the paste. Soak the skewers in water for about 30 minutes. Nip off the stalks of the dried long red chillies, then cut along their length and scrape out the seeds. Soak the chillies in water for about 15 minutes until soft.
- Meanwhile, separately roast the coriander, cumin and cloves in a dry, heavy-based frying pan, shaking the pan, until aromatic. Grind to a powder using an electric grinder or pestle and mortar.
- Thread the ginger and garlic onto individual skewers. Grill all the skewers: the ginger need only be coloured, but the garlic must be charred and the flesh soft. Allow to cool, then peel the garlic.
- Drain the soaked chillies, squeezing to extract as much water as possible, then roughly chop them. Rinse the dried bird's eye chillies to remove any dust. Using a pestle and mortar, pound the long red chillies with the salt and, when reduced to a paste, add the bird's eye chillies. Continue to pound, adding the lemongrass, galangal, shallots, ginger, garlic and shrimp paste, reducing each one to a fine paste before adding the next. Alternatively, puree the ingredients in an electric blender. You will probably need to add a little water to aid the blending, but try not to add more than necessary, as this will dilute the paste and alter the taste of the dish. Halfway through, turn the machine off and scrape down the sides of the bowl with a spatula, then turn it back on and whiz the paste until it is completely pureed. Finally, stir in the ground spices, curry powder and nutmeg.
- Trim the beef and cut into thin slices about 2 cm (1 in) square. Rinse well and dry. In a large saucepan or stockpot, bring the coconut milk, 2 cups of the stock or water and 1 cup of the coconut cream to the boil with the salt. Add the paste and, when it has dissolved, the beef. Simmer gently, stirring occasionally, until the beef is just cooked and beginning to become tender. This could take anywhere between 25 and 45 minutes, depending on the cut and quality of the beef. In a dry heavy-based frying pan, briefly roast the cardamom or bay leaves, cardamom pods and cassia bark, then add them to the beef, along with the pandanus. Simmer for another 5 minutes, skimming occasionally, but not overly scrupulously. Some cooks strain the soup through a coarse sieve to collect the aromatics, although others prefer to leave the aromatics in. You're the cook, you decide!
- Either way, return the soup to the boil and season lightly with the fish sauce, sugar and chilli powder. Add the remaining cup of stock or water and another cup of the coconut cream. Leave to simmer very gently for several minutes, stirring as needed. It improves if left to stand for an hour or so at this point.
- Meanwhile, pour the deep-frying oil into a large, stable wok or a wide, heavy-based pan until it is about two-thirds full. Heat the oil over a medium–high flame until a cooking thermometer registers 180°C (350°F). Alternatively, test the temperature of the oil by dropping in a cube of bread – it will brown in about 15 seconds if the oil is hot enough. Deep-fry the shallots in the oil until golden, stirring so they cook evenly, then drain on paper towels. Deep-fry the dried chillies for a few moments, then drain on paper towels. Pat the bean curd dry and deep-fry it until it has a golden skin. Drain on paper towels and, when cool, cut into 5 mm (¼ in) slices. Reserve the deep-frying oil, in case a little is needed to enrich the laksa.
- When almost ready to serve, reheat the soup and check the seasoning. It should taste rich, spicy and salty, but should not be too thick – it's a soup, not a sauce. The surface should be dappled with an attractive amount of oil. If it is not, I suggest adding a tablespoon or two of the deep-frying oil.
- Bring a large pan of salted water to the boil. Pull apart the rice noodle strands and add them to the boiling salted water, together with 2 cups of the bean sprouts. Simmer for a moment or two then drain and divide among four bowls. Add the beef and ladle over the soup.
- Sprinkle the soup with the ground dried prawns, preserved Chinese vegetable, quarters of hard-boiled egg, roasted peanuts and the remaining cup of bean sprouts. Garnish each bowl with 1 tablespoon of the remaining coconut cream, 1 tablespoon of the deep-fried shallots, and some spring onions and coriander.
- Serve with wedges of lime and roasted chilli powder.

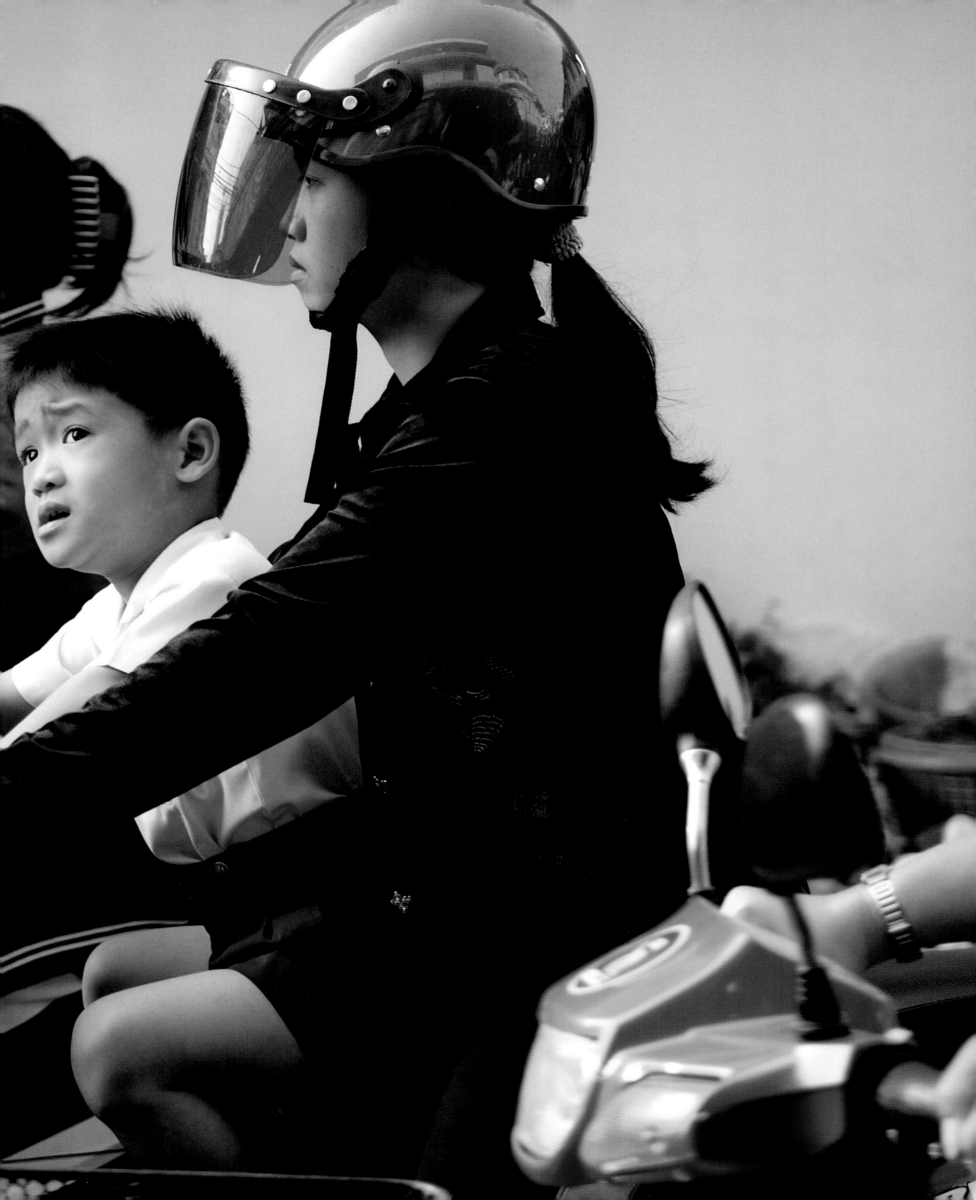

ทัฒนาการเกษตร
035-555561-2

NIG

GHT

IN THE TROPICS, NIGHT FALLS QUICKLY. There is little twilight to separate the day from the night. It is usually dark by about 6:30 p.m. The streets, however, are alive once more. Dinner comes early, with some people wandering out to reconnoitre as soon as 5 p.m. And given that some have probably been up since before dawn, it's time to eat. Night markets are at their busiest for the two hours or so from around 7 p.m. After this time, only the stragglers, those running late or those still hungry and wanting a second round will linger. ○ The range of food is more diverse than at any other time of the day. Many Thais no longer cook at home, finding it easier and more convenient to pick up something on the way home. Others may head out a little later and eat with family or friends. In the evening time is less constrained, and people will spend more time choosing what to have. They will stroll up and down the precinct perusing, appraising the merits of various stalls, considering what is on offer and working out what they might prefer to have tonight. The deciding can be as delicious as the eating! ○ As night descends, stalls ablaze with bare bulbs or stark neon lure customers. Like moths, they are drawn to the lights – on street corners, down narrow but busy alleyways, at petrol stations and near the sites of the morning markets. Wherever there is space, there are stalls crowded with people sitting, eating, talking and drinking. Signs advertise what is cooked, and each stall specialises. Some offer one or two dishes, others propose a range of simple, quickly cooked

Previous page: A wet night at Suan Luang market, Bangkok.

stir-fries 'made to order' (dtam sang). A glance will tell you what is for sale, but for those who don't read Thai, what is on offer becomes very evident on approach: noodles of all kinds, quenching and complex soups, stir-fried minced beef with holy basil, asparagus with prawns or Siamese watercress with shrimp paste, braised pork hocks with five-spice powder and Asian greens, comforting rice congee with its accompaniments. ○ Each night market is known to the locals: they know the stalls, they know the food, and they know the cooks. Most night markets operate where Thais live, and at times that suits them. Some areas are known for certain dishes and there may be three, four or more stalls offering different versions. And there is always a cluster of dtam sang stalls. ○ In tourist areas, the food may be less pleasing. These night markets cater to few known customers, even fewer of whom are likely to return. Hence the care, the quality of the dishes served and the pride taken in their preparation can suffer when compared to areas that cater to locals, where the cooks face their customers nightly and quite possibly have known them for years. ○ Although Chinatown in Bangkok is not as solidly residential, the night markets go on much longer, often into the early hours of the morning, since this is an area where people come to quell their late-night hunger and sober up before returning home. Some stalls remain open until 3 or 4 a.m., just in time to see the morning markets rub their eyes, yawn and begin to open up. The daily cycle begins once more.

ตามสั่ง
MADE TO ORDER
DTAM SANG

Finding a dtam sang stall is easy. They operate mostly at night, their bright lights a beacon to the milling crowds. Normally there is a large glass cabinet containing perishable items – all pertly, even proudly displayed. Some are makeshift stalls, little more than a cart returning every night to the same spot to encourage regular trade, while others are larger and far more established. Carts seem to sprout wherever people need to eat – and in Thailand that means everywhere – at night markets, factories, offices, a junction of busy streets. Now they can also be found in the daytime, in shopping malls and in the basements of buildings.

The menu is usually written on a board above the stall, listing any special dishes – but almost any combination can be ordered as it is up to the customer. Dtam sang means to order as one wants – and that's exactly what you do. Everything is made to order.

The food served is simple, determined by local ingredients and rudimentary equipment. Very little is prepared in advance, maybe some stock (though often just water is used), the meat sliced, the vegetables and seafood cleaned, and the pastes purchased from a nearby market. Most of the food is stir-fried, deep-fried or, occasionally, boiled: stir-fried vegetables and hot and sour soups of all kinds feature, as do deep-fried delicacies – popular, commonplace dishes.

The food from a dtam sang stand is slightly hybridised cooking, a mixture of Chinese and Thai food, cooked mainly by men, the descendants of Chinese immigrants. Initially the menu was very simple and utilitarian: some fried rice, a stir-fried noodle dish or beef stir-fried with holy basil. Later, as the menu expanded, many Chinese ingredients were used, such as roast pork, bean sprouts, Chinese broccoli, dried fish – a reflection of what was eaten at home by these cooks. But Thai elements crept in as chillies in hot and sour soups and brisk stir-fried curries made their way onto the menu.

Originally the cooking was done over charcoal made from mangroves growing along the coast near the mouth of the Chao Phraya River. A few stalls still use this fuel source, but most now cook with gas. One important piece of equipment is a battered pot, usually aluminium, for boiling. But the most important item, reflecting the Chinese heritage of much of this food, is the wok. Round-bottomed, carbon steel woks are the ubiquitous cooking utensil. I prefer the ones with a single wooden handle, which makes the tossing of food much easier than those with a pair of hooped handles.

When a wok is properly seasoned, it is more likely to impart the smoky undercurrent that is so characteristic of a good stir-fry. Tempering a wok is quite an easy process, and once done the wok is primed and ready for use. In Thailand, a few cups of grated coconut meat, usually the stuff that has already been squeezed to extract the cream, is often used. Other people use salt and I have also used oil. The method is easy. Simply heat the part of the wok covered with the grated coconut (or salt or oil) over a medium heat for several minutes, turning the wok, discarding the charred coconut and replacing it with some more, until all parts of the wok have been thus treated and its surface has changed colour and is slightly oily. If using salt or oil, there is no need to replenish it during the tempering process – but be careful not to overheat oil lest it burst into flames. Wipe out the debris, rinse the wok and then return it to the heat to dry and burn it once again. It's now ready. Always make sure the wok is very hot before embarking upon your stir-fry.

After use, wash out the wok with some water, scraping out any recalcitrant bits of food with a bamboo wok brush. These are readily available in any Chinatown and will remove the offending items without scratching the wok and breaking the seal. (To make the bristles pliable, soak the brush in cold water for a few hours before you first use it, and for a few minutes before each subsequent use.) Return the wok to the heat to dry. It is unlikely that you'll use a wok as frequently as a dtam sang cook does, so it might be wise to smear the inside with a little oil before storing it to prevent any rusting or oxidising of the metal. If cooking with it frequently, and I really mean constantly, then this step is not necessary.

The wok needs to be primed each and every time before using it. This is just a matter of heating it, scorching it then scraping off any carbonised residue with the bamboo brush. Wash it out, dry it by heating it and it is ready. By following this method, your stir-fries shouldn't stick to the wok, and they are more likely to have that desirable smoky tang.

Now what to put in the wok . . . in Thailand, you just go up to the stall and have a look at what's there, talk to the cook and then decide. Easy, if you speak Thai – but even if you don't, by indicating what ingredients you would like used, you should get something quite close to what you intended. Clams, mussels and fish – fresh, deep-fried or salted – will certainly be on offer. There is likely to be some roast pork hanging up and some raw meats on ice, all types of vegetables, such as Siamese watercress, asparagus, acacia and other Asian greens. So the clams could be stir-fried with chilli and garlic or with chilli jam, squid with garlic chives, or prawns with asparagus. You simply tell the cook what you fancy and how you want it – or point and mime as best you can.

Whatever is finally ordered, it is cooked and plated then served with rice. Since it is usual for Thai people to eat in a group, several dishes will be ordered to share, and they'll arrivie in no particular order, just as they're cooked. The pleasure of such a place is the immediacy of the cooking – often almost too close for comfort, as tables and stools may be huddled right up to the stove. Given its origins, as a stall serving workers, there is always the possibility of Thai whiskey nearby. Following is just a taste of what would be available, but it should give you some idea.

○ The night market in Samut Sakhon, south-west of Bangkok,
is more than professional – it's truly delicious.

SERVES 2

10 thin asparagus spears
10 medium-sized raw prawns (shrimp)
2 garlic cloves, peeled
pinch of salt
2 tablespoons vegetable oil
5–6 cloud ear mushrooms
¼ cup stock or water
1 tablespoon light soy sauce
a little oyster sauce – optional
pinch of white sugar
pinch of ground white pepper

GUNG PAT NOR MAI

ASPARAGUS STIR-FRIED WITH PRAWNS

This is a simple recipe that can be used as the basis for an array of alternatives, stir-frying snow peas, sugar-snap peas or any Asian greens alone or with scallops, pork or chicken. Thai asparagus is generally young, thin and crisp, so try to find fresh thin spears, which there should be no need to peel, although it will probably be necessary to trim off the tough stem end. If you can only find thicker spears, you will probably need to peel the stems. Fresh cloud ear mushrooms are used in many stir-fries, where their texture plays a refreshing role. They are occasionally available fresh in Asian grocers and some super-markets. The dried version can always be found in Chinese food shops: they need to be rinsed well to remove any mustiness, then soaked in hot water for about 10 minutes and drained before use.

- Wash and trim the asparagus. Remove the tough ends and cut into roughly 4 cm (1½ in) lengths. Peel and devein the prawns, but leave the tails attached; the heads can also be left intact for a more pleasing presentation, but it makes for trickier eating later.
- Crush the garlic to a somewhat coarse paste with the salt – either by pounding it using a pestle and mortar or finely chopping it with a knife.
- Heat a well-seasoned wok over a medium–high heat. When truly hot, pour in the oil and add the garlic paste, asparagus and prawns. Stir-fry, taking care that the garlic does not burn. When the prawns and asparagus are just about cooked – or should the garlic begin to colour too much – add the cloud ear mushrooms then moisten with the stock or water and simmer for a moment. Season with the soy and oyster sauces, sugar and pepper – it should taste nutty and salty.
- Serve with steamed rice.

RED CURRY PASTE

3–5 dried long red chillies

2–3 dried bird's eye chillies – optional, but desirable

2–3 fresh bird's eye chillies (scuds)

good pinch of salt

½ tablespoon chopped galangal

1 tablespoon chopped lemongrass

½ teaspoon finely grated kaffir lime zest

½ teaspoon cleaned and chopped coriander root

1 tablespoon chopped grachai (wild ginger)

2 tablespoons chopped red shallots

2 tablespoons chopped garlic

½ teaspoon Thai shrimp paste (gapi)

3–4 tablespoons vegetable oil

150 g (5 oz) mixed mussels and clams,
    cleaned and debearded

3 large raw prawns (shrimp), peeled and
    deveined but with tails still attached

100 g (3 oz) squid, cleaned, scored and
    cut lengthways into 4 pieces

1–2 tablespoons fish sauce

pinch of white sugar – optional

¼ cup stock or water

2 tablespoons shredded grachai (wild ginger)

2–3 kaffir lime leaves, coarsely torn

3–4 green beans, trimmed and cut
    into 3 cm (1¼ in) lengths

3–4 strands fresh green peppercorns – optional

2 long red or green chillies, sliced on the
    diagonal, deseeded if desired

¼ cup Thai basil or holy basil leaves

Cleaning clams and mussels

Clams usually need to be purged of sand and grit by being left to steep in salted water overnight, although sometimes you can buy clams that have already been cleaned. Mussels don't need purging, but they do require a good scrub to clean the shells and they may need to be debearded – that is, to have the weeds and strands that hang out of their shells pulled out.

ผัดพริกแกงทะเล

PAT PRIK GENG TARLAE

MIXED SEAFOOD STIR-FRIED WITH CURRY PASTE

Stir-fried curries are usually found at a dtam sang stall. Many cooks will use a red curry paste bought from the market, but the one here is more specific, and will produce a sharp, hot and honed result. It makes a difference.

Some cooks will add a smashed clove of garlic to the heating oil and wait for it to colour, to enhance the taste and aroma. Others will blanch the seafood first and then add it to the waiting simmering sauce, for a cleaner-tasting result. Almost any combination of seafood can be used here – the selection given is merely a starting point.

- First make the curry paste. Nip off the stalks of the dried long red chillies, then cut along their length and scrape out the seeds. Soak the chillies in water for about 15 minutes until soft, then drain and roughly chop them. Rinse the dried bird's eye chillies, if using, to remove any dust. Using a pestle and mortar, pound all the chillies with the salt, then add the remaining ingredients in the order they are listed, reducing each one to a paste before adding the next. Include any seeds, flowers or buds you find when cleaning the basil in the paste as well. Alternatively, puree the ingredients in an electric blender. You will probably need to add a little water to aid the blending, but try not to add more than necessary, as this will dilute the paste and alter the taste of the curry. Halfway through, turn the machine off and scrape down the sides of the bowl with a spatula, then turn it back on and whiz the paste again. Some cooks like to leave this paste just slightly coarse, enjoying its texture.
- Heat a well-seasoned wok and pour in the oil, then add the paste and fry over medium heat until fragrant – about a minute. If it threatens to catch, moisten with a tablespoon or two of water. Add the mussels and clams and fry until they are just beginning to open before adding the prawns and then, after a few moments, the squid. Season with the fish sauce and sugar then add the stock or water, grachai, kaffir lime leaves, green beans, fresh peppercorns (if using) and sliced chillies. Simmer for a moment until all is cooked.
- This stir-fried curry should taste rich, hot, salty and slightly oily. Finish with the basil leaves.
- Serve with steamed rice.

SERVES 2

½ long red chilli

pinch of salt

1 large garlic clove, peeled

2 tablespoons vegetable oil

1 teaspoon Thai shrimp paste (gapi)

200 g (6 oz) Siamese watercress (water spinach),
     cleaned, trimmed and cut into 3 cm (1¼ in) lengths

4–7 bird's eye chillies (scuds), bruised –
     an optional surprise

3–4 tablespoons stock or water

PAK BUNG PAT GAPI

SIAMESE WATERCRESS STIR-FRIED WITH SHRIMP PASTE

Siamese watercress – also known as kangkung or water spinach – is a mainstay of Thai food. It is eaten in a variety of ways, and this is one of the more popular on the streets, using a little shrimp paste to perfume the stir-fry without overwhelming it. Make sure the shrimp paste is the best quality you can find: some brands are harsh, salty and acrid, though lightening such paste with a little water should take the edge off it. Yellow beans or even fermented bean curd are alternative seasonings to the shrimp paste. Sometimes a few prawns, fresh or dried, are tossed in as well. And various green fleshy-stalked vegetables could be used in place of the Siamese watercress, such as choy sum or, in a pinch, Chinese cabbage.

- Using a pestle and mortar, pound the chilli to quite a coarse paste with the salt and garlic.
- Heat a well-seasoned wok, pour in the oil and, when hot, add the garlic and chilli paste and fry until slightly golden. Add the shrimp paste and fry for a moment before adding the Siamese watercress and scuds, if daring enough. Then moisten with the stock or water and boil for a moment over a high heat. It should taste quite rich and smooth, oily, spicy and salty.
- Serve with steamed rice.

SERVES 2–3

1–2 garlic cloves, peeled

an equivalent amount of peeled ginger

pinch of salt

3–4 tablespoons vegetable oil

2 heaped tablespoons curry powder

1–2 tablespoons fish sauce, to taste

smallest pinch of white sugar, to taste

200 g (6 oz) fresh crabmeat

1 small bunch Asian celery, cleaned and
    cut into 2 cm (1 in) lengths, about 1 cup –
    optional, but desirable

1 tablespoon shredded ginger

1–2 long orange, red or even green chillies,
    sliced on the diagonal, deseeded if desired

½ small white onion, sliced

3–4 small spring (green) onions, cleaned and
    cut into 3 cm (1¼ in) lengths

1 tablespoon chopped coriander

Cooking fresh crab

To cook a live crab, despatch it humanely by placing it in the freezer for about an hour, then boil or steam the beast for 6–10 minutes per kg (3–5 minutes per lb), depending on the variety. The yield of crabmeat will be in the region of 40–50 per cent of the weight of the crab in its shell.

ปูผัดผงกะหรี่

BPUU PAT PONG GARI

CRAB STIR-FRIED WITH CURRY POWDER

Thais would use a generic curry powder for this, perhaps enlivened with some chilli powder. If you have a favourite blend, feel free to use it, but for the purist there is a recipe for a curry powder on page 356 that works particularly well with crab and other seafood.

Some cooks will enrich this stir-fry with a ladle of coconut cream, while others will thicken it with an egg – it is entirely up to the cook. I like the combination of spring onions and sliced onions, which cuts through the spices and enhances the sweetness of the crab. Mud crabs, sand crabs or blue swimmers are the best ones to use here. Freshly cooked crabmeat is a time-saving blessing: it is sold in Thai markets, and by good fishmongers elsewhere. Otherwise, to ensure a spanking freshness, prepare your own (see above). Allow the cooked crab to cool before cracking the shell gently with the back of a heavy knife then prising and lifting out the sweet meat – try to keep the meat in large hunks, or it will break up into a mash when it is stir-fried. Keep the odd claw to use as a garnish, if you like.

- Using a pestle and mortar, pound the garlic, ginger and salt into a rather coarse paste.
- Heat a well-seasoned wok, add the oil and then fry the paste over a medium heat for a few minutes. Just as it is beginning to colour, sprinkle in the curry powder. Turn down the heat a little and continue to fry for a few moments, stirring constantly. When fragrant, season with fish sauce and sugar and simmer for a moment.
- Now add the crabmeat, along with the Asian celery (if using), ginger, chillies, white onion and spring onion. Allow to warm through for a moment, than check the seasoning. It should taste aromatic, rich and salty.
- Sprinkle with coriander and serve with steamed rice.

SERVES 2

4 garlic cloves, peeled
4–10 bird's eye chillies (scuds)
good pinch of salt
3–4 tablespoons vegetable oil
2 eggs
200 g (6 oz) coarsely minced (ground) beef
about 2 tablespoons fish sauce
large pinch of white sugar
¼ cup stock or water
2 large handfuls of holy basil leaves
chillies in fish sauce (see right), to serve

+ CHILLIES IN FISH SAUCE

¼ cup fish sauce
10–15 bird's eye chillies (scuds), finely sliced
2 garlic cloves, finely sliced – optional but desirable
1 tablespoon lime juice – optional
good pinch of chopped coriander

Combine the fish sauce, chillies and garlic in a bowl and set aside. It keeps for some time – in fact it becomes richer and milder as it settles for a day. Make sure it is covered if you are making it in advance – and if the fish sauce evaporates, add an equivalent amount of water to refresh it. Just before serving, stir through the lime juice and coriander.

NEUA PAT BAI GRAPAO

STIR-FRIED MINCED BEEF WITH CHILLIES AND HOLY BASIL

This is a relatively recent addition to the Thai repertoire, coming onto the streets about 50 years ago. The secret to the dish, I think, lies in the tempering of the wok, which imbues this simple stir-fry with a smoky tinge. Although beef was probably the first meat to be used, now minced (ground) chicken or pork, whole prawns or scored squid, even fish dumplings are cooked in this way. I find a rather coarse mince yields the best result – ideally done by hand, and using a cut of beef with some fat attached, such as flank, rump or shoulder.

Strangely, for this dish I find that mincing or chopping the garlic and chillies gives a better flavour than pounding them. Add as many small chillies as you can bear – head towards 10, as this dish is meant to be hot – the fieriness is offset by the supple richness of the fried eggs. I like the sauce seasoned with fish sauce alone but some cooks will add a little oyster sauce or even some chilli jam. This dish and an egg or two over some steaming rice, with a bowl of chillies in fish sauce alongside, is Thai ambrosia.

- Coarsely chop the garlic with the chillies and salt.
- Heat a well-seasoned wok over a high heat then turn down the heat and add 2 tablespoons of the oil. Crack in one of the eggs and fry gently, shuffling the egg to prevent it from sticking, until it has cooked to your preference – I like mine with a runny yolk but with crispy, frazzled edges. Spoon some of the hot oil over the egg to ensure the yolk cooks evenly. Carefully lift out the egg with a spatula and place it on a warmed plate, then fry the other egg. Keep the eggs warm while you cook the beef.
- Add more oil – you'll need about 4 tablespoons of oil in all in the wok. When the oil is hot, fry the garlic and chillies for a moment, but don't let it colour. Add the beef and continue to stir-fry for a minute until just cooked. Season to taste with the fish sauce and sugar but be careful not to make it too salty.
- Add the stock or water and simmer for a moment. Don't let it boil or stew for too long, otherwise the meat will toughen and too much liquid will evaporate – there should be enough to form a sauce. Stir in the holy basil and as soon as it is wilted, remove from the heat. It should taste rich, hot, salty and spicy from the basil.
- Serve on two plates with plenty of steamed jasmine rice, a fried egg on top and a bowl of chillies in fish sauce on the side.

SERVES 2–3

1 small bunch Chinese broccoli
200 g (6 oz) roast pork, cut into 1 cm
   (½ in) slices
1 tablespoon oyster sauce
a little light soy sauce
a few tablespoons stock or water
pinch of white sugar
1 tablespoon chopped garlic
pinch of salt
2 tablespoons vegetable oil
pinch of ground white pepper

PAT KANAA
MUU GROP

STIR-FRIED CRISPY PORK
WITH CHINESE BROCCOLI

This is a decidedly Chinese dish that has entered the Thai repertoire. The salt and oil content of the pork help to counter the slightly bitter, mineral qualities of the Chinese broccoli. If the broccoli is young, there is no need to peel it. Choy sum or even Chinese cabbage can also be cooked in this way.

Roast pork is available ready-made from most Chinese barbeque shops: its inviting golden crackling distinguishes it from the red-tinged barbeque pork. I've included a recipe on page 296 for those who need or want to make their own.

- Clean the Chinese broccoli then cut the stalks into roughly 3 cm (1¼ in) lengths, peeling them if necessary. Tear or cut the leaves into large pieces.
- Assemble the prepared broccoli and the roast pork, along with the oyster sauce, soy sauce, stock or water and sugar. Crush the garlic to a somewhat coarse paste with the salt – either by pounding it using a pestle and mortar or finely chopping it with a knife.
- Heat a well-seasoned wok and add the oil. When it is fiercely hot, add the garlic and stir-fry briskly until it is coloured then add all the assembled ingredients and continue to stir-fry for a few moments until the broccoli is cooked.
- Sprinkle with the pepper and serve with steamed rice.

300 g (9 oz) pork ribs, trimmed

1 bitter melon

salt

6–8 small dried shiitake mushrooms

4 coriander roots, cleaned

3 red shallots, peeled

boiling stock or water, to cover

3 tablespoons yellow bean sauce

2–4 tablespoons light soy sauce

good pinch of white sugar

2 tablespoons chopped Asian celery

good pinch of ground white pepper

pinch of deep-fried garlic

1 tablespoon chopped coriander – optional

DTUM MARA SII KRONG MUU

PORK RIBS STEAMED WITH BITTER MELON

Double steaming is a Chinese method of slow cooking that is often used to instil food with medicinal properties. You'll need a large metal steamer. Choose carefully when it comes to the bowl the dish will be steamed in: it should be big enough and deep enough to hold all the ingredients, bearing in mind that the stock must cover everything generously, but it also needs to fit into the steamer – check this before you start.

By all means ask your butcher to cut the ribs for you, but don't worry if this can't be done, as it is quite easy to do at home. Pork belly or hock may be used instead of ribs. Some cleaned pieces of chicken or duck would also sit happily in this broth.

The bitter melon needs to be salted to reduce its bitterness, then thoroughly rinsed. Green or ash melon or gourd is a logical replacement but since their flavour is milder, there is no need to treat them beforehand. Blanched shredded bamboo is a good alternative too.

- Cut the pork ribs into 2–3 cm (1–1¼ in) pieces. Blanch from a cold-water start, rinse well to remove any scum, then drain. (Although this really wouldn't be done on the streets, it will give the broth a clear sheen and a clean taste.)
- Top and tail the bitter melon then cut in half lengthways and cut each half into three or four pieces. Scrape out the seeds and the very bitter fleshy white pith. Rub the melon pieces with salt and leave for about 20 minutes in a colander to leach out some of the bitterness, then rinse well. For those who really don't relish bitter tastes, the melon can then be blanched from a cold-water start.
- Rinse the shiitake mushrooms then soak them in hot water for about 10 minutes. Nip off the coarse stems.
- Using a pestle and mortar, pound the coriander roots and shallots to a fine paste with a pinch of salt.
- Place the pork and melon in a large bowl that will fit inside your steamer. Pour over enough boiling stock or water to cover, then stir in the coriander root and shallot paste, yellow bean sauce, soy sauce, sugar and a good pinch of salt. Cover the bowl with foil then place in the steamer and put on the lid. Steam for about 1½ hours, making sure there is plenty of water in the steamer throughout. When the pork is tender, it's ready. It should taste salty and rich yet clean, with just a hint of bitterness.
- Sprinkle with white pepper, deep-fried garlic and some chopped coriander, if desired, and serve with steamed rice.

SERVES 2

4 soft-shell crabs, each about 60–75 g
   (2–2½ oz) – thawed if frozen
6 coriander roots, cleaned and chopped
salt
8–10 garlic cloves, unpeeled – about 3 tablespoons
1 teaspoon black peppercorns
3–4 tablespoons plain (all-purpose) flour
vegetable oil, for deep-frying
1 tablespoon chopped coriander
sauce Siracha, to serve

BPUU NIM TORT PRIK THAI DAM

DEEP-FRIED SOFT-SHELL CRABS WITH GARLIC AND BLACK PEPPER

In a few markets there are vendors who sell soft-shell crabs live – a rare treat – but they are more commonly available frozen. If neither can be found, fish, large prawns, squid or crabs of the hard-shell variety can be used in this recipe.

In Thailand the garlic is less pungent and the cloves much smaller. It is used in abundance and with impunity. The skin is thinner and the flesh is young, soft and moist. Most Western garlic has a peppery sharpness to it, and its larger cloves have tougher skin, so you may need to fish out some of the excess hard shards. Look out for new-season garlic, which is much closer in taste to the Thai variety.

Sauce Siracha is a wonderful chilli sauce that's available in all Asian shops – it is a fairly standard accompaniment to dishes deep-fried with garlic and peppercorns.

- To clean the crabs, lift the shell on each side of the body and scrape out the frond-like gills. Snip off the eyes and mouth. Give the crabs a quick rinse then pat dry with a paper towel.
- Using a pestle and mortar, pound the coriander roots to a paste with a good pinch of salt. Add the garlic and continue to pound into a somewhat coarse paste. Remove excess or tough garlic skin then stir in the peppercorns, crushing them lightly.
- Mix the flour with a large pinch of salt. Dredge the cleaned crabs with the seasoned flour, shaking off any excess, then combine them with the garlic and black pepper paste.
- Pour the deep-frying oil into a large, stable wok or a wide, heavy-based pan until it is about two-thirds full. Heat the oil over a medium–high flame until a cooking thermometer registers 180°C (350°F). Alternatively, test the temperature of the oil by dropping in a cube of bread – it will brown in about 15 seconds if the oil is hot enough.
- Deep-fry the crabs in the hot oil for 3–4 minutes, turning them a few times to ensure even cooking, until they are cooked and the garlic is golden. Should the garlic start to smell bitter and darken too much before the crabs are ready, quickly scoop it out. Lift out the crabs and drain on paper towels.
- Sprinkle with the chopped coriander and serve with steamed rice and a small bowl of sauce Siracha.

SERVES 3–4

500 g (1 lb) small clams

1–2 tablespoons vegetable oil

2–3 tablespoons chilli jam

2 kaffir lime leaves, torn

1 stalk lemongrass, trimmed and bruised – optional

good pinch of white sugar

1–2 tablespoons fish sauce – to taste

generous handful of Thai basil leaves

1 long red or green chilli, sliced, deseeded if desired

HOI LAAI PAT NAHM PRIK PAO

STIR-FRIED CLAMS WITH CHILLI JAM AND THAI BASIL

Although small clams are the molluscs most commonly used for this dish, surf clams, scallops, mussels, prawns or even fish can be used in their place. I also rather like the combination of crispy roast pork and squid stir-fried together with chilli jam, but this is hardly street food.

Clams usually need to be purged of sand and grit by being left to steep in salted water overnight, although sometimes you can buy clams that have already been cleaned.

Most Thais will go to the market to pick up their chilli jam, where they can choose from many varieties: some extra hot, others with or without dried prawns. While commercial chilli jam is generally more acceptable then commercial curry pastes, homemade (see page 354) adds a real depth and quality to the finished dish.

- Purge the clams overnight in salted water, if necessary, then rinse and drain well.
- Heat the oil in a well-seasoned wok then add the chilli jam. Stir in the clams, along with the kaffir lime leaves and the lemongrass, if using. Simmer until the clams have opened, then season with the sugar and fish sauce – but be careful as the clams will be quite salty. You may also need to add a tablespoon or two of water to prevent the chilli jam from catching, especially if the clams are reluctant openers.
- Finish by stirring in the Thai basil and chilli. It should taste rich, slightly oily, sweet and salty, yet not too spicy.
- Serve with steamed rice.

1 large or 2 small coriander roots, cleaned

pinch of salt

3 garlic cloves, peeled

5–10 bird's eye chillies (scuds), to taste

1 tablespoon Thai shrimp paste (gapi)

20 sadtor beans, peeled *or* ½ cup green, runner
    or snake (yard-long) beans, cut into 3 cm
    (1¼ in) lengths

10 small–medium raw prawns (shrimp) in their shells

2 tablespoons vegetable oil

100 g (3 oz) pork shoulder or loin, quite thinly sliced

100 g (3 oz) squid, cleaned, scored and
    cut lengthways into 4 pieces

3–4 tablespoons stock or water

2–3 kaffir lime leaves, roughly torn

good pinch of white sugar

good dash of lime juice or white vinegar – optional

1–2 tablespoons fish sauce, to taste

ก้งผัดสะตอ

GUNG PAT SADTOR

STIR-FRIED SADTOR BEANS WITH PRAWNS, SHRIMP PASTE AND PORK

Sadtor beans are vivid green beans that, when peeled, look a little like broad (fava) beans – but their pungent taste is vastly different. Refined cooks like to blanch the beans in boiling water then refresh them under cold running water to reduce their strong taste and maintain their vivid colour. They are sometimes available from Asian grocers, but green, runner or snake beans make good, more readily available alternatives.

Do not pound the paste to a pulp, as a rather coarse texture is necessary to give some body to the dish. Mussels or scallops can be used instead of the prawns, and chicken can stand in for the pork. Some versions are finished with Thai basil or coriander.

- Using a pestle and mortar, pound the coriander roots to a paste with the salt. Add the garlic and chillies and continue to pound to a somewhat coarse paste, then work in the shrimp paste.
- Briefly blanch the prepared beans in boiling salted water, drain and refresh under cold running water, then drain again. Peel and devein the prawns, but leave the tails attached; the heads can also be left intact for a more pleasing presentation, but it makes for trickier eating later.
- Gently heat the oil in a well-seasoned wok then add the paste and fry until fragrant. Add the prawns, pork, squid and beans and stir-fry until everything is just cooked – about 3–4 minutes. Moisten with the stock or water and add the kaffir lime leaves, then season with the sugar, lime juice or vinegar (if using) and fish sauce. The dish should taste rich, oily, hot and salty.
- Serve with steamed rice.

4 cups chicken stock

good pinch of salt

pinch of white sugar

1 large tomato, cut into quarters and
deseeded – optional

1 dried long red chilli, coarsely chopped

8–12 raw prawns (shrimp) in their shells

3–5 stalks lemongrass, trimmed

4–5 kaffir lime leaves, roughly torn

2–3 slices galangal

5 red shallots, peeled

4–5 coriander roots, cleaned

5–10 green bird's eye chillies (scuds), to taste

200 g (7 oz) straw or oyster mushrooms, cleaned
and trimmed – about 2 cups

1–2 tablespoons tamarind water – optional

2–4 tablespoons lime juice, to taste

1–2 tablespoons fish sauce, to taste

3–10 bird's eye chillies (scuds), bruised

pinch of roasted chilli powder

1 tablespoon chopped coriander

DTOM YAM GUNG

HOT AND SOUR SOUP OF PRAWNS

A ubiquitous classic that, when made well, is understandably so. Prawns of any size can be used. Some cooks will make a stock from the shells, simmering them in water with a few aromatics until some oil from the prawn tomalley dapples the surface, then straining the liquid.

Straw mushrooms are the most common mushroom used in Thailand, but they are not easily available fresh outside of Asia. Oyster mushrooms are a happy alternative.

A dtom yam is a generic style of soup that can be made with fish, mussels, chicken, or even pork hocks, but the stronger the flavour of the fish or meat, the stronger the seasoning of the soup should be. Some cooks will add several slices of galangal to achieve this. When the time comes to decide how many bruised bird's eye chillies to add, taste and capricious bravery should be your guide!

Sometimes a little chilli jam is added to give a smoky depth to the soup, but mostly it is kept clean and clear. One modern innovation that I find baffling and unsettling is the addition of a splash of milk to the soup. However, I do like to add some tamarind water to a dtom yam as it helps to make the sour note deeper and more rounded; and, unconventionally, I like to add a tomato to give the soup an attractive golden hue.

- Bring the stock to the boil, season with the salt and sugar then add the tomato (if using) and dried chilli. Simmer for several minutes until the tomato begins to break up.
- Peel and devein the prawns, but leave the tails attached; the heads can also be left intact for a more pleasing presentation, but it makes for trickier eating later.
- Using a pestle and mortar, bruise the lemongrass, lime leaves, galangal, shallots, coriander roots and green bird's eye chillies. Add these to the simmering stock, then cut or tear the mushrooms and add them too. Simmer for a minute or so until the mushrooms are tender before adding the prawns and tamarind water, if using. Simmer until the prawns are cooked – about 2–3 minutes.
- In a serving bowl, combine the lime juice with the fish sauce, chillies, chilli powder and coriander. Pour in the soup and stir thoroughly. It should taste equally hot, salty and sour – adjust the seasoning accordingly, or to your taste.
- Serve with steamed rice.

SERVES 2

250 g (8 oz) squid

1 bunch flowering garlic chives – about 125 g (4 oz)

1–2 garlic cloves

pinch of salt

1–2 tablespoons vegetable oil

¼ cup stock or water

about 1 tablespoon light soy sauce

pinch of white sugar

pinch of ground white pepper

PLAA MEUK
PAT GUI CHAI

STIR-FRIED SQUID WITH FLOWERING GARLIC CHIVES

A clean-flavoured, straightforward dish. Spring (green) onions, snow peas or almost any Asian green can be used if flowering garlic chives are unavailable. I think leaving the purple-flecked skin on the squid makes for an attractive finish.

If you have a ferocious source of heat – by which I mean one as hot as the wok stalls on the streets of Bangkok – you should stir-fry the squid first for a moment before adding the garlic. This prevents the garlic from burning. But if you have a normal kitchen with a more moderate heat source, then follow the method here.

- First clean the squid. Carefully pull out the firm transparent quill from inside the bodies and separate the tentacles from the bodies. Trim the eyes and hard black beak from the tentacles, as well as the ink sac if still attached. If there are any tough cartilaginous suckers on the tentacles, scrape them away. If the squid are quite small, leave the tentacles whole, otherwise cut them into 2 or 3 pieces.
- Cut along the length of the bodies and drag out the white mushy innards. Holding the knife at an angle, scrape away any residue, then trim the edges of the bodies if tatty and frayed. Turn the squid over and pull off the wings. If the purple membrane is fresh and intact you can leave it on, if you like. Otherwise, simply peel it away.
- Now rinse all the pieces, then drain and pat dry. If the squid are quite large, score the bodies to help them cook evenly. Place the squid bodies on the board, with the inside facing up. Holding the knife at an angle and slicing diagonally, score the squid about every 5 mm (¼ in), taking care not to cut right through. I like my squid scored in one direction only, but many cooks prefer a diamond cut. If you're one of them, turn the squid through 45 degrees and repeat the scoring. Cut into rectangles 4 cm × 3 cm (1½ in × 1¼ in).
- To prepare the garlic chives, trim off the tough lower ends of the stalks. Cut into 3–4 cm (1¼–1½ in) lengths, then rinse well, soaking briefly to wash away any stubborn dirt, and drain.
- Crush the garlic to a somewhat coarse paste with the salt – either by pounding it using a pestle and mortar or finely chopping it with a knife.
- Heat a well-seasoned wok, add the oil and let it heat for a moment before adding the garlic paste and the squid. Stir-fry over a very high heat until the squid is almost cooked – about 30–60 seconds. Add the garlic chives and stir-fry until they have wilted. The wok should be quite dry and starting to smoke a little – if necessary, moisten with a drizzle of oil. Pour in the stock or water, then season with the soy sauce, sugar and pepper. It should taste rich, salty and slightly smoky.
- Serve with steamed rice.

SERVES 2

1 × 300 g (9 oz) whole fish – such as snapper,
    bream, perch or pike – cleaned and scaled
1–2 tablespoons light soy sauce
pinch of white sugar
3 coriander roots, cleaned
good pinch of salt
½ teaspoon white peppercorns
1 large head garlic, broken into cloves
vegetable oil, for deep-frying
1 tablespoon chopped coriander
sauce Siracha or fish sauce with lime juice
    and bird's eye chillies (scuds), to serve

ปลาทอดกระเทียมพริกไทย

PLAA TORT GRATIAM PRIK THAI

DEEP-FRIED WHOLE FISH WITH GARLIC AND PEPPERCORNS

The combination of garlic, coriander root, salt and pepper is a fundamental seasoning used in many Thai dishes – curries, soups, salads and even the occasional dessert. In this dish it is at its most undisguised and elemental. Thai garlic is much smaller and less pungent than the stuff commonly available in the West, so Thais use it with abandon. When pounding the coarser Western garlic, you'll most likely need to remove the hard core and some of the excess skin from the paste. Make sure you don't overcook the garlic: it should be a light honey brown – any darker and you risk burning the garlic and making it bitter, ruining the whole dish.

The fish shown opposite is sheatfish (plaa nahm ngern), a freshwater fish from the Chao Phraya River that flows through Bangkok, but most fish, seafood or meat benefits from being cooked like this. The ubiquitous sauce Siracha, available in Asian supermarkets, is often served with this fish.

- Rinse the fish and pat dry with a paper towel. Score the fish by making three or four diagonal cuts into each side, then place it in a glass or ceramic bowl. Add the soy sauce and sugar and leave the fish to marinate for a few minutes.
- Meanwhile, using a pestle and mortar, pound the coriander roots to a paste with the salt and peppercorns. Add the garlic and continue to pound to a coarse paste, fishing out and discarding some of the excess garlic skin. Mix the paste with the fish.
- Pour the deep-frying oil into a large, stable wok or a wide, heavy-based pan until it is about two-thirds full. Heat the oil over a medium–high flame until a cooking thermometer registers 180°C (350°F). Alternatively, test the temperature of the oil by dropping in a cube of bread – it will brown in about 15 seconds if the oil is hot enough.
- Deep-fry the fish and the garlic and pepper paste, stirring regularly, until the garlic is golden and the fish is cooked, golden and crunchy. Remove and drain on paper towels. Depending on the size of the fish, the garlic may need to be taken out of the oil earlier – if it threatens to burn, scoop out the garlic and drain on paper towels (it will become crisp as it cools).
- Serve sprinkled with coriander, and with a bowl of sauce Siracha or fish sauce seasoned with lime juice and chopped chillies on the side.

SERVES 3

1 cup white sticky rice

3 × 150 g (5 oz) freshwater fish such as perch
    or pike, gutted and thoroughly cleaned *or*
    300 g (9 oz) perch or pike fillets

5 tablespoons sea salt

15 garlic cloves, peeled

3 slices galangal

vegetable oil, for deep-frying

3 tablespoons sliced red shallots

5–10 bird's eye chillies (scuds)

lime wedges, to serve

PLAA SOM TORT

DEEP-FRIED FERMENTED FISH

In Thailand whole fish and fillets are treated in this delectable way, which hails from the north-east of the country. In most Thai markets there will be at least one stall that specialises in this dish, and such stalls will usually sell shrimp paste (gapi) and uncooked fermented fish (plaa raa) as well. Fermenting the fish in rice gives the flesh a deep nutty sourness – a taste that soon becomes addictive. Thais will use only freshwater fish for this, such as the carp in the photo, but Thai carp makes for much more pleasant eating than its Western sister. I'd recommend a freshwater perch or pike.

Some care is needed to make this safely: if using whole fish, rinse it scrupulously, paying particular attention to the stomach cavity. It is worth using good-quality salt for a superior flavour. As the fish cures and its texture changes, it becomes quite crumbly – I suggest chilling the fish, to make it easier to fry without it disintegrating. The Thais themselves wouldn't bother with this step, but then their fish is firmer and holds its own.

- Soak the sticky rice in plenty of water overnight.
- The next day, drain the rice, rinse and place in a steamer; normally the raw grains of rice cling together, so they rarely fall through the holes, but if you're feeling cautious line the steamer with some rinsed muslin (cheesecloth). Make sure the rice is not piled too high in the centre, nor too widely spread, so that it cooks evenly, and keep the water level below the steamer high to ensure there is plenty of steam. Steam the rice until tender (test some grains from the area where the mound of rice is deepest) – this should take 45 minutes–1 hour. Remove the rice and set aside to cool to room temperature, then rinse and drain well.
- Score each fish or fillet three times, being careful not to cut right through. Cover the fish in water with a good pinch of the salt and leave to steep for about an hour.
- Using a pestle and mortar, pound the garlic and galangal to a paste with the remainder of the salt. Work in the rice until you have a somewhat coarse paste, but be careful not to pound it too much otherwise the gluten will get overworked and the paste will become a tough knot, almost unusable. Taste to ensure it is neither over- nor under-salted.
- Drain and dry the fish. Rub the rice paste into the fish and place in a glass or ceramic bowl. Cover closely with plastic film and leave in a warm place, such as in the oven with the pilot light on and the door ajar, to cure – this usually takes a little over a day. The fish should smell rich, and it should certainly smell as if something has fermented. When this stage has been reached, remove some of the excess rice paste, transfer the fish to a clean container and refrigerate for at least a day but no longer than 3 days.
- When ready to cook, pour the deep-frying oil into a large, stable wok or a wide, heavy-based pan until it is about two-thirds full. Heat the oil over a medium–high flame until a cooking thermometer registers 180°C (350°F). Alternatively, test the temperature of the oil by dropping in a cube of bread – it will brown in about 15 seconds if the oil is hot enough.
- Brush the rice paste off the fermented fish then deep-fry the fish until it is cooked and golden, turning often so that it cooks evenly. Drain on paper towels then transfer to a plate.
- Cast the shallots and chillies over the fish and serve with lime wedges and steamed rice.

SERVES 2–4

1 × 400 g (12 oz) fish – such as sea bass,
    barramundi, John Dory, snapper or
    bream – gutted and scaled

CHILLI AND LIME SAUCE
1–2 coriander roots, cleaned
pinch of salt
2–3 garlic cloves, peeled
3–5 bird's eye chillies (scuds) –
    or more, if you wish
1 tablespoon white sugar
3–4 tablespoons lime juice
1–2 tablespoons fish sauce, to taste

1 banana leaf – optional
chopped coriander, to serve

ปลานึ่งพริกมะนาว
PLAA NEUNG PRIK MANAO

STEAMED FISH WITH CHILLI AND LIME SAUCE

On the streets, the fish is usually steamed well in advance, in the interests of quick service at the stall. At home, however, it should be cooked when required. Scoring the fish allows for faster, more even cooking. Some cooks will fill the cavity with a few stalks of lemongrass, a pandanus leaf or a few coriander roots.

Thai diners like their fish completely cooked and will steam this over a furious heat. But as a concession to modern styles of cooking, I suggest you steam it over a moderate heat to ensure a tender texture – steaming over a rolling boil can be harsh and may toughen the flesh.

- Rinse the fish well and pat dry with a paper towel. Score the fish by making three or four diagonal slices on each side.
- Next make the sauce. Using a pestle and mortar, pound the coriander roots to a fine paste with the salt. Add the garlic and chillies and continue pounding to a coarse paste. Season with the sugar, lime juice and fish sauce. The sauce should be hot, sour, salty and more than a little sweet – but this can be altered to taste. Transfer the sauce to a small bowl and set aside.
- Place the fish on a banana leaf or heatproof plate and then into a steamer. Steam over simmering water for about 15–20 minutes or until cooked – the scored flesh should be opaque right to the bone.
- Spoon the chilli and lime sauce over the fish and serve sprinkled with chopped coriander.

SERVES 3–4

400 g (12 oz) bitter melon tendrils – about 4–5 cups
1–2 garlic cloves
pinch of salt
2–3 red bird's eye chillies (scuds) – green will do,
    but they'll be dangerously camouflaged
1 tablespoon vegetable oil
a few tablespoons stock or water
1 tablespoon light soy sauce
pinch of white sugar
pinch of ground white pepper

PAT PAK MAEW

STIR-FRIED BITTER MELON TENDRILS

This a simple dish that can be made with almost any Asian green, including Chinese broccoli, choy sum, Siamese watercress (water spinach) and snow pea shoots.

The best soy sauce to use here is a light Thai variety. These generally have a fine taste and a golden colour, and are not too salty. If none can be found, dilute regular soy sauce with a little water.

On the streets, cooks use Thai garlic, which has very thin, edible skin that doesn't need to be peeled – not unlike new season's garlic. If using regular garlic, it is best to peel the cloves.

- To clean the bitter melon tendrils, trim off the tough ends of the stalks and pick off any motley leaves. Rinse and drain well, then cut into approximately 4 cm (1½ in) lengths.
- Crush the garlic to a somewhat coarse paste with the salt – either by pounding it using a pestle and mortar or finely chopping it with a knife. Bruise the chillies with a mortar and pestle or with the flat of the knife.
- Combine the garlic and chilli with the bitter melon tendrils.
- Heat a well-seasoned wok until quite hot, then add the oil and the vegetables. Stir-fry briskly for a few minutes until just tender – do not allow to burn. Moisten with the stock or water, then season with the soy sauce, sugar and pepper.
- Serve with steamed rice.

SERVES 2–3

½ cup white sticky rice

500 g (1 lb) pork ribs, cut into 2 cm (1 in) pieces

3–4 garlic cloves, peeled

1 tablespoon salt

banana leaves – optional

vegetable oil, for deep-frying

2–3 extra garlic cloves, crushed

handful of coriander sprigs

shredded ginger, sliced red shallots, roasted
    peanuts and bird's eye chillies (scuds),
      to serve – optional

แหนมซี่หมูโครงทอด

NAEM SII KRONG MUU TORT

DEEP-FRIED CURED PORK RIBS

This is a delicious and addictive dish. Although it takes some time to prepare, it is quite easy, and the result is so lip-smackingly good that you may wish to double the recipe.

The best cut of pork to use is from the top end of the ribs, where the cartilage is soft and the meat is sweet (Thais call this 'soft bone'). This cut is more likely to found in a Chinese butcher's shop, but if you can't find it use regular ribs – just ask the butcher to cut the ribs into small pieces. Pork belly is also a possibility, but try to find one that's not too fatty. Traditionally the pork mixture was wrapped in banana leaves to cure. Now, however, a plastic bag is more commonly used. I prefer to use a plastic takeaway container lined with some cut banana leaves as a nod to the traditional.

When deep-frying the pork, do so over a moderate heat so as not to burn the garlic. Drain well and leave to cool somewhat before eating. Have a beer at hand – it's the perfect accompaniment.

- Soak the sticky rice in plenty of water overnight.
- The next day, drain the rice, rinse and place in a steamer; normally the raw grains of rice cling together, so they rarely fall through the holes, but if you're feeling cautious line the steamer with some rinsed muslin (cheesecloth). Make sure the rice is not piled too high in the centre, nor too widely spread, so that it cooks evenly, and keep the water level below the steamer high to ensure there is plenty of steam. Steam the rice until tender (test some grains from the area where the mound of rice is deepest) – this should take about 25–35 minutes. Remove the rice and set aside to cool to room temperature, then rinse and drain well.
- Rinse and dry the pork ribs. Using a pestle and mortar, pound the garlic to a paste with the salt. Add the rice and continue pounding until you have a somewhat coarse paste, but be careful not to pound it too much otherwise the gluten will get overworked and the paste will become a tough knot, almost unusable.
- Combine the rice paste with the pork ribs and wrap tightly in banana leaves or pack into an airtight plastic or glass container to cure, making sure there are no air bubbles that might cause the pork to spoil. The curing normally takes 2–5 days at room temperature – Thai room temperature. In cooler climes, leave the pork in a warm sunny spot, or even in an oven with the pilot light on and the door slightly ajar. Check the meat after 2 days if it is very warm, 3 days if it has been cooler – be careful as there could be a lot of moisture. The aroma should be pungent and sour, but still clean. If not, leave the pork to ferment for another day. The longer it is left, the stronger it becomes. If it smells in any way dubious, throw it out.
- When the pork has successfully cured it will be moist, firm, succulent and sour, but with quite a strong aroma. When it seems ready, test by frying a piece until it is completely cooked – it should taste rich, sour and lip-smackingly good.
- At this stage, the cured pork can be stored in the refrigerator (in fact it is better chilled before deep-frying), where it will keep for a week or so. To be on the safe side, test again before using.
- When ready to cook, wipe the pork clean, removing most if not all of the rice paste. Pour the deep-frying oil into a large, stable wok or a wide, heavy-based pan until it is about two-thirds full. Heat the oil over a medium–high flame until a cooking thermometer registers 180°C (350°F). Alternatively, test the temperature of the oil by dropping in a cube of bread – it will brown in about 15 seconds if the oil is hot enough. Deep-fry the pork, adding the crushed garlic when the pork is almost cooked. Continue to deep-fry until both are golden, then remove and drain on paper towels.
- Sprinkle with coriander and serve. This pork may be accompanied by shredded ginger, sliced red shallots, peanuts and chopped or whole scud chillies. Steamed rice is optional, but I think a beer is not!

DUMPLINGS

100 g (3 oz) minced (ground) pork – I prefer
   slightly fatty
1–2 tablespoons light soy sauce
pinch of white sugar
pinch of ground white pepper

4 cups light chicken or pork stock
pinch of salt
2–3 tablespoons light soy sauce
pinch of white sugar, to taste
150 g (5 oz) silken bean curd
2 sheets dried sea lettuce – about 30 g (1 oz) –
   torn into pieces
2 tablespoons chopped spring (green) onions
pinch of ground white pepper
1 teaspoon garlic deep-fried in oil
   (see page 358)
good pinch of coriander leaves

ต้มจืดเต้าหู้สาหร่าย
DTOM JEUT DTAO
HUU SAARAAI

BEAN CURD, SEAWEED
AND PORK DUMPLING SOUP

This is a smoky soup with a deep, peaty taste from the dried green seaweed, *Ulva lactuca*, which also
goes by the name of sea lettuce. You should be able to find it easily enough in Chinese food shops. The
cool, calm presence of silken bean curd in this soup is welcome, and I often think that a handful of small
prawns, fresh or dried, or some crabmeat would also be a pleasing, if less than pedestrian addition.

○ First make the dumplings by mixing the minced pork with the soy sauce, sugar and pepper in
   a bowl. Combine well, then gather up the seasoned meat and throw or slap it against the side of the
   bowl. Repeat several times. This works the protein in the pork, making it more springy.
○ Bring the stock to the boil then season with the salt, soy sauce and sugar. Pinch the pork mixture
   into small rough dumplings and add to the stock. Simmer for a moment before adding the bean curd,
   breaking it up a little as you do so. Finally, add the seaweed and simmer for another moment until
   it is softened.
○ Remove the soup from the heat and let it sit for a minute. Check the seasoning: it should taste rich,
   salty, nutty and slightly minerally from the seaweed. Ladle into soup bowls and sprinkle with the spring
   onions, white pepper, deep-fried garlic and coriander leaves.
○ Serve with steamed rice.

ชุมชนจีน
CHINATOWN

Before Bangkok became the capital of the Thai kingdom in 1782, it was a village surrounded by orchards, mainly inhabited by Chinese merchants and market gardeners. When the capital was established, the place where the Chinese had settled was deemed to be the most auspicious area – it was certainly the most defensible. As a consequence, the Chinese were moved a little to the south, into a marshy area called Sampeng. And this is where many are still found today.

As their numbers swelled, they broke out of the confines of Chinatown and moved into the surrounding districts, and from there throughout all of Bangkok and beyond onto the central plains and farther up-country. The resultant blending of cultures and changing of customs had a profound effect on the Thais. Noodles and rice congee, pork and duck, fish dumplings and yellow beans entered the Bangkok diet, then the Thai diet in general.

One of the notable culinary differences in those times was that Chinese would often eat outside of the home. This was a custom carried on from China. Thais preferred to eat food prepared at home. To cater to this habit, some Chinese or their descendants sold some simple food, ready to eat or easy to cook, to the workers in the mills and docks nearby. They carried it in bamboo baskets supported by a bamboo pole. Noodles, rice soups and other cooked snacks were thus transported.

Another notable distinction is that most of this food was eaten in the manner of the Chinese, that is, with a Chinese soup spoon and chopsticks.

As the hawkers became more successful a few opened shops; the variety of dishes hawked also expanded to include braised pork hocks, roast duck, duck and vegetable soup (jap chai), and of course noodles of all kinds.

The character of Bangkok's Chinatown changes as the day wears on. Early morning and daytime are hard-working, steamy and crowded with people working, delivering and preparing. The markets start before dawn and are filled with people purchasing goods and foods. The stalls are filled with Chinese ingredients not often seen in those catering to Thais: dried spices, teas, various styles of bean curd, jellyfish and seaweed, roast duck and pork, bitter greens and fleshy gourds. Coffee and tea shops are filled with men as they read newspapers and discuss the news, gossip, sip and while away some time. Later, as the shops open, Chinatown is full of shoppers – especially for gold. Down the smaller streets are an impossible number of engine shops.

At night the many streets are lined with food stalls with bright lights and waiters beckoning to prospective diners with the choice of steamed fish; deep-fried crabs; rice soup plain, with minced (ground) pork or with fish, served with knots of deep-fried bread; simple clear soups with pork, assorted offal and bitter herbs, or with bean curd and seaweed; and roast pork and duck, served alone, over rice or in noodle soups.

Chinese merchants are everywhere, in neon lights and on the streets in their singlets, cooking, hawking and living.

○ Pork hocks braised with star anise (see next page)
for sale on the street in Yaowarat, Bangkok's Chinatown.

4 coriander roots, cleaned and chopped

good pinch of salt

3–4 garlic cloves, peeled

8–10 white peppercorns

about 2 tablespoons vegetable oil

1 heaped tablespoon five-spice powder

2 tablespoons shaved palm sugar

2–3 tablespoons fish sauce

6 cups stock or water

2 tablespoons oyster sauce – optional

1 pork hock – about 750 g–1 kg (1½–2 lb)

1 small head garlic or a few cloves, bruised
    but unpeeled – optional

2 cm (1 in) piece ginger, bruised – optional

SAUCE

1–2 long yellow or red chillies,
    deseeded if desired

1 scant teaspoon salt

2–3 garlic cloves, peeled

1–2 slices galangal – optional

⅓ cup white vinegar

1 bunch Chinese broccoli – about 200 g (6 oz)

chopped coriander, ground white pepper and
    sauce for pork parlow (see above), to serve

KHAA MUU
PARLOW

PORK HOCKS BRAISED WITH FIVE-SPICE POWDER

In the markets and along the streets, great brass woks proudly display this solidly Chinese dish. A rich dark stock simmers away, while two or three plump golden hocks hang on a trellis above, waiting to be served. Some blanched Chinese broccoli leaves may be wrapped wantonly around the mahogany-coloured meat.

It was Teochew migrants from southern China who gave this dish its name in Thailand (parlow is a Teochew word for five spice), and who now form the largest Chinese group in the country. This way of cooking is also referred to as red-braising, on account of the rich and inviting sheen that develops as the meat braises.

There are quite a few variations to this dish. Some stalls braise their hocks and serve them with blanched Chinese broccoli alone. Some versions add whole peanuts or pickled mustard greens, while others might add a few shelled hard-boiled eggs and perhaps a cake or two of firm bean curd about halfway through the cooking. All have as their base a parlow or five-spice powder, which is readily obtainable – but may be stale – or can be made from scratch (see page 357).

Pork hocks are usually sold free of bristles, but sometimes you'll find a few stray tufts that need to be burnt off: simply grasp the hock firmly with a pair of tongs and pass it over an open flame three or four times to remove the recalcitrant fuzz. Rinse it well afterwards. I like to blanch the hock once, or even twice, from a cold-water start. This is certainly not something a street vendor would do, but it does clean the pork and give the stock an admirable clarity.

Parlow of pork is always served with rice, and there is usually some chilli and vinegar sauce at hand to help cut the sumptuous richness of the pork. The sauce can be used immediately but it improves over time. Store in an airtight container. In Thailand it would be left unrefrigerated (and certainly kept this way it mellows quickly), but if you wish to keep it longer than 3 days it may be wise to refrigerate it.

- Using a pestle and mortar, pound the coriander roots to a paste with the salt, garlic and peppercorns. Heat the oil in a large pan and fry the paste until light golden and fragrant. Add the five-spice powder and, after a moment, season with the sugar and fish sauce and continue to fry for a few more moments, then add the stock or water and oyster sauce, if using. Bring to the boil, add the pork hock and simmer for 1 hour or until the meat is tender, skimming regularly throughout. Test the hock by pressing the flesh, but don't cook it for too long – that is, until the meat falls off the bone. Remove from the heat. Add the bruised garlic and ginger to the pan, if using, then leave to rest for 30 minutes to allow the flavours to mature.
- Meanwhile, make the sauce. Using a pestle and mortar, pound the chillies to a fairly fine paste with the salt, garlic and galangal, if using. Moisten with the vinegar. It should taste sour, salty and hot.
- Prepare the Chinese broccoli. Trim off the tough lower stalks then separate the stems and cut into 4 cm (1½ in) lengths. Rinse well and drain. Bring a pan of salted water to the boil and blanch the broccoli for about 30–60 seconds, depending on the thickness of the stalks. Lift out and refresh under cold water. Leave the pan of water over the heat, simmering.
- When ready to serve, gently warm the braised pork – it doesn't need to be too hot. Take out the hock and lift the meat and skin off the bone, trying as much as possible to keep the muscles and skin intact – hopefully it should come away in three or four largish pieces. Cut each piece into quite thin slices across the grain.
- Ladle some of the braising liquid into each bowl then place the sliced pork on top. Plunge the broccoli into the simmering water to reheat, then quickly drain it before arranging it around the pork.
- Sprinkle with chopped coriander and pepper then serve with a bowl of sauce alongside and plenty of steamed rice.

SERVES 3–4

6–8 large raw prawns (shrimp) – approximately
    400–500 g (12 oz–1 lb) in total
150 g (5 oz) dried glass (bean thread) noodles
50 g (2 oz) pork back fat (fatback)
4 coriander roots, cleaned
3 garlic cloves, unpeeled
10 white peppercorns
1 cup light stock
2 tablespoons oyster sauce
1 tablespoon light soy sauce
1 teaspoon white sugar
ground white pepper and coriander leaves,
    to serve

GUNG OP WUN SEN

PRAWNS WITH GLASS NOODLES

This is a silken dish, simple yet very pleasing. It is one of the few occasions when noodles may be eaten with rice. Pork back fat adds a rich smoothness to the noodles – a defining characteristic. Prawns are the most popular seafood for this dish. A close second is small mud crabs, broken into segments, but these take a little longer to cook.

The noodles were traditionally cooked in a rustic earthenware pot, and they still are occasionally, but more often a heavy aluminium pot is used. Similar clay pots can be found in most Asian shops. The pot and its lid must be soaked in water for several hours before being used for the first time so it will not crack over direct heat. Metal pots of a similar design are more common on the streets. These are more practical as they don't break but they can become discoloured, which is less attractive than the speckled patina of a well-used clay pot. Whatever the receptacle, the dish should be started in a hot pot and then simmered gently until cooked. Some stalls will transfer the pot to a makeshift oven.

Glass noodles are made from mung bean flour and look like stringy fishing lines. In their dried form they are truly tough, but they become much softer and easier to handle after they have been soaked in water for about 15 minutes. They are sold packaged in small bundles, and are readily obtainable in Asian food shops. They really are one of my favourite types of noodles.

- Rinse and drain the prawns. Peel and devein them, but leave the tails attached; the heads can also be left attached to impart a deep flavour to the noodles, as well as giving the dish an attractive appearance.
- Soak the noodles in warm water for about 15 minutes or until soft. Drain well and cut with scissors into manageable lengths – that is, about 7 cm (3 in) or so.
- Preheat the oven to 200°C (400°F). Warm the pot in it for 10 minutes.
- Meanwhile, cut the pork back fat into thin slices about 3 cm × 1 cm (1¼ in × ½ in).
- Using a pestle and mortar, bruise the coriander roots and garlic and coarsely crush the peppercorns.
- In a small pan, heat the stock then stir in the oyster and soy sauces and the sugar.
- Carefully take the hot pot out of the oven and place it over a low heat. Spread the sliced back fat over the bottom of the pot. Place the noodles on top of the back fat then scatter over the coriander roots, garlic and peppercorns. Pour the seasoned stock over the noodles and place the prawns on top. Stir to make sure everything is evenly distributed. Turn up the heat to high and quickly bring to the boil, then cover with a lid and place in the oven for about 10 minutes. The finished dish should be quite dry and, of course, the prawns should be red, cooked and tempting.
- Serve sprinkled with pepper and coriander leaves.

MAKES ABOUT 200 G (6 OZ)

250 g (8 oz) pork belly
2 teaspoons white vinegar
1 teaspoon salt
vegetable oil, for deep-frying

หมูกรอบ
MUU GROP

ROAST PORK

It is the crisp and bubbly crackling that makes this pork such an alluring prospect as it hangs wantonly at street stalls waiting to be eaten. This is quite an easy dish to prepare but it does take a little time as the pork must absorb some of the salt and vinegar if its crunchy crust is to develop in the hot oil. Just be careful when you fry it – it can really explode – and leave it to cool afterwards.

If it is served solo, slices of it always sit on rice and there is usually a bowl of chillies in soy sauce (see page 302) nearby. However the pork is served in many other guises, especially in stir-fries with Asian greens, such as with Chinese broccoli (see page 264), but asparagus, Chinese cabbage, snake (yard-long) beans or sugar snap peas could also be used. It also bobs up in a few noodle soups. But wherever it is, it is a welcome find.

- Trim the pork belly and blanch in simmering water until it is tender to the touch but still slightly springy – this should take about 15 minutes. Drain and allow to dry, then cut the pork into two or three 3 cm (1¼ in) strips. Mix together the vinegar and salt then rub into the rind of the pork. Allow to dry on a wire rack in a warm and airy place for about 3 hours.
- Pour the deep-frying oil into a large, stable wok or a wide, heavy-based pan until it is about two-thirds full. Heat the oil over a medium–high flame until a cooking thermometer registers 180°C (350°F). Alternatively, test the temperature of the oil by dropping in a cube of bread – it will brown in about 15 seconds if the oil is hot enough.
- Deep-fry the pork strips over a medium heat, turning them often, until the skin begins to crackle and bubble. Be careful – the slight splutter can turn into a searing eruption that always seems to hit home. Once the pork is done, lift it out and drain on the rack. Allow to cool before slicing.

100 g (3 oz) chicken breast fillet, with or
    without skin as preferred

a drizzle of light soy sauce, plus 2 tablespoons extra

1 garlic clove, peeled

pinch of salt

3 tablespoons vegetable oil

75 g (2½ oz) cured squid (plaa meuk chae) or fresh
    squid or cuttlefish, scored and finely sliced

ground white pepper

1–2 teaspoons preserved Chinese vegetable
    (dtang chai), rinsed and drained

2 heaped tablespoons chopped spring
    (green) onions

2 heaped tablespoons chopped Asian
    celery – optional

250 g (8 oz) fresh wide rice noodles

1–2 teaspoons dark soy sauce, to taste

good pinch of white sugar

2 eggs, ideally duck

1 cup loosely packed, very coarsely cut
    Chinese lettuce

pinch of deep-fried garlic

1–2 tablespoons chopped coriander

sauce Siracha, to serve

GUAY TIO KUA GAI

FRIED CHICKEN AND SQUID RICE NOODLES

This is a very Bangkok-style noodle dish, one that has increased in popularity over the last 30 years. The noodles are almost dry-fried or roasted ('kua' in Thai), so that they char and become smoky – if there is too much oil in the wok at this stage, the noodles will shrivel, gnarl and clump together.

Fresh noodles are best for this dish – fresh and at room temperature. If the noodles have been refrigerated, steam them briefly to soften them, then allow to cool before using. Dried rice noodles really do not work well here.

Cured squid is available in every market in Thailand, and often in Chinatowns throughout the world. It is made by steeping prepared cuttlefish in a mild caustic solution for one or two days, during which time it expands and becomes crunchy. It is then cleaned and rinsed to remove any chemical residue. Although sold fresh, it doesn't keep well, so should you come across it, freeze it and thaw what you need. Fresh squid or, better, cuttlefish, is an easy and natural alternative. Of course it needs to cleaned, but I tend not to peel it as the purple-coloured skin is rather attractive.

Sauce Siracha is a wonderful chilli sauce that is available in all Asian shops.

- Slice the chicken and briefly marinate it in a drizzle of light soy sauce. Crush the garlic to a somewhat coarse paste with the salt – either by pounding it using a pestle and mortar or finely chopping it with a knife.
- Heat the wok then add 2 generous tablespoons of the oil. Add the chicken and the cured squid and lightly stir-fry until golden and almost cooked. Stir in the garlic paste, a pinch of white pepper, the preserved Chinese vegetable and 1 tablespoon each of the spring onions and Asian celery (if using). By now most of the oil should have been absorbed; drain off any excess.
- Pull apart the rice noodle strands and add to the wok, spreading them over the contents of the wok and onto the surface of the wok itself. Leave undisturbed for a moment – up to 30 seconds – then gently begin to stir and shuffle the noodles and the wok. It is important not to break the noodle strands while doing this. Drizzle the noodles with the extra 2 tablespoons of light soy sauce, the dark soy sauce and the sugar. Sprinkle them with most of the remaining Asian celery and spring onions, along with a good pinch of white pepper. Turn up the heat slightly to caramelise the noodles, stirring occasionally and carefully. After a minute or two, push the noodles to one side of the wok and add the remaining tablespoon of oil. Turn up the heat, crack in the eggs and fry until they are just beginning to set and the edges of the whites are beginning to brown. Lightly break up the eggs, then gently stir and fold in the noodles, simmering them for a few minutes so that they caramelise and char slightly. Finish with the Chinese lettuce and the remaining Asian celery.
- Serve the noodles sprinkled with the deep-fried garlic, the remaining spring onions, the coriander and a pinch of white pepper.
- Accompany with a bowl of sauce Siracha.

100 g (3 oz) fresh egg noodles
> or 75 g (2½ oz) dried egg noodles

vegetable oil, for deep-frying

3 garlic cloves, peeled

pinch of salt

1 teaspoon cleaned and chopped coriander roots

good pinch of white peppercorns

2 tablespoons yellow bean sauce

8–10 medium-sized raw prawns (shrimp),
> peeled and deveined but with tails left intact

1 cup Chinese broccoli trimmed and
> cut into 3 cm (1¼ in) lengths

3 cups light chicken or pork stock

1–2 tablespoons light soy sauce

2 tablespoons oyster sauce

good pinch of white sugar

good pinch of ground white pepper

2 tablespoons tapioca flour, mixed with
> 4 tablespoons water to make a slurry

roasted chilli powder, white sugar, fish sauce
> and chillies steeped in vinegar (see page 355),
> to serve

ราดหน้ากุ้งบะหมี่กรอบ
RAAT NAR GUNG BA MII GROP

PRAWNS WITH CRISPY EGG NOODLES

This is a Thai chow mein! The egg noodles can be deep-fried a couple of hours in advance – they certainly would be in Thailand. The best egg noodles to use for this are the round, quite thin ones: try and form each skein of noodles into a nest or raft of strands a little smaller than the size of the serving plates.

The sauce, however, must be served the moment it is ready, just as the flour thickens it. If it sits for too long, the tapioca slurry breaks down and the sauce returns to a watery, somewhat broken state.

Chicken, pork, squid or a medley of all of them would also go swimmingly with these noodles.

- Tease and separate the egg noodles. Pour the deep-frying oil into a large, stable wok or a wide, heavy-based pan until it is about two-thirds full. Heat the oil over a medium–high flame until a cooking thermometer registers 180°C (350°F). Alternatively, test the temperature of the oil by dropping in a cube of bread – it will brown in about 15 seconds if the oil is hot enough. Deep-fry the egg noodles until golden and crunchy (they will frazzle and sizzle and expand slightly). Drain on paper towels. This can be done an hour or two beforehand. Keep the oil for later.
- Using a pestle and mortar, pound the garlic, salt, coriander roots and peppercorns into a somewhat coarse paste.
- Heat 2–3 tablespoons of the oil in a wok and fry the paste until it is beginning to colour. Add the yellow bean sauce and after about a minute, when fragrant, add the prawns. Fry for a moment then add the Chinese broccoli. When the prawns and broccoli are just about cooked, pour in the stock and bring to the boil. Season with the soy and oyster sauces, sugar and pepper, but be careful not to make the sauce too salty. Stir in the tapioca slurry and simmer for 15–20 seconds until the sauce has thickened.
- Place the noodles on the plates, then spoon over the prawns, Chinese broccoli and sauce.
- Serve with roasted chilli powder, white sugar, fish sauce and chillies steeped in vinegar.

MARINADE

4–5 spring (green) onions
3–4 coriander roots, cleaned
2–3 red shallots, peeled and bruised
10–15 slices galangal, bruised
20 slices ginger, bruised
1 star anise
2 cm (1 in) piece cassia bark
2–3 cloves
good pinch of five-spice powder
1 piece dried tangerine peel – optional
3–4 tablespoons light soy sauce
1 tablespoon dark soy sauce
2–3 tablespoons Chinese rice wine
¾ cup white sugar
2 tablespoons fermented bean curd liquid – optional
1 tablespoon red food colouring – optional

2 kg (4 lb) pork butt, neck or shoulder

BASTING SYRUP

generous ¼ cup maltose
¼ cup white sugar
1 tablespoon light soy sauce
about 1 tablespoon honey
1 tablespoon hoisin sauce
dash of red food colouring – optional

+ SAUCE FOR BBQ PORK AND RICE

1 teaspoon sesame seeds
1 cup light stock
good pinch of ground white pepper
good pinch of five-spice powder
½ star anise
2 tablespoons leftover basting syrup
2 tablespoons light soy sauce
1 teaspoon dark soy sauce
2 teaspoons cornflour (cornstarch)

In a small, heavy-based pan, dry-roast the sesame seeds over a low heat until they are golden. Remove from the pan and set aside. Pour the stock into the pan, add the five-spice powder and star anise and simmer gently for about 5 minutes. Strain the stock then return to the boil. Add the basting syrup and soy sauces and simmer for 5 minutes. Make a slurry by mixing 2 tablespoons of water into the cornflour. Stir this into the sauce and simmer, stirring constantly, for about a minute until the sauce thickens, then add the roasted sesame seeds. It should taste rich, salty and nutty. Serve at room temperature.

+ CHILLIES IN SOY SAUCE

4 tablespoons dark soy sauce
2 tablespoons white vinegar
¼ long red chilli, finely sliced

Mix the soy with the vinegar and 2 tablespoons water. Stir in the sliced chillies. Pour into a small bowl. It will keep for several hours.

หมูแดง
MUU DAENG

BARBEQUE PORK

If you walk through any Chinatown, there will always be a few shops selling barbequed meat, with ducks and pork behind sheets of glass, tempting customers. I'm easy prey for these sirens – I can't resist their call. It takes years to master the Chinese method of barbequing meats, and few shops will disclose their secret techniques. The following recipe has been gleaned from many years of furtive glimpses into this dark, smoky world.

The marinade and basting syrup can both be made well in advance. The fermented bean curd liquid adds richness and colour to the marinade – the red sort is preferable since it will imbue the pork with its colour. I have struggled with suggesting the use of red food colouring – but that's what street cooks do, so it is included here. If you share my qualms, you should be able to find some natural food colouring online. (Unfortunately, beetroot [beets] won't do, as it imparts a heavy and earthy flavour; it tastes of itself, normally a good thing for an ingredient to do but quite unacceptable here.) The maltose gives a glistening sheen and a slight crunch to the caramelised crust of the meat – try to find the darker, amber-coloured maltose, rather than the paler sort.

Originally the pork was cooked over wood, but now it is mostly done in large gas-fired kettles. Since it is unlikely you'll have one of these contraptions hanging around in your kitchen cupboards, I suggest you improvise by moving one of your oven shelves to the topmost slot, then hanging the meat hook from it. Hopefully the meat won't reach the bottom of the oven, but if it does, trim it to fit. Make sure there is space between each strip of pork so that they cook, colour and caramelise evenly. If your oven is not big enough to hang the pork, then lay it on a rack in a roasting tin and turn it often. I like to turn the heat up a bit near the end of the cooking so there are lots of delectable black crunchy bits – the best part, I think. Not every cook thinks like me, though, and some prefer a lighter colour and flavour.

Barbeque pork is rarely eaten alone. It is used in soups and noodles, but on the streets is mostly sliced across the grain and perched on top of steamed rice accompanied with cucumber, and with some dark, rich sauce (see left) spooned over the meat. A smaller bowl of chillies in soy sauce (see left) is always at the side.

- To make the marinade, simmer the spring onions, coriander roots, shallots, galangal and ginger in 1½ cups of water for about 5 minutes.
- Meanwhile, separately roast the star anise, cassia and cloves in a dry, heavy-based frying pan, until lightly toasted and aromatic. Add them to the simmering stock, along with the five-spice powder and the tangerine peel, if using. Stir in the soy sauces, rice wine and sugar – and the bean curd liquid and food colouring, if using – and continue to simmer for a few minutes longer. Allow to cool.
- Trim the pork and cut it into strips about 4 cm (1½ in) wide, following the muscle structure as far as possible. (If you plan to hang the pork strips in your oven to cook them, it might be wise to see if they will fit at this stage, when they can be easily trimmed.) Add the pork to the marinade, making sure it is completely immersed, and refrigerate for about 4 hours or overnight.
- Make the basting syrup by adding the maltose and sugar to ⅓ cup of water in a small pan and boiling until dissolved. Stir in the soy sauce, honey, hoisin sauce and red food colouring (if using), along with the star anise, cassia and cloves from the marinade, if you like, then simmer for a moment. Set aside to cool and thicken.
- Preheat the oven to 140°C (275°F) and remove the pork from the marinade. If the meat is to be suspended inside the oven to cook, pierce one end of each strip with a small butcher's hook, making sure it is securely placed so it will hold throughout the cooking. Hold it for a few moments to let the excess marinade drip off, then carefully hang the free end of the butcher's hooks over the topmost oven shelf. Have a solid tin sitting underneath it to collect anything that drips off the pork as it cooks. (Alternatively, lay the strips of pork on a rack set over a roasting tin.) Roast the pork for 10 minutes, then remove and brush with the basting syrup for a few minutes before returning to the oven for a further 5 minutes. (Now is the time to turn up the oven if you want the pork deliciously caramelised.) Baste the pork again and return to the oven for a final 5 minutes. Check that the pork is cooked (it must be well done) by pressing, almost pinching it: it should feel firm and resilient. If you are uncertain, then cut a little slice of meat to check – apart from the coloured crust, the pork should be matt ivory, just like regular roast pork. When it is cooked, take the meat out and let it cool, keeping the tin underneath to collect any drips. Barbeque pork will keep for several days in the refrigerator.
- Serve with the sauce spooned over the meat and a bowl of chillies in soy sauce.

SERVES 2

2–3 garlic cloves, peeled
good pinch of salt
1–1½ tablespoons vegetable oil
200 g (6 oz) fresh wide rice noodles
2–3 teaspoons dark soy sauce
150 g (5 oz) barramundi or sea bass fillet
vegetable oil, for deep-frying
1 tablespoon yellow bean sauce
1½ cups light stock
150 g (5 oz) Chinese broccoli,
    cut into 2–4 cm (1–1½ in) lengths
1 tablespoon light soy sauce
2–3 teaspoons oyster sauce
½ teaspoon ground white pepper
½ teaspoon white sugar
2 tablespoons tapioca flour, mixed with ¼ cup water
    to make a slurry
ground white pepper, fish sauce, white sugar,
    roasted chilli powder and chillies steeped
    in vinegar (see page 355), to serve

RAAT NAR PLAA GRAPONG

SEA BASS AND RICE NOODLES IN THICKENED 'GRAVY'

Don't worry too much if the noodles break up as you fry and colour them with the garlic and dark soy. They'll still taste good and you can cover your sins with some of the sauce! Mostly these noodles are served at room temperature, so they can be done in advance – just keep them covered in a warm place. The fish can also be cooked a little ahead of time, leaving only the sauce to be made just before serving.

Any white-fleshed fish makes a good alternative to the sea bass – try some dory or snapper. Prawns or squid are very agreeable candidates too, and there is no need to deep-fry them. Simply add the cleaned pieces to the wok when you are cooking the garlic, just before you add the yellow bean sauce.

- Crush the garlic to a somewhat coarse paste with the salt – either by pounding it using a pestle and mortar or finely chopping it with a knife.
- Heat the 1–1½ tablespoons of oil in a wok. Fry half of the garlic paste until just beginning to colour. Add the noodles, along with the dark soy sauce, and fry until aromatic and beginning to colour. Make sure the garlic doesn't burn, or it will ruin the dish. Remove the noodles from the wok, cover them and set aside in a warm place.
- Next deep-fry the fish. Cut the fish into pieces about 4 cm × 2 cm (1½ in × 1 in). Pour the deep-frying oil into a large, stable wok or a wide, heavy-based pan until it is about two-thirds full. Heat the oil over a medium–high flame until a cooking thermometer registers 180°C (350°F). Alternatively, test the temperature of the oil by dropping in a cube of bread – it will brown in about 15 seconds if the oil is hot enough. Deep-fry the fish until cooked and golden – this should take 3–4 minutes – then drain on paper towels.
- Pour off all but a tablespoon of the oil from the wok and fry the remaining garlic paste in it until fragrant. Add the yellow bean sauce and fry for a minute before pouring in the stock. Add the broccoli, season with the light soy sauce, oyster sauce, pepper and sugar and simmer for about 30 seconds.
- Add the tapioca slurry and simmer until thickened, stirring constantly. Check the seasoning: it should taste salty, slightly peppery and smoky.
- Divide the noodles between two plates. Place the fish on top of the bed of noodles and spoon over the sauce. Sprinkle with white pepper and serve with fish sauce, white sugar, chilli powder and chillies in vinegar.

200 g (6 oz) minced (ground) pork – preferably fatty
salt
3–4 tablespoons light soy sauce, to taste
ground white pepper
5 cups prepared plain rice congee (see below)
about 1 cup light pork or chicken stock
2 eggs
3–4 tablespoons shredded ginger
1 tablespoon chopped spring (green) onions
deep-fried Chinese bread (see page 40),
     to serve

โจ๊กหมูบะช่อใส่ไข่

JOK MUU BACHOR SAI KAI

RICE CONGEE WITH MINCED PORK AND EGG

This is a gentle and comforting dish that heals and salves the soul. All is forgiven or forgotten after eating this suave silken potage. It is eaten for supper, a dinner alone or occasionally for breakfast. It is especially kind to those who are feeling unwell.

Deep-fried Chinese bread is a regular accompaniment – I love to let pieces of it steep in the soup for a few minutes. Congee is eaten with a Chinese soup spoon and chopsticks.

- Mix the minced pork with a pinch of salt, 2 tablespoons of the light soy sauce and a good pinch of pepper. Leave for 10 minutes.
- Combine the rice congee with the stock and a very good pinch of salt then bring to the boil, stirring regularly, until thoroughly incorporated and smooth. Cover and let it simmer very gently for about 10 minutes, stirring regularly to ensure it doesn't catch – it may be necessary to add a few tablespoons of water.
- Roll or roughly pinch the seasoned minced pork into small rough dumplings – about 1 cm (½ in) in diameter – and add to the congee. Simmer for the minute or so they will take to cook. Crack in the eggs and let the congee sit tremulously for a few moments, without stirring. Sprinkle over the ginger and about a tablespoon of the light soy sauce, then stir once or twice to fold in the eggs, ginger and soy sauce. Check the seasoning: if it needs to be more salty, add some soy sauce.
- Sprinkle with the spring onions and a good pinch of pepper, and serve with deep-fried bread.

2 cups broken rice – about 500 g (1 lb)
3 tablespoons broken sticky rice – optional, but
     it makes for a thicker, more textured congee
1 teaspoon salt – or more, to taste
1 pandanus leaf, knotted

โจ๊กเปล่า

JOK PLAW

PLAIN RICE CONGEE

Broken rice is simply the grains of rice that break and shatter during the milling process. These kernels are separated from the premium whole grains and are usually sold separately, although some of the lesser grades of rice will contain a small percentage of the damaged goods. Broken rice cannot be used to make steamed rice as the starch spills out of the broken grains as they cook, making a gluggy, gluey mass. Terrible for steamed rice, but wonderful for rice soup! Some Thai cooks prefer new season's rice for congee, saying it makes a more supple soup, while others incline to old rice, saying it has more character and aroma. I plump for the latter.

Broken rice is easily bought in Thailand, and is usually available in Chinese grocery shops. It is also very easy to make: just lightly grind or pound the required amount of rice.

The congee must simmer very, very gently, and it should not be too thick or dry – you may need to add more water as it cooks. Once done, it is ready to use as a base for other, more complex congees. Plain congee is really invalids' food, but Thais and Chinese love its bland taste and easy-to-digest texture.

- Combine the rices, rinse well and drain. Soak in plenty of cold water for 2–3 hours – no longer or the cooked congee will be a thin, dull gruel with no perfume.
- In a large, heavy-based pan, bring 8 cups of water to the boil with the salt and the pandanus leaf, then gradually pour in the rice, stirring gently and constantly as the water returns to the boil. If the uncooked rice sticks to the pan and scorches, the congee will be ruined. When the rice begins to swell, turn down the heat to very low, cover with a lid and simmer as gently as possible, stirring regularly and adding more water if needed, until the rice grains have almost dissolved – about 45 minutes–1 hour. Put to one side, covered, and use within a few hours.

+ YELLOW BEAN SAUCE

3 tablespoons yellow bean sauce

1 tablespoon white vinegar

1 teaspoon white sugar

2 cm (1 in) piece long red or yellow chilli, sliced
    or 2–3 bird's eye chillies (scuds)

Combine all the ingredients in a small bowl. The sauce should taste salty, sour and slightly sweet.

SERVES 2–3

1 cup jasmine rice – preferably old (see page 359)

150 g (5 oz) sea bass fillet

2 cups light pork or chicken stock

2 tablespoons light soy sauce

salt, to taste

good pinch of preserved Chinese vegetable
    (dtang chai), rinsed and drained

good pinch of galangal powder

Asian celery or coriander leaves, chopped spring
    (green) onions, garlic deep-fried in oil (see page
    358), yellow bean sauce (see right) and ground
    white pepper, to serve

ข้าวต้มปลา

KAO DTOM PLAA

SEA BASS WITH RICE SOUP

This too is a comforting and calming soup, one that can assuage the cares of the world. Once cooked, the rice is softer than normal since it is simmered in a greater proportion of water. While some places will serve the rice straight from the pot, other more diligent stallholders will quickly plunge the cooked rice into a pot of boiling water to reheat before it is strained and spooned into the waiting serving bowls.

White-fleshed fish, such as sea bass, snapper, dory or barramundi, are ideal for this soup – just make sure it is really fresh, firm and not oily. Prawns, oysters, clams, scallops or sliced lobster are also welcome additions. I've even had one made with crunchy jellyfish. Some versions of this soup use fish stock, but I find this can make the soup too strong and fishy, so I prefer to use pork or chicken stock. In fact, some stalls will even poach the fish separately in order not to have a fishy soup!

A bowl of yellow bean sauce (see above) and one of chillies steeped in vinegar (see page 355) can also be served. This soup should be eaten with chopsticks and a Chinese soup spoon.

○ Rinse the rice three or four times until the water runs comparatively clear. Place in a heavy-based pan, cover with enough water to reach from the surface of the rice to just past the first joint of your index finger and simmer, covered, until the rice is cooked, tender and has absorbed most of the water – about 25 minutes. Remove from the heat and leave to sit for at least 30 minutes.

○ Rinse the fish fillet and remove any stray bones. Cut into elegant slices about 3 cm × 5 mm (1¼ in × ¼ in). Bring the stock to a simmer, seasoning it with the soy sauce and salt. Add the fish slices and poach for about 2 minutes or until just cooked.

○ Ladle the prepared rice into bowls. Now ladle over the fish and some of its stock and sprinkle with the preserved vegetable and the galangal powder. Garnish with the celery or coriander leaves, spring onions, deep-fried garlic and pepper, and serve with a small bowl of yellow bean sauce.

1 bitter melon, peeled, deseeded and
    cut into 3 cm (1¼ in) pieces

1 Chinese cabbage, coarsely chopped

1 bunch Siamese watercress (water spinach),
    trimmed and cut into 2–3 cm (1–1¼ in) lengths

1 small bunch Chinese broccoli, trimmed
    and cut into 2–3 cm (1–1¼ in) lengths

1 daikon (mooli), peeled and cut into
    2–3 cm (1–1¼ in) slices

3 tablespoons dried lily stalks, knotted – optional

5–6 garlic cloves, peeled and bruised

3–4 tablespoons yellow bean sauce

400–500 g (12 oz–1 lb) pork belly, cut into
    2 cm × 1 cm (1 in × ½ in) pieces

1 tablespoon salt

4 tablespoons light soy sauce

large pinch of white sugar

pinch of ground white pepper

JAP CHAI

MIXED VEGETABLE AND PORK BELLY SOUP

In the Teochew dialect, jap chai means many vegetables mixed together, and that's exactly what this soup is: a collection of leafy green vegetables, daikon and mushrooms. I like to add some dried lily stalks, which taste a little bit like sultanas and can be found in most Chinese food shops. They need to be rinsed before being added to the soup, and many cooks will also tie a knot in each one.

Pork belly is the cut of meat most commonly used in this soup. Don't worry if there are any small bones in the meat – they'll improve the flavour of the soup. Ribs can also be used, and I have occasionally seen pieces of duck pop up amid the vegetable medley too.

The soup is really not at its best when just cooked. Of course you can eat it, but it keeps on getting better. This recipe makes quite a few servings, but I think you'll find you'll want to have another bowl. After two days in the refrigerator, this soup really comes into its own – just remember to boil it every second day to keep it sweet.

- Scrape any white pith from the bitter melon, rub the pieces with some salt and leave for about 20 minutes in a colander to leach out some of the bitterness, then rinse well. Place the melon and all the vegetables, lily stalks (if using), garlic and yellow bean sauce in a stockpot or a large, heavy-based pan. Add the pork belly and cover everything generously with water. Season with the salt, soy sauce, sugar and pepper, then bring to the boil and simmer gently for 2–3 hours, skimming as needed. Top up with water from time to time and stir occasionally to prevent from catching. Allow to cool then place in the refrigerator overnight.

- The next day return the soup to the boil. (If the soup has jellied slightly, then add a few tablespoons of water to prevent anything from catching as the soup melts and heats up.) Check the seasoning: it should taste rich with a natural sweetness and slightly salty. Should it lack saltiness, add some extra soy sauce.

- The flavour of this soup improves over several days – it keeps well refrigerated, but if keeping it for longer than a day or two, it should be brought back to the boil every other day.

- Serve in soup bowls accompanied with plates of steamed rice. You should feel it doing you good each and every time you have it.

ของหวาน
DESSERTS
KORNG WARN

Desserts are beloved by the Thais. They will eat them contentedly as a snack; for breakfast, lunch, dinner or supper; to conclude a meal or in its place; to stave off hunger or to while away the time. Any time is the right time for a sweet. They are the national succour.

Thai desserts can be substantial, weighty even; they are so because they are not necessarily considered as part of a meal but can be eaten separately, at any time, day or night. In the morning, the preference is for slightly sweet and rich snacks, such as corn steamed with coconut or Thai cup cakes, but as the day progresses this taste changes and by the afternoon the desserts become richer and are more likely to contain coconut cream. Desserts also change according to the season, not only due to availability of ingredients but because of the weather – during the hot season, syrup desserts with ice are understandably popular.

On the streets and in the markets, there is a blurred boundary between sweet and savoury. Some desserts contain pepper, garlic, coriander and even prawns, dried fish or pork. And some savoury snacks are decidedly sweet. To the Western palate many of them are an acquired taste, but once that taste is acquired it is very hard to forgo. The sugar and soothing coconut cream help to calm the palate after the onslaught of chillies and other spices.

Of all Thai foods, desserts are the most specialised and technically demanding. They require attention, time and practice, but they are addictive. Desserts are not often cooked at home, although most home cooks will have a few recipes up their sleeves. For anything more elaborate, they will generally resort to the experts and head to the streets and markets to satisfy their craving.

There it is mostly women, jovial, gossipy and plump, who prepare desserts and run the stalls. Each stall specialises, often selling only one or perhaps two varieties, or they may specialise in a particular method, offering steamed, churned or deep-fried sweetmeats. But in every market there is at least one stall selling a selection of steamed puddings or desserts presented in a tray. Usually there are more.

Dessert cooks go to the market in the morning: how early depends on when they must start their preparation. If the stall opens early, then they are up before dawn, heading to the market before starting the day's work.

Some of the kitchens specialising in desserts have changed little over a hundred years. Charcoal fires the stoves, and baking is done inside a metal box with a door that is placed over the coals before embers are placed on top to create an even, oven-like heat. Coconut cream is freshly squeezed then diluted with freshly made perfumed water. Pastry is made and kneaded, eggs cracked and whisked, and the air is filled with the clean, sweet fragrance of jasmine and the resinous aroma of pandanus. The kitchen is normally open and airy, yet quite hot with various sugar syrups simmering, pastes churning and charcoal glowing. Of course there are also more modern kitchens. They are far more practical but have little of the charm of those older rustic kitchens.

Once the desserts are made, they are taken to the stalls to be sold. When a dessert is ordered, it is cut into portions and then wrapped in a banana leaf. This is a deft art. The leaves are trimmed and then cleaned with a slightly damp cloth before they are cut into strips, depending on the size of the sweet, with each end cut and rounded. The dessert is wrapped quickly and elegantly, then secured with small bamboo skewers. Passed over to the expectant customer, it is ready to go.

○ Desserts play an important role in ceremonies and rituals – here they are waiting to be eaten after the final chant of a merit-making ceremony.

1 cup white sticky rice

6–8 Thai jasmine flowers – optional, but desirable

2–3 pandanus leaves – optional

½ cup castor (superfine) sugar

1½ teaspoons salt, to taste

½ cup thick coconut cream

2 tablespoons yellow mung beans

2 ripe mangoes

sweet coconut cream (see right), to serve

+ SWEET COCONUT CREAM

½ cup coconut cream

½ teaspoon rice flour, mixed with a little water or coconut cream to form a paste

good pinch of salt

½–1 pandanus leaf – optional, but desirable

2 tablespoons white sugar – perhaps more to taste

Mix the coconut cream with the flour paste in a small saucepan or brass wok, stirring rigorously to incorporate. Add the salt and pandanus leaf, if using, then bring to the boil, stirring constantly to ensure the cream does not separate. When the coconut cream has thickened, add the sugar and immediately remove the pan from the heat. Stir until the sugar has dissolved. Allow to cool before serving.

ข้าวเหนียวมะม่วง
KAO NIAW MAMUANG

WHITE STICKY RICE WITH MANGO

Peeling mangoes the Thai way

Thais do things differently. For instance, when they peel fruit they always peel away from themselves – in the opposite direction to most Western cooks. It's difficult to jump cultures, but try it. Cup the mango in the palm of one hand and hold a small sharp knife in the other, with the blade facing outwards. Now pull the mango towards you slightly while moving the knife slowly away, peeling or shaving off the skin. Continue, moving and angling the mango as you go, until one side is peeled, then cut the cheek away from the stone. Repeat with the other side. Skilled cooks can lift the skin off seamlessly, with no cut marks evident, but I always leave a trail.

Thais will very often use a brass knife to cut their fruit, as it does not react with the sugar or acids and so will not taint it. Some scrupulous cooks will use brass woks and trays for the same reason.

Perfuming coconut cream

This enhances the taste and aroma of coconut cream. If making your own, use jasmine water (see page 358) when extracting the coconut cream. Alternatively, use water perfumed with pandanus: add 3–4 pandanus leaves to 1 cup of water and simmer for a few minutes, then leave to cool to about blood temperature and remove the leaves before using.

If you're using canned coconut cream, pop in a few Thai jasmine flowers – the effect won't be as pervasive as using perfumed water or as subtle as making your own coconut cream, but it will still add an agreeable note.

This dessert is a favourite of the Thais – and quickly becomes so to anyone who tastes it.

I think it is wise to scrub the steamer just before using – even though it is doubtlessly already clean – as it is surprising how easily the rice picks up hints of flavours past as it cooks in the steamer. In fact, every utensil should be washed just before use. The coconut cream must be thick and creamy. Making your own is best, of course (see page 355), but if you use the canned stuff, don't shake the can and use the solid plug of coconut cream at the top.

Yellow mung beans lend a crunchy texture and nutty flavour to the finished dish. You can buy them in most Asian shops – try to find ones that are already cracked or coarsely crushed, to save you having to do it. Be careful, though, as they can play havoc with the molars if crunched inopportunely!

- Rinse the rice carefully to remove any excess starch without breaking the grains. Soak it overnight – with 2–3 Thai jasmine flowers, if possible.
- The next day, drain the rice, rinse and place in a metal steamer; normally the raw grains of rice cling together, so they rarely fall through the holes, but if you're feeling cautious line the steamer with some rinsed muslin (cheesecloth). Make sure the rice is not piled too high in the centre, nor too widely spread. Add a pandanus leaf or two to the water in the base of the steamer, if you like, then steam the rice until tender (test some grains from the area where the mound of rice is deepest) – this should take about 45 minutes–1 hour. During this time, make sure that there is plenty of water in the steamer; if you need to top up the water level, use boiling water so as not to interrupt the steaming. When you check on the rice, wipe dry the inside of the steamer lid before replacing it.
- Meanwhile, stir the sugar and salt into the coconut cream until dissolved. When the rice is cooked, remove from the steamer and place in a glass or ceramic bowl, then pour over the prepared coconut cream and stir to incorporate fully. (It is important that the rice is still piping hot, so it will more completely absorb the coconut cream and become rich and glistening.) If you like, you can plunge a knotted pandanus leaf into the rice and dot the surface with a few Thai jasmine flowers. Cover and set aside in a warm place for 15 minutes before serving. Some cooks like to swaddle the bowl in a towel to keep it warm and snug!
- While the rice is settling, soak the mung beans in water for about 5 minutes then drain well. Dry-roast the mung beans over a low heat in a small, heavy-based pan or a wok, shaking often, until they are golden brown and smell nutty. Remove from the heat and, if necessary, crush coarsely using a pestle and mortar or an electric grinder.
- Peel the mangoes with a sharp knife, then cut the flesh away from the central stone into cheeks. Cut each cheek crosswise into five or six slices.
- Divide the rice among four bowls, then place a sliced mango cheek alongside and cover with a spoonful or two of sweetened coconut cream. Sprinkle with the mung beans and serve.

SERVES 4–6

2–3 pandanus leaves, knotted
200 g (6 oz) cassava
pinch of salt
2 tablespoons white sugar – more or less, to taste

COCONUT TOPPING
2 tablespoons rice flour
1 cup coconut cream
1 pandanus leaf, cut into 3 or 4 lengths
very good pinch of salt

Cassava

This long and comparatively slender tuber with rough dark brown skin can be found fresh and as frozen, peeled pieces in most Asian and Pacific Islander shops. When buying fresh cassava, look for firm roots with white flesh. The longer cassava has been out of the ground, the harsher its taste as the root develops acids that make it dark and bitter and can irritate those with sensitive innards. Some cooks will rinse the grated meat in water then squeeze it dry, but this is only necessary with old and dark roots, or with frozen cassava.

TAKO MANSAPALANG

CASSAVA PUDDING
WITH COCONUT TOPPING

The Thai term tako covers a whole range of layered desserts steamed in trays or banana leaves then topped with rich thickened coconut cream. The lower layer is usually based on a starchy ingredient such as tapioca, water chestnuts, corn, taro or cassava. This type of dessert is steamed in a small square tray – the older the stall, the more battered the tray from daily use. Swank places use one made from brass, but any heatproof container about 8–10 cm (3–4 in) square and 2 cm (1 in) deep will do.

Cassava pudding is at its best on the day it is made, but will keep for several hours. On the street, it is scooped out with a small spatula and wrapped in banana leaves (see page 196) to take away, but you can simply serve it straight onto waiting plates.

- Place the pandanus leaves in a small pan with ¾ cup of water. Bring to the boil and simmer for a minute or so, then leave to cool before fishing out the pandanus leaves.
- Bring water in a metal steamer to the boil.
- To prepare the cassava, peel then cut in half crossways. Just below the surface, you should see a thin black line that encircles the root: this contains irritants, so pare it all away. Rinse the root well, then grate the creamy flesh very finely, avoiding the tough central core, if there is one – you should have about 125 g (4 oz) grated cassava. Place this in a small bowl and work in the salt, sugar and 3 tablespoons of the pandanus-infused water. Pour into a heatproof container about 8 cm (3 in) square and 2 cm (1 in) deep and steam for about 45 minutes or until translucent. Make sure that there is plenty of water in the steamer – if you need to top up the water level, use boiling water – and when you lift the lid to check on progress, wipe it dry before replacing it.
- Meanwhile, make the coconut topping. Place the rice flour in a bowl and gradually add 2 tablespoons of the pandanus-infused water, working it in with the back of a spoon to form a dough. Leave to rest, covered, for about 30 minutes. Transfer the rested dough to a small saucepan and work in about another 3 tablespoons of the pandanus-infused water to form a batter. Bring to the boil, then simmer over a low heat for 3–4 minutes, stirring constantly and moistening the batter with 1–2 tablespoons of the pandanus-infused water as the flour cooks, to prevent it from becoming too dry. Add the coconut cream and the pandanus leaf then continue to simmer very gently for another 3–4 minutes, stirring regularly so the coconut cream does not separate. (If it threatens to do so, take the pan off the heat and add a tablespoon or two of pandanus-infused water.) Season with the salt. The coconut topping should be rich, creamy and discernibly salty. Pass through a sieve into a small glass or ceramic bowl and then pour it over the warm, but not too hot, cassava pudding.
- Allow to cool and set for at least an hour. To serve the pudding, cut into 3–4 cm (1¼–1½ in) squares or rectangles. Make sure you cut right through before lifting out the pieces, otherwise they will stick. If the first piece comes out sloppily, reshape it with a spatula dipped in hot water; the others should be easier.

SERVES 4–6

400 g (12 oz) taro – about 1 medium-sized taro
3 duck eggs *or* 4 chicken eggs, lightly beaten
1½ cups coconut cream
¾ cup shaved palm sugar
1 tablespoon rice flour
6–8 red shallots, very finely sliced lengthways
vegetable oil, for deep-frying

MOR GENG PEUAK

TARO PUDDING

Phetchaburi, to the south-west of Bangkok, is an ancient city where Siamese kings had their summer palaces, and where sugar palm trees grow in abundance. It is famous for its food, especially its desserts, and this pudding is one of the specialties.

Taro has a coarse dark-brown skin and creamy white flesh that may be flecked with black or purple spots. Raw taro contains calcium oxalate, which can irritate the skin, so it may be wise to wear gloves when preparing it. Once cooked, it is no longer bothersome.

Duck eggs are used to give greater depth and texture to this dessert, but chicken eggs can of course take their place. In more traditional kitchens, the pudding is cooked over charcoal. The mixture is poured into the heated tray, which is placed over the embers before being covered with another tray that is then covered with more embers. 'Baked' this way, the top of the pudding develops a wonderful crusty, caramelised top. To replicate this, I suggest you place the pudding under a hot grill for about 5 minutes before putting it in the oven. The garnish of deep-fried shallots seems downright bizarre to Western sensibilities, but to Thais their nutty taste and crisp texture are a welcome addition. Try them – you'll be surprised how fitting they are.

Taro pudding keeps well for several hours, but is best eaten on the day it is made.

- Peel the taro then rinse thoroughly. Cut into quarters and rinse once more. Steam or boil for about 15–20 minutes until tender. Remove and allow to cool, then pass the taro through a coarse sieve into a large bowl – you should have about ½ cup of taro puree. Add the eggs, coconut cream, sugar and flour and mix well. Pass through a fine conical sieve twice, pressing any recalcitrant bits firmly with the back of a spoon.

- Preheat the oven to 90–100°C (190–210°F), then place a heatproof container about 8–10 cm (3–4 in) square and 2 cm (1 in) deep in the oven to heat for about 5 minutes. Remove the container from the oven and pour in the mixture – it will sizzle for a moment. Place under an overhead grill (broiler) on low for 3–4 minutes until the pudding has a golden-brown skin, then transfer to the oven and bake for 30–40 minutes until just firm to the touch: a skewer inserted in the centre should come out clean. Remove from the oven and allow to cool for about an hour.

- Meanwhile, make the deep-fried shallot garnish. Pour the deep-frying oil into a large, stable wok or a wide, heavy-based pan until it is about two-thirds full. Heat the oil over a medium–high flame until a cooking thermometer registers 180°C (350°F). Alternatively, test the temperature of the oil by dropping in a cube of bread – it will brown in about 15 seconds if the oil is hot enough. Carefully add the shallots (the oil will bubble up) and deep-fry, stirring constantly with tongs, until the shallots are golden, nutty and fragrant. Drain on paper towels.

- When the pudding is cool, sprinkle with the deep-fried shallots. To serve, cut into 4 cm (1½ in) squares and gently lift out with a spatula.

KANOM DTOM DAENG

RED TOPKNOT LOLLIES

SERVES 6

3–4 pandanus leaves, knotted
½ cup white sticky rice flour
1½ teaspoons arrowroot flour
½ cup shaved palm sugar
good pinch of salt
1 cup grated coconut

This rich dessert was considered an auspicious sweetmeat to serve during the topknot-cutting ceremony for young children of the Kingdom of Siam when they came of age, at about 12. Hence the English name I give it, though the more prosaic literal translation is 'red boiled pastry'. This practice – and the ceremony that went with it – has fallen into decline, although you will still occasionally see young kids in the countryside with a telltale tuft of hair.

- Place the pandanus leaves in a medium-sized pan with 4–5 cups of water. Bring to the boil and simmer for a minute or so, then leave to cool slightly before fishing out the pandanus leaves.
- Sieve the rice and arrowroot flours into a bowl, then gradually work in about 2 tablespoons of the pandanus-infused water and knead for a minute or so until you have a malleable dough – you may need more or less water, depending on the flour. Roll into a cylinder about 3 cm (1¼ in) in diameter, wrap in plastic film then leave to rest for about an hour.
- Meanwhile, caramelise the coconut. In a small pan, heat the palm sugar with a pinch of salt and simmer over a medium heat for 3–4 minutes until it begins to caramelise and turns a golden nutty brown. Add about 4 tablespoons of the pandanus-infused water then the coconut. Cover and simmer over a medium heat for about 5 minutes: the coconut meat should be translucent and there should be plenty of caramel.
- To cook the topknot lollies, bring the remainder of the pandanus-infused water to the boil with the good pinch of salt. Unwrap the dough and cut into 5 mm (¼ in) discs. Slip the lollies into the water and boil for about 5 minutes until they float to the top. Scoop them into a large bowl of warm water and leave to steep for 5 minutes. Add the lollies to the caramelised coconut then let them sit for half an hour or so, covered.
- Serve in small bowls.

KAO NIAW DAENG

CARAMELISED WHITE STICKY RICE WITH SESAME SEEDS

SERVES 6

½ cup white sticky rice
⅓ cup shaved palm sugar
pinch of salt – optional
1 teaspoon sesame seeds

Caramelising palm sugar

Most palm sugar available outside Thailand is mixed with white sugar, which means it will crystallise when it is heated to make a caramel, unlike pure palm sugar. To help prevent this, add a tablespoon of maltose, glucose or corn syrup. I also like to add a pinch of salt to the caramel, although I know this would not happen on the streets. Be careful when caramelising palm sugar – it can burn quickly, due to the impurities that give it its rich broad taste.

This is a sticky and slightly crunchy confection with a deep golden colour that can be found in every market and on most streets. In Thailand, this dessert is set in a mould and cut into squares, but it can simply be left to harden in a bowl then spooned out.

- Soak the sticky rice in plenty of water for at least 3 hours or overnight.
- Drain the rice, rinse and place in a steamer; normally the raw grains of rice cling together, so they rarely fall through the holes, but if you're feeling cautious line the steamer with some rinsed muslin (cheese-cloth). Make sure the rice is not piled too high in the centre, nor too widely spread, so that it cooks evenly, and keep the water level below the steamer high to ensure there is plenty of steam. Steam the rice until tender (test some grains from the area where the mound of rice is deepest) – this should take about 25–35 minutes.
- Remove the rice from the steamer and spread it out on a plate to cool for about 20 minutes, turning and breaking it up into smaller pieces so it doesn't become one large soggy clump. Once the rice is cool, carefully crumble the pieces without breaking the grains.
- Heat the palm sugar (with a pinch of salt, if you want) in a small saucepan or brass wok and simmer over a medium heat, stirring vigilantly, until it caramelises to a rich dark brown. Be careful not to let it scorch – you'll smell it when it approaches that stage.
- When the caramel is the colour of dark honey, remove from the heat and quickly add the rice, working it in with a wooden spoon and making sure that every grain of rice is separated and coated with caramel. It is important to do this quickly before the caramel cools and hardens – if this starts to happen, return the pan to the heat for a moment. Spoon the caramelised rice into a mould or bowl and leave to cool.
- Meanwhile, dry-roast the sesame seeds in a tiny pan over a low heat until they are golden and aromatic, shaking the pan to prevent them from scorching.
- To serve the caramelised rice, either cut it into 2 cm (1 in) squares – you'll need a hot knife to achieve this – or scoop out spoonfuls and shape into squares or leave free-form. Sprinkle with the sesame seeds. As it cools the rice develops a crunchy, almost crispy texture. Make sure you keep it covered as it dries out quickly.

SERVES 4–6

1 large or 2 small Japanese pumpkins
1 egg, at room temperature
3 tablespoons shaved palm sugar
⅓ cup thick coconut cream
pinch of salt, to taste

STEAMED PUMPKIN AND COCONUT CUSTARD

In Thai, sangkaya means custard, which is the basis of quite a few Thai desserts. One of the most popular of these is a coconut custard steamed inside a pumpkin. Thai pumpkins are small and squat with knobbly blue-green skin and light golden flesh. Japanese pumpkins are quite close to them in both taste and texture. If you can't find a small enough pumpkin you can make the custard separately, steaming it in a small tray and serving it with slices of steamed pumpkin. It is also often served with steamed white sticky rice (see page 314).

Make sure you use the thickest coconut cream, otherwise the custard could split and it will never really set firmly once it has cooled. Thai cooks like to steam this over quite a high heat, which can also cause the custard to split and will certainly leave pock marks as the air expands and forms bubbles under such duress. I plump for a gentler approach, which makes for longer cooking but a better result. The custard should taste of palm sugar, and the texture should be rich and velvety.

- Cut the top off the pumpkin and carefully scoop out the seeds, then rinse well. Place the pumpkin upside down in a steamer and steam for about 15 minutes until partly cooked. Remove and turn upright to allow any steam to escape.
- In a small brass wok or pan, mix the egg with the sugar and coconut cream and salt. Gently warm this mixture over a low heat to a little above room temperature, then strain it. Pour into the pumpkin and steam gently for about 15–20 minutes until the custard is cooked: it should be softly set, with a light wobble if you nudge the pumpkin. If you find that the custard needs a little more time, wipe dry the inside of the steamer lid before replacing it, so that no water drips onto the custard as it steams.
- When it is done, lift off the entire steamer basket and place on a large plate. Leave the custard-filled pumpkin to cool completely before cutting into wedges to serve.

ลูกชินปลารสเยียม 丸魚製特龍
เย็นตาโฟ่รสเด็ด ปลอดสารทุกชนิด
อร่อย ลูกชิ้นทำเองเต้นได้จริง ๆ ปลีก - ส่ง
02 - 2151905 (สวนหลวง)

INGREDIENTS AND BASIC PREPARATIONS

Like any great cuisine, Thai food relies upon its ingredients for its quality: they form the basis of cooking. Thailand is a fertile country with an imaginative people, a complex history and a propensity for good food. As a result, its culinary repertoire contains many unusual ingredients and preparations – even in the simplified world of the street – that require some explanation beyond the brief introductions to the recipes.

Some of these ingredients may seem exotic but you might be surprised by how many are becoming available. The best place to look for them is at Thai specialty shops. In major cities 'Thai-towns' are taking root to cater to the needs of the local Thai community – a little like the markets described in this book, they not only supply food and ingredients but also help to maintain cultural connections in a strange new world. Of course they also help us even stranger farangs (Westerners) on our addled forays into Thai cooking.

In smaller cities Chinese or Asian shops should have quite a few of the necessary ingredients, however I must suggest that wherever possible you purchase items produced in Thailand. This is not from any adopted chauvinism, but because many Thai ingredients – such as shrimp paste, fish sauce, chillies and tamarind – taste quite different to the versions from neighbouring countries.

Finally, there is a whole world of specialist ingredients available online, which can be delivered to your door. And so distance is no longer an excuse for poor renditions of exotic food. Go and exploit the ever-increasing availability of once-elusive ingredients. Your cooking, this cooking, will be the better for it.

ASIAN CELERY keun chai ขึ้นฉ่าย

This looks more like stalky, lime-green parsley than celery. It has a strong, cleansing, mineral flavour and is generally added to dishes just before serving.

ASIAN PENNYWORT *see under* PENNYWORT, ASIAN

AUBERGINE *see* EGGPLANT

BANANA BLOSSOMS hua bplii หัวปลี

These are the flower buds of the banana tree, most commonly from the sugar banana variety. The large sheaths are what you use; the immature bananas within are very bitter and must be discarded. The best way to clean the blossoms is to peel off the tough russet-coloured outer layers until you reach the softer paler layers. Cut the blossom lengthwise into quarters and place in water soured with lime juice or vinegar to prevent discoloration. Cut away the hard core from the base of each quarter and shake out those bitter little bananas. Return to the acidulated water and repeat with the remaining quarters. Slice or shred as required. Try to do all of this as close to serving as conveniently possible, as the soured water only delays discoloration – it does not prevent it.

BANANA LEAVES bai dtong ใบตอง

The best banana leaves are quite young, green and fresh. As they get older, they become tough and tattered, making them difficult to handle. Some cooks will blanch the more recalcitrant leaves in boiling water to soften them – a quick dunk should make them yield. You will normally find banana leaves in Asian shops, sold as rolls of cut leaves, which need to be trimmed and wiped with a damp cloth before use.

BASIL

There are three main kinds of basil used in Thai cooking. Thai basil is usually available in Asian grocery shops, while holy and lemon basil are generally found in Thai shops alone. If keeping basil for a day or so, there is no need to refrigerate it – just keep it wrapped in a damp cloth. If keeping it for longer, then it is better to keep it in the fridge, but over time its perfume will become dull. The leaves should be picked just before using.

Thai basil bai horapha ใบโหระพา

This looks very much like Italian basil, but it has deep purple stalks and buds with white flowers. When fresh, it has a rich, resonant, aniseed-like taste and aroma.

holy basil bai grapao ใบกระเพรา

This basil is much sharper in taste than Thai basil, with a clove-like pepperiness to it.

lemon basil bai manglaek ใบแมงลัก

The soft green leaves and stalks of lemon basil have the most alluring and sweet taste of lemon zest. Sadly it doesn't last well – after a day or so, most of its perfume will have dissipated.

BEAN CURD dtao huu เต้าหู้

This is the pressed curd or solid protein made from soy beans pureed with boiling water then coagulated using a salt such as gypsum. There are various types of bean curd.

silken bean curd dtao huu orn **เต้าหู้อ่อน**

This is the softest curd, delicate and tender to eat but sometimes tricky to handle without it breaking up – it is worth the care.

yellow bean curd dtao huu leuang **เต้าหู้เหลือง**

This is a firmer curd, pressed and then dipped into a yellow dye. Often it is stamped with a little red Chinese logo. It is not too common outside of Asia, so if you can't find it, use firm bean curd.

fermented bean curd dtao huu yii **เต้าหู้ยี้**

This pungent product is made by curing blocks of firm bean curd in Chinese rice wine, spices and sometimes rice mould. There are two varieties, red and white – both readily available in Chinese shops. I generally prefer the white version, which is creamy, rich and agreeably musty; I find the red type, however colourful and exotic, too strong.

BETEL LEAVES bai champluu **ใบชะพลู**

Closely related to true betel, these large, tender green leaves are often known outside Thailand as betel or sometimes piper leaves. They are indispensable when making miang, a perennially popular snack. Torn leaves are also added to some curries.

BITTER MELON mara **มะระ**

These are bitter beasts. Some people love their strength – it's an acquired taste – but I believe they must be treated first to make them palatable. Cut the bitter melon in half, scraping out the seeds and especially the white fleshy pith, then rub with salt and leave for about 20–30 minutes to leach out some of the bitterness. Rinse well before continuing with the recipe. Some cooks prefer to steep them in heavily salted water. Other bolder cooks, with sterner tastes, will not bother with any of these niceties.

CARDAMOM

Several types of cardamon are used in Thai cooking.

Thai cardamom luk grawarn **ลูกกระวาน**

The cardamom of choice in this book, this is a small, round, off-white ridged shell containing black seeds. It is usually roasted before being husked, leaving the aromatic seeds to use. You should be able to find it at Thai food shops or Chinese medicine suppliers. More common green or Indian cardamom is an acceptable alternative, however I find it stronger and spicier in taste, so I suggest you use about a half to a third less.

Chinese black or brown cardamom luk chakoo **ลูกชักโก**

Sometimes known as amomum, black or brown cardamom is a musty, dark, ridged seed that adds a smoky, slightly tart taste. It is readily available in the spice section of most Chinese grocers.

cardamom leaves bai grawarn **ใบกระวาน**

These are mainly used in Muslim curries, and are not too common beyond the south of the country. Outside Thailand, you may find them in Asian food shops under their Malay/Indonesian name of daun salam, but dried bay leaves can be substituted.

CASSIA BARK op cheoi **อบเชย**

Cassia bark is occasionally referred to as poor man's cinnamon, but I find it richer and sweeter than its more common and affluent cousin. The quill is usually larger and thicker, with a fuller aroma and an opulent taste.

CHICKEN STOCK nahm soup gai **น้ำซุปไก่**

I find it best to use freshly made stock, as it has a sweetness and aroma that older stocks do not have. If you find it more practical to make stock in advance, it should keep well refrigerated for 2–3 days or frozen for a month or so. When reheating the stock, add a little fresh ginger and garlic to revitalise the taste and aroma. I like to use chicken bones but in Thailand a stock made with pork is equally popular – use leg or hip bones for a sweeter stock if you are going with the hog.

MAKES 2–3 LITRES (2–3 QUARTS), DEPENDING ON SIZE OF PAN

2 kg (4 lb) chicken bones – of course, a whole chicken could be used
large pinch of salt
a little ginger and garlic
any offcuts from spring (green) onions, cabbage,
     coriander stalks – whatever is to hand
1 small daikon (mooli), peeled and sliced

Wash the chicken bones then crush them slightly with a pestle or heavy object. Place in a large pan or stockpot, cover with cold water, add salt and bring to the boil. Add the vegetables and simmer for about 2 hours, skimming as necessary, then strain.

CHILLI JAM nahm prik pao **น้ำพริกเผา**

Chilli jam is a versatile, smoky preparation made from deep-fried shallots, garlic, chillies and dried prawns, pleasingly seasoned and not especially hot. It is worthwhile having a jar in the fridge, where it will keep indefinitely.

While ready-made chilli jam can be found in most Asian food shops, and is generally more acceptable then commercially produced curry pastes, homemade adds real depth of flavour.

MAKES ABOUT 1 CUP

5–10 dried long red chillies, to taste
¼ cup dried prawns
vegetable oil, for deep-frying
2 cups sliced red shallots
1 cup finely sliced garlic
2 slices galangal – optional
2–3 tablespoons shaved palm sugar
3 tablespoons tamarind water
good pinch of salt *or* 1–2 tablespoons fish sauce

Nip off the stalks of the chillies, then cut along their length and scrape out the seeds. Soak the chillies in water for about 15 minutes until soft, then drain, squeezing to extract as much water as possible. Rinse the dried prawns, then soak them in water for a few minutes to soften.

Pour the deep-frying oil into a large, stable wok or a wide, heavy-based pan until it is about two-thirds full. Heat the oil over a medium–high flame until a cooking thermometer registers 180ºC (350ºF). Alternatively, test the temperature of the oil by dropping in a cube of bread – it will brown in about 15 seconds if the oil is hot enough.

Deep-fry the shallots, garlic, galangal (if using) and chillies separately, one after the other, stirring with tongs or chopsticks to ensure even cooking, until each is golden. Be careful when adding the shallots and garlic as the oil will froth up: add a little at a time but quite swiftly. And watch out when adding the chillies – they will splutter and spit as the water hits the oil.

Drain the deep-fried ingredients on paper towel and allow to cool. Using a pestle and mortar, pound them and the drained prawns to quite a fine paste. Alternatively, puree the ingredients in an electric blender, moistening with a little of the oil used for deep-frying to facilitate the blending – add only as much as necessary, and no more than 3–4 tablespoons. Halfway through, turn the machine off and scrape down the sides of the bowl with a spatula, then turn it back on and whiz the paste until it is completely pureed.

Transfer the paste to a small saucepan and bring to the boil, then season with the palm sugar, tamarind water and salt or fish sauce. It should be quite oily – it may be necessary to add a few tablespoons of the deep-frying oil. If, however, it threatens to catch, add a few tablespoons of water. Simmer until quite thick, stirring regularly, but do not cook for too long otherwise the sugar may burn: 3–4 minutes should do it.

The resulting 'jam' should be thick with a good layer of oil, and it should taste smoky, sweet, sour and salty.

CHILLIES prik พริก

Chillies litter the streets and markets of Thailand. There are always several varieties hanging around, ready to be thrown with abandon into waiting pots, pans and woks. Fresh chillies come in various colours, but dried chillies can only be made from ripe red fruits – they are smokier and richer in taste than fresh. Try to buy dried chillies imported from Thailand, as they do have a slightly different flavour.
see also ROASTED CHILLI POWDER

long chillies prik chii faa พริกชี้ฟ้า

These are the commonplace workaday variety. They come in either red or green and, apart from aesthetic considerations, are pretty much interchangeable. The difference is simply due to the degree of ripeness: the green ones are unripe with a slightly tart flavour, and they turn red as they mature. Some people like to remove the seeds and inner white membrane: it is a cooling refinement. I used to do this but now I prefer them as they are, real and gutsy with their sharp pointed heat.

yellow chillies prik leuang พริกเหลือง

These are quite uncommon – well, outside of Thailand at least. They are stubbier, hotter and tarter than their longer cousins, but frankly long green or red chillies can be used in their place.

banana chillies prik yuak พริกหยวก

These large, thin yet fleshy chillies have a lime-green skin and are not too spicy. They are very similar to small capsicums or bell peppers, which can be used instead.

bird's eye chillies prik kii nuu suan พริกขี้หนูสวน

These are small, green and can be mean – I affectionately call them scuds. Intensely hot, aromatic and utterly addictive, they are delightful weapons in the Thai kitchen armoury. They are usually available in Thai food shops and Asian supermarkets.

dried long red chillies prik chii faa haeng พริกชี้ฟ้าแห้ง

Sometimes these chillies are used whole, but if they are being used in pastes, especially ones for curry, the stalks should be nipped off and the seeds and slivers of white membrane taken out. Those with more tender hands might be wise to wear gloves while doing this, as the dust can irritate. Then the chillies are soaked in water to soften their flesh and reduce their pungency.

dried bird's eye chillies prik kii nuu haeng พริกขี้หนูแห้ง

These really only need a rinse. Rarely would any cook try to deseed them – certainly no street cook worth their marbles would bother. They are hot, piercing and memorable.

CHILLIES STEEPED IN VINEGAR prik nahm som พริกน้ำส้ม

This is a crucial component of the seasoning condiments for noodles. Long red, green or yellow chillies are sliced then steeped in white vinegar for at least 30 minutes. The longer this sits, the better and more mellow it becomes.

CHINESE LETTUCE
pak gart horm ผักกาดหอม

This green, slightly crunchy lettuce has a mild taste. It is also known as celtuce and looks like a cross between fresh mustard greens and butter lettuce. It can be found in Asian food shops and markets, but most sturdy-stalked green lettuce can be used as a sly substitute.

CHINESE RICE WINE lao jin เหล้าจีน

This is rarely used in Thai cooking, where its use generally denotes a dish of Chinese origin. It is readily available in Chinese food shops.

CILANTRO *see* CORIANDER

COCONUT mapraow มะพร้าว

When buying a fresh coconut, always choose one that is quite heavy for its size. Weight suggests age, and an older coconut is best for the purposes of making cream. As the coconut matures, the white wall of meat that lines the shell develops and thickens, becoming rich and opaque, and so the yield of cream will be greater.

However, the coconut must be fresh. Improbable as this sounds, try shaking the coconut: if there is water inside, the meat is less likely to be fermented. If it has started to ferment, the cream will be tainted and, depending on the extent, may be unusable. Another telltale sign of spoilage is white mould around the eyes of the coconut.

To crack a coconut, place it in the palm of your hand, with its eyes facing your thumb or little finger. Holding it over a bowl to catch the coconut water, use the back of a heavy cleaver to crack the coconut deftly down the centre with a hefty whack. Hit it and then lift the cleaver quickly, so as to shatter the husk. Repeat the wallop, turning the coconut about 90 degrees after each strike – three, four or five times should do it. Once there are cracks in the coconut, be careful to hold it with the tips of your fingers so it is not touching your palm, as the cracks in the shell can nip as it is struck – and no one expects or likes to be bitten by a coconut! Rinse the coconut halves, removing any parts that are mouldy or discoloured.

The traditional Thai coconut grater called a 'rabbit' is a small stool with a sharp-pronged grater at one end. However, a hand-cranked spindle grater or even a zester works. For long strands, drag the utensil along the coconut half, at right angles to the shell. For shorter shreds, start from the centre of the coconut half and work your way to the rim. Turning the coconut regularly helps to ensure even strands. If using the grated coconut to make coconut cream, try not to include any of the brown skin that lies between the shell and the meat, as it will mute the sweetness of the cream and muddy its colour.

The long strands are mostly used to garnish desserts. If such grated coconut is called for, Thai cooks use a semi-mature coconut (mapraow teun teuk), which yields a soft yet full-flavoured meat. This type of coconut is hard to find outside Thailand, and should not be confused with a young green coconut, the meat of which is too immature to be grated.

COCONUT CREAM hua gati หัวกะทิ
AND COCONUT MILK hang gati หางกะทิ

The taste of fresh coconut cream is incomparably luscious and rich, with a depth of flavour that, I think, justifies the effort required to produce it. Traditionally, grated coconut is worked by hand with an equal amount of warm water – and, depending on the dish, may be perfumed with Thai jasmine flowers or pandanus leaves – for a few minutes, although some cooks extract cream directly from the grated coconut. This gives the richest and thickest of creams, but requires a strength in the hands and wrists that I simply don't have – unlike those market girls! However, I have found success with a blender: place the grated coconut in a blender and process with warm water (do not use coconut water, as it will sour the coconut cream or milk) for a few minutes.

Always extract the cream and milk from the grated or blended coconut by squeezing it through muslin (cheesecloth) into a glass, china or plastic bowl (metal taints the cream). Squeeze murderously, therapeutically, to obtain as much of the creamy goodness as possible. Leave to settle and separate for at least 20 minutes: the cream is the thicker, opaque liquid that separates and floats on top of the thinner liquid, which is the milk. No matter how much water is added, the yield of cream will always be approximately the same, as the cream separates from the milk. Normally one good coconut yields about a cup of coconut cream. Often the squeezing process is repeated, with more warm water being added to the grated coconut, but this second pressing will yield more milk than cream.

Both cream and milk are best used within a few hours. They can be kept refrigerated, which extends their life considerably, but the cream will solidify, making it hard to incorporate and difficult to use – especially for desserts. So on balance it's probably best to make it just before you need it.

All of the above is for those who want to make their own coconut cream and milk. I will always recommend that you should, but then I have the luxury of cooks in various kitchens doing that for me, or I can go down to a market when I am in Thailand – which you probably don't or can't. For many, the canned stuff will be a more realistic option: try to find a variety with no stabiliser in it, especially if you are making a curry that requires separated coconut cream; another trick is to not shake the can, then use the thicker part of the cream that sits on the top. When Thai cooks resort to cans, they will often use a tablespoon of oil to fry the curry paste first before adding the coconut cream. This will give the curry its requisite oiliness, which is then enriched with the cream.

CORIANDER pak chii ผักชี

All parts of this herb are used in Thai cooking. After washing and drying it well, tear off the root with some of the stalk then chop the leaves and stalks. Few but the most precious of cooks will bother to pick the leaves and use them alone.

But be sure to keep the roots. They are used in pastes of all kinds and in soups. I always peel them, though it's not essential if the skin is thin. Scrape away the skin and wash the roots well: it might help to steep them in water to dissolve and dislodge any soil lurking among them. Drain well before use.

CURRY POWDER pong gari ผงกระหรี่

Frankly most Thais buy prepared curry powder from a market. You can too – just make sure it is quite mild and store it in the refrigerator, where it will keep its vigour for longer. For those who want to make their own . . .

curry powder for beef pong gari samrap neua ผงกระหรี่สำหรับเนื้อ

MAKES ABOUT ½ CUP
5 long pepper (sold in Indian shops as pipalli or peepar) – optional
1 teaspoon black peppercorns
1½ tablespoons coriander seeds
1 tablespoon cumin seeds
1 teaspoon cloves

1 teaspoon fennel seeds
7 Thai cardamom pods *or* 4 green cardamom pods, husked
2 tablespoons turmeric powder
1½ tablespoons ground ginger

Grind the whole spices to a powder using an electric grinder or a pestle and mortar. Add the turmeric and ginger, then pass the powder through a sieve. Store in the fridge.

curry powder for chicken pong gari samrap gai ผงกระหรี่สำหรับไก่

MAKES ABOUT ½ CUP
2 dried long red chillies – optional
1 tablespoon coriander seeds
1 tablespoon cumin seeds
2 teaspoons fennel seeds

5 Thai cardamom pods *or* 3 green cardamom pods
5 cloves
3 cm (1¼ in) piece cassia bark
½ nutmeg, grated
2 tablespoons ground ginger
1 tablespoon turmeric powder

If using chillies, nip off the stalks then cut along their length and scrape out the seeds. Soak the chillies in water for about 15 minutes until soft, then leave to dry. In a dry, heavy-based frying pan, separately roast the whole spices, shaking the pan to prevent them from scorching, until aromatic. Husk the cardamom. Grind the roasted spices and dried chillies to a powder using an electric grinder or a pestle and mortar. Add the nutmeg, ginger and turmeric, then pass the powder through a sieve. Store in the fridge.

curry powder for seafood pong gari samrap arharn tarlae ผงกระหรี่สำหรับอาหารทะเล

MAKES ABOUT ¾ CUP
1 tablespoon white peppercorns
1½ teaspoons coriander seeds
1½ teaspoons cumin seeds
1½ teaspoons fennel seeds
5 Thai cardamom pods *or* 3 green cardamom pods
2 cm (1 in) piece cassia bark or cinnamon
½ nutmeg, grated
3 tablespoons ground ginger
4 tablespoons turmeric powder

In a dry, heavy-based frying pan, separately roast the whole spices, shaking the pan to prevent them from scorching, until aromatic. Grind to a powder using an electric grinder or a pestle and mortar, then add the nutmeg, ginger and turmeric. To obtain a truly fine powder, pass it through a sieve. This is tedious, but rewards with a result where the tastes sing, unmuffled by the chaff. Store in the fridge.

DEEP-FRIED GARLIC *see under* **GARLIC**

DEEP-FRIED SHALLOTS *see under* **RED SHALLOTS**

DRIED CHILLIES *see under* **CHILLIES**

DRIED PRAWNS gung haeng กุ้งแห้ง

These little beauties are delicious and savoury, if they are fresh. Commercially they are produced by steaming peeled small prawns over salted water and then leaving them to dry. However, if stored for too long, they become stale and pale, often with a faint whiff of ammonia. Sometimes they are just plain rank. Look for ones that are kept refrigerated: they should be pink in colour and sweet-smelling. Even better, make your own and be assured of their freshness and quality.

30 small raw prawns (shrimp)
½ teaspoon salt
about 1 tablespoon fish sauce or light soy sauce
pinch of white sugar

Peel, devein and rinse the prawns. Combine the salt, fish sauce or soy sauce and sugar, then pour over the prawns and leave to marinate for 2 hours.

Place the prawns on a cake rack over a foil-lined tray (this makes for easier cleaning). Ideally, they should be dried for a day or two in direct sunlight, covered by muslin (cheesecloth) to prevent anything untoward enjoying them before you do. Otherwise, dry the prawns overnight in an oven with just the pilot light on until they are dried but not brittle.

Dried prawns will keep for several weeks refrigerated. Grind or pound them as needed.

DRIED TANGERINE OR ORANGE PEEL
peu som haeng ผิวส้มแห้ง

This can be found in most Asian food shops. To make your own, simply dry strips of tangerine, mandarin or orange peel – with the white pith removed – in a warm place for a day or so. Store in an airtight container.

EGG NOODLES sen ba mii เส้นบะหมี่

These are made by kneading strong wheat flour and eggs into a stiff dough that is then rolled and cut into strands – flat or rounded, depending on the origin of the dish and its requisite noodle. For instance, egg noodles for Chinese dishes are usually thin and can be either flat or rounded, but noodles destined for Chiang Mai noodles (kao soi) are much thicker and are generally flat.

When purchasing fresh egg noodles, make sure they are dusted with flour. They keep for 3–4 days refrigerated. They are generally blanched before use – careful cooks will often blanch the noodles twice, rinsing them in warm water in between.

If using dried egg noodles, follow the manufacturer's instructions.

EGGPLANT makreua มะเขือ

Many types of eggplant are used in Thai cooking, but perhaps the most common are the apple and pea varieties – and these are the two that are called for in this book.

apple eggplant makreua pok มะเขือเปาะ

Used mainly in curries and salads, this eggplant is so called because of its shape: it is a small round fruit, usually with a green and white marbled skin. When fresh its flesh is white and very crisp, but the taste is not so pronounced. It should only be sliced as needed, since it oxidises and browns quickly. Some cooks will steep the cut eggplant in salted water to retard this discoloration.

pea eggplant makreua puang มะเขือพวง

These small olive-green eggplants look just like large peas. They grow in clusters, and must be picked from their stems then washed. I suggest steeping the eggplants in water for several minutes to dislodge any buds, which tend to stick to them. When they are really fresh, they are sweet yet starchy – but as they become older, like so many things, they become solely bitter. They are used mainly in curries, especially those based on coconut cream. Some cooks like to add them just before serving to retain their pleasingly bitter crunch, while others like to simmer them until cooked so they develop a drawn, tea-like flavour. Since they'll probably be quite old in the Asian food shops where you're most likely to find them, I think it is best to let them stew a little.

FERMENTED BEAN CURD see under BEAN CURD

FISH SAUCE nahm plaa น้ำปลา

This condiment is the lifeblood of Thai cooking. It is made by fermenting small fish with salt. The liquid is matured for several months before being strained and left in the sun, effectively pasteurising it. Once almost every household, certainly every village, made their own heady brew, but now most homes buy it from the market. In Thailand there are many types available and even some regional variations resulting from the specific fish used in each province.

Outside of Thailand, two or three companies dominate the market, and they offer quite a good product. Some companies are now offering organic or high-end quality fish sauce. Whatever brand you decide upon, buy a small bottle as you are more likely to use the sauce before it oxidises and becomes flat. After opening, evaporation may occur, causing salt crystals to form at the bottom of the bottle – don't worry, they're not shards of glass! If the sauce becomes too salty or stale, I have found that adding a little water helps to refresh it somewhat. While it stores well in the larder, I think it is better kept refrigerated.

Some Thais, especially from the north-east, are fond of fish sauce perfumed with giant water bugs (*Lethocerus indica*), called maengdtaa in Thai. Rife in rice paddies, these insects are collected and cleaned, and parts of them are added to fish sauce. It sounds horrendous but tastes delicious, and the resulting sauce has the most haunting of aromas. It may be found in very small bottles near the fish sauce. Use sparingly.

FIVE-SPICE POWDER pong parlow ผงพะโล้

Five-spice powder is a cornerstone of the Chinese kitchen, helping to balance the richness of fatty meats, especially pork and duck. It is not called five-spice powder because it uses five spices alone (many blends include six or seven spices), but rather because it contains at least one spice that represents each of the five elements that pervade all of Chinese culture: earth, wind, metal, fire and water. This need for balance is reflected in the culinary world with the judicious use of ingredients that promote harmony in the body. Five-spice powder then is a blend of spicy, sour, bitter, sweet and salty components in accord with the Chinese pharmacopoeia. Some cooks suggest the addition of a few other spices, such as white pepper, liquorice, coriander seeds and brown cardamom pods.

You can buy five-spice powder easily, but I am afraid it will probably be stale. Making your own is simple and quick – and it is more likely to promote a better taste, and maybe even health too.

MAKES ABOUT ½ CUP
1 tablespoon Sichuan peppercorns
10 star anise
2 cm x 8 cm (1 in x 3 in) pieces cassia bark
1½ teaspoons fennel seeds
3 cloves
1 teaspoon white peppercorns

Lightly roast the Sichuan peppercorns, star anise, cassia, fennel and cloves separately in a dry, heavy-based frying pan until aromatic, shaking the pan often to prevent scorching. Grind to a powder, along with the white peppercorns, using an electric grinder or a pestle and mortar. Pass the powder through a sieve then store in an airtight container, preferably refrigerated.

GALANGAL khaa ข่า

Galangal looks similar to ginger, but tastes quite different, with a peppery, musty taste and a sharp aroma. When it is young the skin is thin and white, tinged with the occasional pink blush, and the flesh is a bone colour. This is when it is best for soups. As it ages it becomes stronger in taste, the skin turns golden or even red and the flesh becomes harder. At this stage it is best for curry pastes. Fresh galangal can be found in most Asian grocers.

GALANGAL POWDER khaa bon ข่าป่น

This can be bought from most Asian food shops, but it is often old and stale. It is easy to make your own and the taste will be immeasurably better. Simply slice peeled galangal and leave it in the sun to dry – or in a warm place, such as the oven with the pilot light on and the door ajar. When completely dried, grind to a fine powder using an electric grinder or a pestle and mortar. Store in an airtight container in the refrigerator.

GARLIC gratiam กระเทียม

Thai garlic is much smaller and sweeter than the garlic that is generally available in the West – it reminds me of new-season or 'wet' garlic. Naturally regular garlic will do, but if your garlic is pungent and peppery it might be wise to cut down the amounts recommended in the recipes. As well as being used extensively in its natural state, there are a couple of garlic preparations that find their way into many dishes.

deep-fried garlic gratiam jiaw กระเทียมเจียว

While this can be bought in Asian grocery stores, the commercial stuff is generally stale, riddled with preservatives and useless. I recommend you make your own: it is cheaper, fresher and better.

Cut garlic cloves lengthwise into thin, even slices – the slices should be as fine as possible, almost paper-thin. Pour enough oil for deep-frying into a small wok or heavy-based pan, then heat over a medium–high flame until a cooking thermometer registers 180°C (350°F). Alternatively, test the temperature of the oil by dropping in a cube of bread – it will brown in about 15 seconds if the oil is hot enough. Add the garlic and reduce the heat a little. Deep-fry, stirring constantly with tongs or chopsticks, until the garlic turns a light honey-gold and smells nutty. Remove the deep-fried garlic from the oil and drain on paper towel. When cool, it will keep for 2–3 days in an airtight container. Pass the garlic-infused oil through a sieve to collect any scraps before re-using it for deep-frying or stir-frying.

garlic deep-fried in oil or with pork scratchings
gratiam jiaw gart muu กระเทียมเจียวกากหมู

This is used with noodles of all kinds – a dab meaningfully enriches a dish. The traditional fat to use is pork fat, which makes a suave and velvety condiment, however modern cooks tend to use oil. The garlic is effectively preserved in the oil or fat and will keep for at least a week. Most Thais have no qualms about leaving it unrefrigerated, but I worry and cannot help but sneak it into the fridge. It must be reheated before use.

MAKES ABOUT 1/3 CUP

about 100 g (3 oz) pork fat – ideally back fat (fatback) – minced
  (roughly ½ cup) *or* 1 cup vegetable oil

salt
2–3 garlic cloves, peeled

If using pork fat, rinse it then place it in a small pan with a good pinch of salt. Cover with water and bring to the boil, then simmer until the water has evaporated, stirring regularly to prevent the pork from catching. Fry – it should be frying by now, all the water having evaporated – until golden and invitingly aromatic, stirring often. Be careful not to let the pork fat colour too much or burn, otherwise it will be tainted and unusable. Carefully strain, keeping both the rendered pork fat and the crispy scratchings.

Crush the garlic to a somewhat coarse paste with a pinch of salt – either by pounding it using a pestle and mortar or finely chopping it with a knife.

Heat the rendered pork fat or oil in a small pan, then add the garlic and fry until golden. Take off the heat and stir in about 3–4 tablespoons of the pork scratchings, if using (keep the rest of the scratchings to have with a beer). Store covered, refrigerated or not – it's your call.

GINGER king ขิง

Ginger is widely used in dishes of Chinese origin, especially stir-fries – it helps to clean up oily or fishy tastes and so is often combined with seafood. As it ages, the rhizome's taste becomes sharp and peppery and this can sometimes be too strong. To soften the blow, rinse the chopped ginger in water to remove some of its pungency.

GLASS (BEAN THREAD) NOODLES wun sen วุ้นเส้น

These are made from mung bean flour and look like stringy fishing lines. In their dried form they are truly tough, but they become much softer and easier to handle after they have been soaked in warm water for about 15 minutes. They are sold packaged in small bundles, and are readily obtainable in Asian food shops.

GRACHAI (WILD GINGER) กระเทียม

There are many names for this rhizome – Chinese keys, wild ginger and finger root, among others. The names are quite descriptive, as its finger-like roots sprout from a small russet cross-root. It has a muddy camphor ginger-like flavour and is used to combat gamey or fishy tastes in curries and stir-fries. Although it is quite uncommon, it is sometimes available fresh in Thai shops. It is, however, usually available pickled in a jar: drain and rinse before using.

GREEN ASIAN MELON fak ฟัก

Several varieties of this fleshy melon are available in Chinese grocers. Also known as Asian gourd, it is quite cooling and offers a pleasant respite from chillies. Chayote – common old choko – can be used in its place.

HOISIN SAUCE sauce prung rot hoisin ช้อสปรุงรสฮ้อยชิน

Readily available in Asian food shops, this sauce is made from fermented soy beans, sesame seeds, brown sugar, garlic and vinegar. Choose carefully – some versions are harsh, thin and full of preservatives.

JASMINE WATER nahm dok mali น้ำดอกมะลิ

Thai jasmine flowers are used to impart an alluring perfume to many desserts. If you can find Thai jasmine (*Jasminum sambac*) in a nursery, then grow it – it is a small shrub that flowers prolifically in warm weather. I'm afraid regular jasmine won't do. Despite its haunting aroma, it makes for a dull, vegetal water.

The best flowers to use are ones that are unopened, as their perfume is more intense. Open the jasmine flowers by pressing each one between the palms of your hands. You'll need about 10–20 jasmine flowers to perfume 4 cups of water. Float the jasmine flowers face down in water and leave to steep overnight, covered. Remove the flowers and strain the water. The jasmine water needs to be used within a day as it loses its perfume quickly.

If you don't have access to Thai jasmine flowers, perfume some water with pandanus leaves (see opposite). Otherwise, Asian stores sometimes sell jasmine essence – but it can be coarse and harsh, so use with caution. I somehow think a better-quality rose or orange flower water might be a more subtle substitute.

KAFFIR LIME LEAVES bai makrut ใบมะกรูด
Widely available, these are an important ingredient in Thai cooking, seasoning salads, soups, curries and stir-fries with a haunting perfume.

KAFFIR LIMES luk makrut ลูกมะกรูด
These dark green, knobbly-skinned fruit have the most heady perfume. The zest is used in curry pastes, although the pith is very bitter and should be assiduously removed. The sour and soapy juice is occasionally used in salads and curries. Kaffir limes are generally available in Asian food shops.

KANOM JIN NOODLES sen kanom jin เส้นขนมจีน
These are the only truly Thai noodles, made from pureed fermented rice that is extruded into vats of simmering water. They are served at room temperature with various sauces and an array of vegetables. Fresh ones are not too common outside of Thailand, but there are some Vietnamese rice noodles called banh canh or rice starch that are quite similar – they are thicker and are not fermented, but they will do. Dried kanom jin noodles are also increasingly available from Thai and Asian food shops.

LEMONGRASS dtakrai ตะไคร้
Used in curry pastes and soups, lemongrass is widely available. To prepare it, peel off the outer leaves and trim off the base and top third of the stalk – all these are tough and comparatively tasteless, though they make a very pleasant tea.

LIME PASTE bun daeng ปูนแดง
This paste, which is made from cockle shells, is also known as quicklime. It is used when making pickles and for adding crispness to flour-based batters and desserts. It is also one of the ingredients in betel quid for chewing – an ancient but increasingly uncommon Thai pastime. The pink or white paste is available in small jars in Asian stores: most Thais prefer the pink; the white is used to add to the mix for chewing betel nuts. When using lime paste for culinary purposes, it must be dissolved in water then left to precipitate, which takes about 15 minutes. Once there is a fine white or red sludge at the bottom of the container, it is ready to use. The water should be clear or a faint pink colour, depending on the colour of the paste you have. Use all the water, but none of the residue.

MACE dork jaan ดอกจัน
This is the outer sheath that covers a nutmeg. When fresh it is a flaming-red colour, but it mellows with age to a honey brown. Mace has a lighter, sweeter, more floral aroma than nutmeg, but once ground it deteriorates rapidly. Unless you can buy the spice whole and from a reputable spice shop, use nutmeg instead.

MALTOSE bae sae แบะแซ
This by-product of cereal fermentation comes in two versions: clear and amber – the latter has a more pronounced, nutty flavour. You'll find both in tubs in Chinese shops. Corn syrup or glucose can be used as alternatives.

MUNG BEAN FLOUR blaeng tua kiaw แป้งถั่วเขียว
Available from most Chinese grocers, this is simply dried green mung beans ground into flour. It makes pastries lighter and cooks to a translucent paste.

NOODLES see EGG NOODLES; GLASS (BEAN THREAD) NOODLES; KANOM JIN NOODLES; RICE NOODLES

PALM SUGAR nahm dtarn bip น้ำตาลปีบ
Pure, freshly made palm sugar is a wonderfully rich, fudge-like confection with a supple texture – in fact, I suspect that palm sugar just like this was one of the original Thai desserts. Unfortunately most of the palm sugar available outside Thailand is mixed with white cane sugar, but its mellowness is still a welcome enrichment to the savoury and sweet dishes it seasons. Palm sugar is widely available in Asian shops and some supermarkets.

PANDANUS LEAVES bai dtoei ใบเตย
Available from Asian grocers, these verdant blade-like leaves are used to perfume a host of Thai desserts and are occasionally used to dispel strong and disagreeable odours – in boiled dishes and some stocks, as well as curries that will be left to stand for some time. The leaves have little aroma when raw but on heating they exude an enchanting nutty perfume.

To make perfumed, pandanus-infused water for use in Thai desserts, add 3–4 pandanus leaves to 1 cup of water and simmer for a few minutes. Leave to cool to about blood temperature before removing the leaves.

PENNYWORT, ASIAN bai bua bok ใบบัวบก
These green, fleshy, clover-like leaves are occasionally used in salads or as a side dish for a spicy *nahm prik* relish, but mostly are juiced and served with sugar and ice as a delicious, quenching and cooling drink.

PICKLED MUSTARD GREENS pak gart dong ผักกาดดอง
These are made by pickling fresh mustard greens in brine. Two versions are available from most Chinese grocers: one sweet and the other salty – go for the latter.

PRESERVED CHINESE VEGETABLE dtang chai ตั้งฉ่าย
This chopped cabbage is preserved in salt, brown sugar, pepper and galangal. It can be easily bought in most Asian stores, however I find the commercial version very salty and coarse-tasting. To mitigate this, rinse and drain it well then work in a little brown sugar, ground white pepper, galangal powder and Chinese rice wine.

RED SHALLOTS horm daeng หอมแดง
These small pink shallots have a finer taste than the grey or brown versions. They are used in pastes, particularly those for curries, or sliced in salads, where their rosy finesse shines. They can be found in most Asian food shops, but if you can't find them, regular shallots may be substituted. At a pinch you could even use red onions, despite their coarser taste: cut them into quarters before slicing them very finely. Thais almost always slice their shallots lengthwise, which better preserves the elegant shape of the shallot.

deep-fried shallots horm jiaw หอมเจียว

These can be purchased in Asian shops but will most likely be stale. To make your own, cut shallots lengthwise into very thin, even slices. Pour enough oil for deep-frying into a small wok or heavy-based pan, then heat over a medium–high flame until a cooking thermometer registers 180°C (350°F). Alternatively, test the temperature of the oil by dropping in a cube of bread – it will brown in about 15 seconds if the oil is hot enough. Turn the heat up slightly and add the shallots – be careful, the oil will bubble up. Deep-fry, stirring constantly with tongs or chopsticks, until the shallots begin to colour. Make sure the oil remains quite hot throughout, otherwise the shallots will absorb oil and become soggy. Remove the deep-fried shallots from the oil and drain on paper towel. When cool, they will keep for 2 days in an airtight container.

RICE kao ข้าว

The cultivation of rice created Thai society, culture and cuisine. When Thais use rice it must be Thai rice – no exceptions. Thais believe their rice is the best in the world and while this might be disputed by some (though not me), it is unquestionably the only rice to use when cooking Thai food. It has a different fragrance and properties that make it distinct. There are a few varieties that are called for in this book.

jasmine rice kao horm mali ข้าวหอมมะลิ

Long, slender and versatile, this is the main rice used in Thailand. It is harvested once a year, and most is sold and consumed within a year of its harvest. Old rice, which is rice from the previous year's harvest, is preferred for a few dishes, most notably chicken and rice (kao man gai). It is stronger in taste and slightly, agreeably musty. It can be found in most Chinese grocers, but you'll probably need to ask for it. The best way to cook any type of long-grain rice is by the absorption method: the rice is rinsed, covered with water and brought quickly to the boil; the pan is then covered and the heat turned to very low, leaving the rice to simmer gently for about 10–15 minutes. It is then removed from the heat and left to rest and settle for a further 10 minutes. The way to measure the depth of water needed when cooking rice (regular pan or rice cooker, it doesn't matter) is to rest the tip of your index finger on the surface of the rice and then pour in water until it comes up to the first joint of your finger.

white sticky rice kao niaw ข้าวเหนียว

Also known as glutinous rice, this variety has shorter and plumper grains, and becomes sticky when cooked. It needs to be soaked overnight before being steamed. White sticky rice is the staple grain of the north and north-east of Thailand, and is also used in many desserts.

black sticky rice kao niaw dam ข้าวเหนียวดำ

Black sticky rice retains its bran layer, which gives the grain a dark aubergine colour. It also prevents the cooked rice from becoming as sticky as white sticky rice grains.

rice flour blaeng kao jao แป้งข้าวเจ้า
and sticky rice flour blaeng kao niaw แป้งข้าวเหนียว

Rice flour is a fine, pure white flour used mainly in desserts to add crispness. Sticky rice flour is ground from white sticky rice, and is mostly used to give desserts a rich, gluey texture. Both can be found in Asian grocers.

RICE NOODLES sen guay tio เส้นก๋วยเตี๋ยว

These are made from rice flour and water: the batter is spread onto muslin (cheesecloth) to form sheets and then steamed before being smeared with a little oil to prevent the sheets – and later the noodles – from sticking together. Almost opaque, with a filmy sheen, they are best kept at room temperature and eaten fresh within a day or two. While they can be refrigerated to prolong their life for as long as 3–4 days, this toughens them and makes them too brittle to use easily. If the noodles have been chilled, I find it is better to steam them for about a minute to soften them, and then let them cool to room temperature before use.

If using dried rice noodles for stir-fries, they should be soaked in cold water for about 15 minutes, then drained well before being added to the wok. I find they can break up and clump when stir-frying. To help prevent this, briefly plunge the noodles in boiling water, draining them well before adding them to the wok. Dried noodles destined for soups can be added straight from the packet.

Rice noodles come in various thicknesses:

wide rice noodles sen yai เส้นใหญ่

Cut into approximately 2 cm (1 in) wide strips, these noodles are mostly stir-fried or added to soups.

thin rice noodles sen lek เส้นเล็ก

Also known as rice sticks in their dried form, these noodles are used in soups and stir-fries, including pat thai.

rice vermicelli sen mii เส้นหมี่

These very thin rice noodles are used in soups, laksa and stir-fries. I like them, though some find them a little dusty in taste.

ROASTED CHILLI POWDER prik bon พริกป่น

This powder made from ground dried chillies is used to season sauces, curries, noodles and stir-fries. To make it, roast a cup of dried bird's eye or dried long red chillies in a dry wok or frying pan over a medium heat, stirring regularly to prevent scorching, until they have changed colour. Cool, then grind to a coarse or fine powder, as preferred, using a pestle and mortar or an electric grinder. This chilli powder keeps well if refrigerated in an airtight container.

SALTED DUCK EGGS kai kem ไข่เค็ม

These are made by steeping duck eggs in a brine for a month. They can be purchased in most Chinese grocery shops.

SALTED RADISH hua chai po หัวไชโป๊ว

This is made from daikon (mooli) cured in salt and brown sugar. It is readily available whole, sliced, shredded or minced in Chinese food stores. I think it is best rinsed well and left to drain before use.

SAUCE SIRACHA sauce prik Siracha ซ้อสพริกศรีราชา

This wonderful chilli sauce is available in all Asian food shops. It is made by simmering dried chillies with garlic, salt, sugar and vinegar for several hours. It takes its name from a seaside town of the same name on the eastern coast of the Gulf of Thailand, where it was created to accompany the seafood that is so prevalent and so delicious in that region. I recommend you buy one produced in that area – try a few to see which you prefer.

SHIITAKE MUSHROOMS het horm **เห็ดหอม**
These are used fresh and dried in Thai cooking. To reconstitute the dried variety, soak in hot water for 10 minutes or simmer for about 5 minutes in water seasoned with a little oyster sauce. Fresh shiitake mushrooms can be found in Asian food stores and some supermarkets. The dried version is always available in Chinese food shops – look for larger ones with fleshy caps and wrinkled and cracked skin. The tough stems should be removed from both fresh and reconstituted dried shiitakes, though they can be used to flavour stocks.

SHRIMP PASTE gapi **กะปิ**
Gapi, as this paste is known in Thai, is the soul of Thai food. In Thailand, each coastal region has their version, but elsewhere I'm afraid there is little choice and its purity is often adulterated with flour. Try to find one that is rich, soft, aromatic and not too salty. Thai shrimp paste is readily available in Asian food shops.

SIAMESE WATERCRESS (WATER SPINACH) pak bung **ผักบุ้ง**
Also known as ong choi or kang kung, this green vegetable with hollow stalks and elongated leaves is used throughout Asia. It is sold in large bunches at Chinese markets and food shops.

SNAKE BEANS (YARD-LONG BEANS) tua fak yaow **ถั่วฝักยาว**
Also known as Chinese long beans, these crunchy green beans are used to add crunch to salads and the occasional curry. Regular green beans or runner beans can be substituted.

SOY SAUCE nahm si iew **น้ำซีอิ๊ว**
Soy sauce is an ancient condiment that has been made in Thailand for hundreds of years. Soy beans are steamed and dried before being fermented with water in vats for several months. As it ages, the water evaporates, producing various densities of sauce. Generally I like to use a lighter grade – one that is salty yet slightly sweet, subtle and versatile. The darker sauces are thicker, smokier and more intense; their use is limited to sauces and the occasional noodle dish. Several varieties and brands are available in all Asian food shops.

STICKY RICE *see under* **RICE**

STOCK *see* **CHICKEN STOCK**

TAMARIND PULP makaam bliak **มะขามเปียก**
Most of the tamarind crop in Thailand is cured in the sun until its flesh is a dark-brown pulp and the skin is brittle. The skin is removed and the pulp is dissolved to make tamarind water, which is used in sauces and soups.

Outside of Thailand tamarind comes as blocks of pulp and plastic tubs or jars of concentrate – but don't be misled by convenience: buy the pulp. It is easy to make tamarind water from the pulp, and it will have a much better taste at half the price.

TAMARIND WATER nahm makaam bliak **น้ำมะขามเปียก**
To make tamarind water, break off the required amount of pulp: ½ cup of pulp and ½ cup of water will yield a little more than ¾ cup of tamarind water. Rinse the pulp to remove any surface yeasts, then cover with a similar volume of warm water and leave for a few minutes to soften. Squeeze and work the pulp to dissolve, then strain the liquid to remove any fibre or seeds. It is best to make it quite thick, as it can always be diluted later, whereas very thin tamarind water will dilute whatever it is added to. Any leftover tamarind water will last for a day or two in the refrigerator.

TAPIOCA FLOUR blaeng man **แป้งมัน**
This processed cassava meal is used to thicken some sauces, giving them a sticky glutinous texture. It also brings a rich crunchiness to pastry and cakes.

TARO peuak **เผือก**
Available in most Asian shops, taro has a coarse dark-brown skin and creamy white flesh that may be flecked with black or purple spots. Raw taro contains calcium oxalate, which can irritate the skin, so it may be wise to wear gloves when preparing it. Once cooked, it is no longer bothersome.

THAI CARDAMOM *see under* **CARDAMOM**

THAI SHRIMP PASTE *see* **SHRIMP PASTE**

TURMERIC kamin **ขมิ้น**
This small vivid orange rhizome has a pungent aroma and an intense, slightly medicinal taste. Used mainly in curry pastes of southern Thai or Muslim origin, it should be available in some Asian shops, especially those that cater for Indian cooks.

TURMERIC POWDER pong kamin **ผงขมิ้น**
Choose carefully when buying turmeric powder – often it is mixed with cornflour to extend it, but its flavour suffers. It is easy enough to make your own if you can get the fresh rhizome. Simply peel and finely slice then leave to dry in the sun – or in a warm place, such as an oven with the pilot light on and the door ajar. When it is completely dried, grind to a powder using an electric grinder or a pestle and mortar. Store in an airtight container in the refrigerator to maintain its haunting perfume and prevent it from tasting dusty, like so many of the commercial powders.

VINEGAR nahm som **น้ำส้ม**
Thais generally use a white vinegar made from rice. It is readily available in Asian shops, but try to find one that is naturally fermented.

WATER MIMOSA pak grachet **ผักกะเฉด**
An aquatic, fern-like plant. The only edible part, the fronds, is slightly sour and crunchy. It has a high iron content, which gives it a distinctive taste, and is used in stir-fries and especially in sour orange curries.

WONTON SKINS paeng gio **แป้งเกี๊ยว**
These are made from a dough similar to that used for egg noodles, but with a higher percentage of flour. The dough is rolled out into thin 4 cm (1½ in) squares and dusted with flour. They come in packets of 100 and will last for several days in the refrigerator. Although they will keep for several months frozen, on thawing they may tear very easily and develop a mottled appearance when deep-fried.

YELLOW BEAN SAUCE dtao jiaw **เต้าเจี้ยว**
Made from fermented yellow soy beans, this sauce has a nutty, rich and attractive aroma. It is easily found in Asian food shops.

I prefer the versions containing whole beans, so I can crush them, puree them or leave them whole. For some dishes, I like to rinse my beans to reduce their saltiness and pungency, leaving a cleaner taste. Not every cook will, however, so it is up to you.

YELLOW ROCK SUGAR nahm dtarn gruat **น้ำตาลกรวด**
You'll find a packet of this sugar in almost every Chinese grocer – it is believed to help calm sore throats. In cooking, it is used in braises, where it adds a sheen but not too much sweetness.

ACKNOWLEDGEMENTS

This stroll through the markets and streets was not done alone. I had many companions who helped me along the way.

The original idea for this book came from Julie Gibbs, my stalwart publisher, whose unfailing vision and firm guidance ensured a honed book trimmed of any irrelevant digressions that might have deflected the focus and dulled the reader's interest.

Alison Cowan, my editor, gave the book clarity and managed to tease some sense from my rambling, desultory text. Her sharp mind and red pen have been tempered with gentle patience, forgoing intrusion while striving to give the text a greater sense of my voice.

Earl Carter's wonderful photographs so clearly outshine my writing. They manage to capture the life, humour, people and feeling of the markets so concisely and elegantly – illustrating what my words struggle to describe.

Daniel New, the book's designer, has given palpable form to the book, conveying the chaotic and colourful nature of Thailand's streets and markets while maintaining some order – quite a juggling act.

Fran Moore, my agent, lent an assuaging ear, a canny eye and a comforting glass of wine when I needed it most.

Jane Alty put up with my cantankerous frustration as she worked hard and cheerfully on testing recipes. Robert Danhi and Ari Slatkin were also patient cooks – playing, testing, toying, mixing drinks and eating. Gobgaew Najpinij and her daughter Ning were welcome advisers on the taste of many of the dishes. The Yordwai family, Lek, Dtaa, Nok, Nuu and New, put up with many intrusions as we used their home to shoot the food photographs. Dylan Jones assisted affably and ably with the food for these photos.

Those who helped me most, however, were the people of the streets and markets themselves, who put up with my prolonged inquisitive stares, baffled looks and naïve questions. They are the source and inspiration of this book.

Lastly and most importantly, Tanongsak Yordwai, my partner, has been my unerring guide not only to the streets and markets of Thailand but to all aspects of Thai culture. Without his insight and explanations I would have been lost. But then without Tanongsak's gentle wisdom and kind patience, my life too would be somewhat wayward.

Therefore I dedicate this book to my darling, Tanongsak Yordwai.

○ Tanongsak, Khun Pranom, me and Khun Gobgaew
rolling the dumplings and chewing the fat.

○ Stir-frying on the street in Yaowarat, Bangkok's Chinatown.

○ The morning market at Samut Sakhon, south-west of Bangkok.

○ Crab noodles (see page 138) being cooked and dressed in Chanthaburi market, on the east coast of the Gulf of Thailand.

○ As dawn breaks, the market at Samut Sakhon is primed and waiting for shoppers to arrive.

○ Small boats meander through quiet canals on the outskirts of Bangkok and into the countryside beyond.

○ At any time and anywhere, it's always good to have a snack.

○ Thai markets are always welcoming.

○ A food vendor with her cart at a market in Suphanburi, in Thailand's central plains . . .

○ . . . and with her regular customers, whom she has most likely known since she – and they – were much younger.

○ Alert and at the ready at Samut Sakhon market.

○ The king is revered in Thailand, and all members of the royal family, past and present, bask in that reflection.

○ Sharing a table at Suan Luang night market in Bangkok.

○ Markets in Thailand are always full of good humour.

○ Monks eat after a merit-making (tam bun) ceremony in Phetchaburi, which lies on ancient trade routes to the south-west of Bangkok.

○ Braised duck, chicken and pork waiting expectantly for customers in Samut Sakhon.

Left: Small frigate mackerel (plaa tuu) are Thailand's favourite fish; these silver beauties are available in every market. Right: The fish is good at the market in Chanthaburi, on the east coast of the Gulf of Thailand.

People come and go at Samut Sakhon market, south-west of Bangkok.

By all means, and of all ages, people head to the markets.

Pork butchers toying with soft rib bones in Samut Sakhon market.

Monks share a meal after a morning merit-making ceremony in Phetchaburi, a city famed for its temples.

Offerings to the spirits of the land (jao tii) are not forgotten.

The day's shopping is a pleasant affair when the purchase is concluded with a smile and a chat.

Left: Two types of steamed corn for sale on the street. Right: Sweet chilli sauce is as popular in Thailand as it is abroad.

On a canal in outer Thonburi, on the opposite side of the Chao Phraya River from Bangkok, a farmer heads to market with her harvest of mangoes.

Betel leaves ready to be sold are bundled into boats.

As one of the original ways noodles were sold beyond the confines of Chinatown, 'boat noodles' have a legendary status among the Thai. And once sold, they are ready to be seasoned and eaten.

Shrimp paste is made by curing small prawns with salt for several months in large earthenware pots, then the wet paste is spread out and dried in the sun for a few days. It must be raked and turned regularly – an unenviable job.

A longtime seller of pineapple and dried prawns with kanom jin noodles (see page 68), near Phetchaburi market.

Along most streets in the vicinity of markets there will be one or two stalls selling deep-fried bread (see page 40). This one is in Phetchaburi.

The dough is prepared the night before, and in the early morning it is spread across a well-floured makeshift bench. As soon as it is fried, it is eagerly purchased by waiting customers.

NOON

○ **Left:** Snacks for sale in the market at Phetchaburi, on the Gulf of Thailand. **Right:** A vendor of bean curd in ginger syrup on the way to work – under his own steam – in Samut Sakhon, south-west of Bangkok.

○ All in a day's work at the market in Phetchaburi, which spills along several streets of the bustling old town.

○ Every market will have a stall that sells deep-fried fish – here some serpent-head fish (plaa chorn) . . . and there'll be cats nearby, alert or asleep, but always dreaming.

○ A stand selling braised chicken and duck in Samut Sakhon market.

○ Yellow bean curd and David Beckham assume equal importance at this market stall.

○ In Phetchaburi, the way to school is through the market.

○ Surveying the scene at the market in Phetchaburi amid pickled and shredded bamboo.

○ **Left:** A young boy with a traditional tuft or topknot of hair, which will be cut off in a year or two – an occasion marked by a ceremony where a special dessert (see page 320) is eaten. **Right:** Bamboo baskets of steamed small frigate mackerel (plaa tuu).

○ **Left:** Pig on a bike! **Right:** Single-plate food (arharn jaan dtiaw) means literally that, eaten by itself and not shared – as seen here in the market at Phetchaburi.

○ The eccentrically decorated interior of a small shophouse in Suphanburi, in Thailand's central plains.

○ **Left:** Irresistibly fresh daikon and cucumbers in Phetchaburi market. **Right:** A dog and his friend.

○ Fish – live, cleaned, filleted and sliced – for sale in the backstreets of Phetchaburi.

○ **Left:** A pile of glacé bael fruit – sweet and pickled fruits and vegetables are a popular way to overcome the midday heat. **Right:** Noodles fried and ready to be sold for the remainder of the day.

○ Down one of the aisles in the market at Samut Sakhon.

○ Making fish dumplings in Siracha, south-east of Bangkok. The fish is pureed then worked with a cleaver to ensure a silken quality. The dumplings are deftly moulded with hand and spoon then poached, ready to go into curries or stir-fries.

NIGHT

Left: Selecting with care from the curries on offer at the Samut Sakhon night market. Right: A tuk tuk on the move.

Ready to go or to eat there and then, Thai fast food reigns supreme.

Siamese watercress (water spinach) goes into a fiery stir-fry in Yaowarat, Bangkok.

Deep-frying nuggets of sour pork sausage (see page 188) at Phetchaburi night market.

Enjoying bowls of noodles at Bangkok's Suan Luang night market.

A typical shophouse with its eclectic wares at Don Wai market, in Nakhon Pathom province, to the west of Bangkok.

Stir-fried noodles prepared en masse in Chinatown.

Silhouettes and neon at Suan Luang night market.

Even though it's meant to be single-plate food, sometimes it's too good not to share.

A noodle shop at Suan Luang night market.

Taro pudding (see page 318) and steamed sticky rice are wrapped in banana leaves at a large dessert stand in Phetchaburi.

Making sauce for charred rice noodles (raat nar – see pages 140 and 304).

Making palm sugar in Samut Sakhon province. The sap is collected every morning from nearby orchards before being simmered until it begins to crystallise and caramelise slightly. The palm sugar is then spooned into small muslin (cheesecloth)-lined moulds.

Cakes of palm sugar are removed from their moulds before being sent to market.

Bangkok's Suan Luang night market is always busy.

INDEX

STANDARD MEASUREMENTS

1 teaspoon	**5 ml**
1 tablespoon	**15 ml (3 teaspoons)**
¼ cup	**60 ml (4 tablespoons)**
⅓ cup	**80 ml (about 5 tablespoons)**
½ cup	**125 ml (about 8 tablespoons)**
1 cup	**250 ml (about 16 tablespoons)**

SOME USEFUL QUANTITIES

Fresh long chillies	
1 tablespoon = ¼ fresh chilli	12 g
1 cup = 4 fresh chillies	100 g
Dried long red chillies	
1 tablespoon = 1 dried chilli, deseeded and soaked	2 g
1 cup = 15 dried chillies, deseeded and soaked	25 g
Bird's eye chillies (scuds)	
1 teaspoon = 3 bird's eye chillies	6 g
1 cup = 30-odd bird's eye chillies	90 g
Lemongrass	
1 tablespoon = ⅓ small stalk of lemongrass	6 g
1 cup = 6–10 small stalks of lemongrass	90 g
Galangal, ginger, turmeric	
1 tablespoon = 10 thin slices	10 g
1 cup	150 g
Red shallots, chopped or sliced	
1 tablespoon = 2 small shallots or 1 large shallot	10 g
1 cup = approximately 15 small or 8 large shallots	150 g
Deep-fried shallots	
1 tablespoon = 4 small or 2 large shallots	15 g
Garlic, chopped or sliced	
1 tablespoon = 2 medium cloves of garlic or 5 cloves of small Thai garlic	10 g
Deep-fried garlic	
1 tablespoon = 3 medium cloves of garlic	15 g
Coriander root, cleaned and chopped	
1 teaspoon = 1 medium coriander root	4 g
1 tablespoon = 3–4 medium coriander roots	12 g
Kaffir lime zest, grated	
1 teaspoon = zest of approximately ¼ kaffir lime	8 g
Shrimp paste	
1 tablespoon	22 g
White peppercorns	
1 teaspoon = 7–8 peppercorns	3 g
1 tablespoon = 20 peppercorns	10 g
White sugar	
1 tablespoon	16 g
1 cup	230 g
Palm sugar, shaved	
1 tablespoon	22 g
1 cup	340 g

Author's note
The official transliteration of Thai to English is based on a system devised by King Rama VI. My transliterations are phonetic; I believe it is more important to pronounce the Thai words correctly, which is not always possible when following the accepted version. However, when a dish, word or place is well known, the familiar transliteration is used.

Copyright © 2009 by David Thompson
Photographs copyright © 2009 by Earl Carter

All rights reserved.
Published in the United States by Ten Speed Press, an imprint of the Crown Publishing Group, a division of Random House, Inc., New York.
www.crownpublishing.com
www.tenspeed.com

Ten Speed Press and the Ten Speed Press colophon are registered trademarks of Random House, Inc.

Originally published in Australia by Penguin Group (Australia), Camberwell, in 2009

Library of Congress Cataloging-in-Publication Data
Thompson, David, 1960–
  Thai street food : authentic recipes, vibrant traditions / David Thompson. — 1st American ed.
    p. cm.
  Includes index.
  Summary: "The definitive guide to Thailand's diverse, vibrant street food and culture"—Provided by publisher.
  ISBN 978-1-58008-284-6
  1. Cookery, Thai. 2. Cookery—Thailand. 3. Snack foods—Thailand. I. Title.
  TX724.5.T5T4922 2010
  641.59593—dc22
                        2010009133

ISBN 978-1-58008-284-6

Printed in China

Design by Daniel New

10 9 8 7 6 5 4 3 2 1

First American Edition

○ Inside a commercial dessert kitchen in Phetchaburi, a city renowned for its sweetmeats.